LF

D1237136

A History of Japanese Economic Thought

Economics in the modern sense of the word was introduced into Japan in the second half of the nineteenth century. However, Japanese thinkers had already developed, during the seventeenth and eighteenth centuries, a variety of interesting approaches to issues such as the causes of inflation, the value of trade, and the role of the state in economic activity. Later, Western economic ideas were grafted onto these roots to provide the basis of debate between Marxist and neo-classical economists in early twentieth-century Japan.

This book provides the first comprehensive English language survey of the development of economic thought in Japan. It considers how the study of neo-classical and Keynesian economics was given new impetus by Japan's 'economic miracle' while Marxist thought, which is particularly strong in Japan, was developing along lines that are only now beginning to be recognized by the West. The book concludes with an examination of the radical rethinking of fundamental economic theory currently occurring in Japan and outlines some of the exciting new approaches that are emerging from this 'shaking of the foundations'.

The Author
Tessa Morris-Suzuki is Senior Lecturer in Economic History at the University of New England, Armidale, Australia. Her previous books are *Showa: An Inside History of Hirohito's Japan* (1984) and *Beyond Computopia: Information, Automation and Democracy in Japan* (1988).

THE NISSAN INSTITUTE/ROUTLEDGE
JAPANESE STUDIES SERIES

Editorial Board:

J.A.A. Stockwin, Nissan Professor of Modern Japanese Studies, University of Oxford and Director, Nissan Institute of Japanese Studies.

Teigo Yoshida, formerly Professor of the University of Tokyo, and now Professor, The University of the Sacred Heart, Tokyo

Frank Langdon, Professor, Institute of International Relations, University of British Columbia, Canada

Alan Rix, Professor of Japanese, the University of Queensland

Junji Banno, Professor, Institute of Social Science, University of Tokyo

Titles in the series:

A History
of
Japanese
Economic
Thought

TESSA MORRIS-SUZUKI

London and New York
and
NISSAN INSTITUTE FOR JAPANESE STUDIES
University of Oxford

ALBRIGHT COLLEGE LIBRARY

First published 1989
by Routledge
11 New Fetter Lane, London EC4P 4EE
29 West 35th Street, New York, NY 10001

Reprinted 1990

© 1989 Tessa Morris-Suzuki

Phototypeset in 10pt Times by
Mews Photosetting, Beckenham, Kent
Printed and bound in Great Britain by
Antony Rowe Ltd, Chippenham, Wiltshire

All rights reserved. No part of this book may be reprinted or
reproduced or utilized in any form or by any electronic, mechanical, or
other means, now known or hereafter invented, including photocopying
and recording, or in any information storage or retrieval system, without
permission in writing from the publishers.

British Library Cataloguing in Publication Data

Morris-Suzuki, Tessa, *1951–*
 A History of Japanese Economic Thought. – (The Nissan
 Institute/Routledge Japanese studies series)
 1. Japan. Economics. Theories, 1600–1988
 I. Title II. Nissan Institute of Japanese Studies
 330.1
  ISBN 0–415–01264–3

Library of Congress Cataloging in Publication Data

Morris-Suzuki, Tessa.
 A History of Japanese Economic Thought / Tessa Morris-Suzuki.
  p. cm. – (The Nissan Institute/Routledge Japanese studies
 series)
 Bibliography: p.
 ISBN 0–415–01264–3
 Economics – Japan – History. I. Title. II. Series.
 HB126.J2M67 1989
 330′.0952 – dc19   89–3484
                                                           CIP

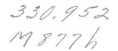
330.952
M877h

225825

Contents

Acknowledgements

My thanks go to all the many people who gave help and advice during the researching and writing of this book: in particular to Mr Koizuka Fumihiro of Mainichi Newspapers, Ms Miki Chiaki of Sophia University, Professor Miyamoto Kenichi of Osaka City University, Professor Murakami Yasusuke of Tokyo University, Mr Nasu Masaki of the National Diet Library, Professor Alan Rix of Queensland University, Mr Shuji Shimamoto of Shogakkan Publishers, Mr Peter Sowden of Routledge, Professor Arthur Stockwin of Oxford University and Professor Uzawa Hirofumi of Tokyo University. Advice, of course, is not synonymous with agreement, and the responsibility for opinions, interpretations (or misinterpretations) in the book is mine alone. I should also like to thank Mrs Naomi Bell and Mrs Fay Hardingham for their assistance in typing the manuscript. Special thanks are due to Mrs Louise Wissman and all the staff of the inter-library sections of the Dixson Library, without whose help in pursuing elusive references this book could not have been written.

* * * * *

Names in this text are given in the normal Japanese order: family name first and given name second, except in quoted references where the Western order is used in the original.

Introduction

Japanese and Western economic thought

Let us begin this study of the evolution of economics in Japan by considering the stark words of Takeuchi Kei, a perceptive analyst of contemporary economic ideas:

> When we speak of 'Japanese economics' we do not of course mean some 'Japanese economics' which is different from the economics of the rest of the world. Such a thing does not exist, and it would be meaningless to attempt to construct it.
>
> (Takeuchi 1987: 39)

Some writers, it is true, have attempted to define enduring characteristics of the Japanese, or even of the Asian, economic tradition. Not so many decades ago, it still seemed plausible for an American writer to contrast a 'Western' with an 'Oriental' mode of economic thought, the latter being based on 'conceptions of logic [which] differ markedly from those of the West' (Kirby 1952: 417).

Japanese writers, although more careful to distinguish their own traditions from those of other 'Oriental' countries, have also at times perceived a discontinuity between the economic thought of Japan and the West. Yamazaki Masukichi, for example, suggests that the most truly Japanese (*nihonteki*) approach to economics is to be found in the writings of certain pre-Meiji Confucian philosophers. These writings, he implies, are a closed book to most Western observers and admirers of Japan (Yamazaki 1981: 190).

In such contrasts between Japanese and western thought, however, 'the West' often becomes no more than an idealized antithesis – either a heaven or a hell – which is used (according to the preconceptions of the author) to damn or to glorify the existing state of affairs in Japan. Thus for Japanese nationalists, Western materialism and

1

individualism have provided an antipole to their own nation's spirituality and social cohesion. Some liberal Japanese writers, on the other hand, have seen Western civilization as characterized rather by altruism and a sense of individual responsibility, and have used these characteristics to highlight the narrow, materialistic nationalism which they perceive as inherent flaws in Japanese culture (see, for example Morishima 1982: 194–7). In this book, I shall make no attempt to define a unifying theme or essence within Japanese economic thought. Instead, I shall try to follow an approach to economics that in some ways resembles the approach to religion set out by Nakamura Hajime in his thought-provoking *Comparative History of Ideas*. As Nakamura observes,

> human beings face much the same problems of life and have demonstrated comparable responses to these problems. In some cases what may be compared is a view of life, or a response to life, which is that of a minority in one tradition while it may be the view or response of a majority in another. Thus it may be held that the religious response indicated by doctrines of self-help is more prevalent in the Buddhist tradition than in the Christian, where the response indicated by acceptance of doctrines of Divine Grace (other help) is more general. Nevertheless, *both responses can be observed in each of these traditions, with tensions between them, as different aspects of the human situation are encountered.*
>
> (Nakamura 1986: 475, italics added)

Religious thought, in other words, fulfils a number of essential social functions – providing consolation, inspiration, ethical guidance, support for the existing social order, and yet sometimes also legitimation for social dissent – but the importance of these functions, and the manner in which they are expressed, varies according to time and place. Similarly, we can say that economic ideas play a variety of important roles in modern society. At one level, they offer explanations for specific, perplexing phenomena such as inflation or unemployment. On another, rather more complex, plane they also attempt to provide coherent models of the whole system of wealth creation and distribution. These models may be eminently practical in purpose – designed to guide the decisions of planners and policymakers – or they may be highly abstract conceptions whose logical elegance is of more importance than their practical use. They may attempt to reveal the inner harmony and perfection of the existing economic order, thus rendering it immune from criticism, or they may seek to expose injustice and exploitation concealed beneath an apparent commonality of interests. They may focus on the physical and material aspects of the economy (the flows of goods and services), on the individual and psychological (the motives of entrepreneurs and consumers), or on the social structural (the problems of supply of labour, distribution of wealth, and so on).

These varied patterns of economic thought are constantly recreated in different countries and in different periods of history. Their relative importance, however, is influenced by local and temporal circumstances. First, the questions asked and the answers given by economic thinkers will clearly depend on the structure and the problems of the society in which they live. Indeed, as we shall see in Chapter 1, it is only when the social and economic system reaches a certain degree of complexity that we can begin to observe the emergence of something that may be termed 'economic thought'.

Second, the scope of new economic ideas will to some extent be restricted by the intellectual heritage from which these ideas spring. The economic thinker, like Goonatilake's scientist, normally perceives a 'worm's-eye view' as he (or she) 'crawls through the tunnel that he and others before him have built and sees what is immediately ahead' (Goonatilake 1984: 83). In this case, the intellectual tunnel is constructed not only of all the earlier economic theories from which the thinker draws inspiration, but also of the ethical, philosophical, and scientific traditions that, consciously or otherwise, mould his or her way of thought. The structure and direction of the tunnel may be dramatically altered when (as happened in Meiji Japan) a whole body of unfamiliar thought is imported from abroad. Gradually, however, these foreign ideas become incorporated into the corpus of 'tradition'. Thus Karl Marx's *Capital* is now just as much a part of the Japanese as it is of the British, American or Soviet intellectual tradition. More accurately perhaps, one might speak, not of a single 'Japanese tradition' but of many traditions, for Japanese thinkers may derive inspiration from the Confucian nationalism of Ogyū Sorai, the radical nationalism of Satō Nobuhiro, or the anarchism of Andō Shōeki, just as they may derive inspiration from Adam Smith, Friedrich List, or Pierre Joseph Proudhon.

Last, the nature of economic thought will also be influenced by the position of the economic theorist in the social structure. It is not surprising to find that the perspective of Tokugawa Confucian writers on economic problems was very different from that of Meiji economic journalists or the Taishō radical intelligentsia. In twentieth century, and particularly in post-Second World War Japan, the role of economists has probably not differed greatly from their role in other industrialized nations. However, the extensive growth of higher education and of mass-volume semi-serious media has enabled Japan to sustain a rather large stratum of economists whose livelihood is relatively independent of the state.

It is not possible, then, to define a characteristically 'Japanese' approach to economic thought. But it is possible to observe how groups of economists in Japan have responded to particular problems in distinctive ways: ways that have been influenced by the Japanese economic environment, by indigenous intellectual traditions, and by the status of the economist in Japanese society.

As one would expect, the differences between Japanese and Western approaches to economic problems are most marked in the Tokugawa period, when the exchange of ideas between Japan and the rest of the world was severely limited. But even at this time, one is often struck by the way in which similar economic problems in Japan and Europe generated analogous economic answers. The rise of commerce and small-scale manufacturing, for example, forced thinkers in Japan, as in Europe, to reassess the notion of agriculture as the source of all wealth, while the spread of the money economy led in both places to speculations on the relationship between the money supply and the movement of prices.

With the opening of Japan to the West in the mid-nineteenth century, the focus of analysis alters: the main problem now is to understand why certain types of Western theory took root and flourished in Japan while others fell on stony ground. Clearly an important influence here is the nature of Japanese economic development itself. Where the state played a vital role in initiating and protecting business enterprise, it is hardly surprising that the theories of *laissez-faire* should have rather less appeal than the state-centred theories of the German historical school. But Japan's intellectual heritage may also have played a part in the process of selection. As we shall see, the original Japanese notion of 'economy' as 'administering the nation and relieving the sufferings of the people' continued to influence the attitudes of Japanese thinkers well into the twentieth century, and perhaps made it particularly hard for Japanese economists to accept the emerging neoclassical view of economics as a purely positivist science.

In these speculations, however, it is important to beware of assuming an Anglo-American norm to which Japan is the 'exception'. When we compare Japanese with British and US intellectual history, it is easy to be surprised at the weakness of neo-classical thought, and the strength of Marxism, in early twentieth-century Japan. But a broader perspective, which includes Eastern and Southern Europe as well as the less developed world, may well lead us to the conclusion that it is Britain and the United States, rather than Japan, that were the exceptions. It was, perhaps, only in countries which attained such high levels of prosperity with so little political upheaval that the assumptions of a harmonious and self-regulating economic system could become so very widely accepted.

The post-war reconstruction of the Japanese social and political system, and subsequent rapid economic development, created a firmer foundation for the expansion of neo-classical economic thought in Japan, but even then neoclassicism failed to attain the overwhelming ascendancy that it had achieved in much of the English-speaking world. Instead, Japanese economics bifurcated into, on the one hand, a 'modern' path which drew inspiration particularly from the US synthesis of neo-classical and Keynesian ideas, and on the other, a somewhat more isolated and inward-looking Marxian path. This two-sided evolution, however, had certain advantages. The number of economists who were able to integrate insights from both traditions, although small, was probably greater in Japan than in many other countries, and it was these economists who were often able to adopt the most innovative approaches to economic theory.

Since the collapse of high growth in the early 1970s, economic thought in Japan, as elsewhere, has entered into a period of crisis, a crisis that affects both modern and Marxian theory with equal severity. There is no reason to think that Japanese economics, any more than US or British economics, will provide a clear and unequivocal solution to this crisis. But because of Japan's particular economic and intellectual environment, contemporary Japanese economists are able, as we shall see, to offer a number of original perspectives on the problems that currently assail economic theory. A better two-way flow of ideas between Japan and other countries might therefore help us in the process of defining directions out of the present theoretical quagmire.

Before taking this exploration of the history of Japanese economic thought any further, it is first necessary to include three brief explanations. The first concerns the use of the terms 'Western' and 'the West'. These expressions are not only geographically vague, but also tend to attribute a spurious cultural unity to a diverse group of nations. Our language, however, offers no other convenient shorthand for such clumsy phrases as 'the countries of Western Europe and North America' or 'the industrialized market economies of the northern hemisphere (excluding Asia)'. 'The West' will therefore be retained here, albeit with some reluctance.

Second, names will be given in the normal Japanese order – family name first and given name second. As is the usual Japanese practice, Tokugawa scholars are referred to by their given (pen) names, while Meiji and post-Meiji scholars are referred to by their family names.

The third explanation is a more significant one which concerns the scope of this study. A relatively short book-length survey of 300 years of economic thought must inescapably be selective – and selection means omission. Many readers may be able to point to an individual theorist whose work, they feel, has received short shift here. My purpose in general has been to single out those scholars whose works give an indication of the main currents in Japanese economic thought: scholars who not only attracted interest in their own day but also influenced those who came after them. In some cases I have also paid particular attention to a theory or debate which offers interesting analogies with economic debates in other countries. If this brief survey encourages others to explore some of the byways of Japanese economic thought which it has neglected, then it will have served its purpose.

1

Economic thought in Tokugawa Japan

The rule of the Tokugawa shoguns (1603–1868) coincided with the age of European intellectual ferment from which economics emerged as an independent discipline. During these two-and-a-half centuries, although certain branches of Western scientific thought were assimilated and propagated by Japanese scholars, the introduction of Western philosophical, political, and economic ideas into Japan was severely restricted. At the same time, though, the evolution of an increasingly complex Japanese economy was creating some of the phenomena which had inspired the speculations of European economic thinkers from Munn to Quesnay and Adam Smith. These phenomena included the expansion of commerce, the fluctuation of prices, and the growing sophistication of the division of labour.

Because economic development in Tokugawa Japan took place in an environment of relative cultural isolation, a study of the period offers particularly fascinating insights into some of the most profound questions in the history of economic thought. How far are economic theories shaped by metaphysical, ethical, and philosophical traditions, and how far by economic circumstances? Do thinkers from diverse traditions, when confronted with the same economic problem, pose similar questions and devise similar answers? The outline of Tokugawa ideas presented in this chapter will, I think, show that although Japanese scholars' concept of the 'economic' was often very different from those of modern economists, their intellectual enquiries sometimes led them along paths curiously similar to those explored by their European contemporaries.

A HISTORY OF JAPANESE ECONOMIC THOUGHT

THE ECONOMIC ENVIRONMENT

Economics as a distinct field of study is a modern phenomenon, but economic ideas in J.S. Mill's sense of the word – ideas about 'the nature of wealth, including the laws of its production and distribution' – have existed in various epochs and in many different societies.

The texts attributed to the Chinese philosopher Confucius, but probably written by his disciples in the fifth century BC, contain frequent references to prosperity and poverty. Before the third century BC Chinese philosophers of the Mohist school had developed a theory on the relationship between prices and the quantity of money, while the fourth-century *Book of Mencius* includes arguments on the advantages of the division of labour (Hu 1984: 13–14, 21–3). Similar discussions on economic exchange, price, and value are to be found in Indian writings of the fourth century BC, including those of Kautilya and Sūkra (Rangaswami 1934). In classical Greece, Plato and Aristotle debated, amongst other issues, the uses of money and the relative merits of communal and private property systems (Spiegel 1971: 14–30).

The common thread connecting these economic ideas is the fact that they evolved in societies with well-developed divisions of labour, complex commercial systems, thriving cities, and widespread use of money. In societies of this type, political and social relationships increasingly acquired an economic form. Prosperity and status were no longer determined purely by military might or political custom, but could be influenced by mysterious and apparently impersonal forces such as the level of prices or the scarcity of specific commodities. Philosophers and administrators who were concerned with questions of social order and justice were, therefore, more and more often forced to turn their attention to unmistakably 'economic' issues.

These historical considerations help to explain the vitality of economic thought in Tokugawa Japan. The Tokugawa social order was, in principle, a highly conservative system. The policies devised by the first Tokugawa shogun, Ieyasu, were designed to restrict or reverse the expansion of domestic and overseas commerce that had been occurring during the previous two centuries, and to create a society that would be not only stable, but static.

The foundations of the system rested on rice. Japan was divided into domains whose importance was measured in terms of the amount of rice they yielded, with the central area remaining under direct control of the shogun. The *daimyō* who ruled the domains obtained revenue mainly through the imposition of a rice tax on the peasants

8

in their fief, and disbursed this rice as stipends to their substantial retinues of samurai officials and retainers.

Individual status was, in theory, fixed within one of four major status groups: warriors (*shi*), farmers (*nō*), artisans (*kō*), and merchants (*shō*). Excluded from this system were outcasts, who were engaged in so-called 'unclean' occupations such as the butchering of animals, or who had been outlawed as a punishment for crime. The functional distinction between the status groups was sharpened by the physical separation of the ruling class from the land. In earlier centuries, the aristocracy had possessed their own estates which they farmed using local peasant labour, but by the Tokugawa period they had withdrawn to castle towns, and the rice tax in effect provided their only link with agriculture. Farming, nevertheless, was recognized as the basis of national wealth. The low position of merchants on the status ladder reflected the ruling-class view that commercial activities were parasitic rather than productive.

Because of its close connections with missionary activity and foreign political influence, overseas trade was regarded by the Tokugawa shoguns as a potentially destabilizing influence. The Portuguese and other Westerners who had established commercial links with Japan were excluded, and the only channels of external trade allowed to survive after the 1630s were a small Dutch trading post on the island of Deshima (off Nagasaki) and the Ryūkyū Islands, which maintained loose political and economic ties both with China and the southern Japanese province of Satsuma.

Paradoxically, however, the very political stability of the Tokugawa system provided the conditions for economic development and this development ultimately eroded the structure of the system itself. Although there were frequent regional peasant revolts, particularly in the second half of the period, the Tokugawa age was a remarkably peaceful one by comparison with both the century it preceded and the one it followed. Prolonged peace encouraged the extension of internal trade networks and the establishment of new markets, and these developments in turn wrought gradual but significant changes in rural life. Farmers were increasingly able to purchase items such as fertilizer and firewood, which they had previously produced for themselves. Trade stimulated the exchange not only of goods but also of ideas, enabling knowledge of the best contemporary farming practices to become widely diffused, and so increasing yields. At the same time the evolution of the exchange economy encouraged farmers to specialize in the production of those goods that were best suited to the climate and soils of their region (Smith 1959: Chaps 6 and 7).

9

Perhaps the most spectacular symptom of the expanding exchange economy was the growth of Japanese cities. The shogun's capital, Edo (where all *daimyō* were obliged to maintain a residence and spend a considerable part of their time), probably had a population of some 1.4 million by the second half of the eighteenth century, making it perhaps the largest city in the world, while the populations of Osaka and Kyoto exceeded 300,000 (Yazaki 1968: 134). Concentration of wealth in the hands of a substantially urbanized ruling class created demand for a wide variety of non-agricultural goods and services: clothing, furniture, construction services, wholesale and retail trade, inns, and theatres. The economic and social consequences of urban growth impinged directly on the personal experience of the economic thinkers of the Tokugawa era. The philosopher Ogyū Sorai, for example, reflecting on the rising price of land in the capital, could recall that

My grandfather owned a piece of land in Ise which had been cultivated for generations by his ancestors. He sold it and bought a house in Edo for only 50 ryō. I understand that the house was sold in my fathers' time for a sum of more than 2,000 ryō.

(Ogyū 1973: 327)

Fluctuations in prices, whether caused (as in this case) by the forces of supply and demand or by changes in the quantity of money, were a central concern of Tokugawa economic debates. As in medieval Europe, the increasing use of money, combined with a general lack of understanding of monetary problems on the part of the political authorities, caused repeated currency crises. The situation was compounded by the complexity of the money system in Japan, where gold, silver, and copper coins circulated side by side and were supplemented by merchants' bills of exchange and by inconvertible paper notes issued in various domains.

Inevitably, the expansion of agricultural and handicraft production, the growth of regional specialization, rise of the cities, monetarization of the economy, and fluctuation of prices gave rise to conflict between the Tokugawa ideology of social stability and the realities of the economic world. In the cities, the theoretically rigid social hierarchy was giving way to a more fluid and ephemeral order, marvellously captured in the art and literature of the period. By the late seventeenth century, the writer Ihara Saikaku could observe that

as a rule, a well-to-do person in Osaka is not the heir to generations of wealth. He is more often some humble clerk — a 'Kichizō'
or 'Sansuke' – who has a quick rise in the world and comes into
money. Gradually as opportunities offer, he acquires the elements
of Chinese and Japanese verse composition, kickball, archery, the
koto, the flute, the drums, incense blending and the tea ceremony,
and by associating with the best people he even loses his old
vulgarities of speech. In life, it is training rather than birth which
counts, and it is not unknown for the unwanted offspring of noble
families to earn their living by hawking home-made paper flowers.
                                                    (Ihara 1959: 23–4)

Discussions of economic issues in Tokugawa Japan were almost
always inseparably entwined with discussions of this erosion of
the hereditary social order, and, not surprisingly, the contrasting
views put forward by contemporary philosophers frequently reflected
their own position in the social hierarchy. The important point,
however, was that social change forced the leading intellectual figures
of the period to confront issues such as the economic basis of the
status system and causes of the changing distribution of wealth.
In this way, the frontiers of philosophical enquiry were broadened
to include an increasing range of economic issues. Thomas Kuhn,
in his analysis of scientific revolutions, observes that 'discovery
commences with the awareness of anomaly' (Kuhn 1970: 52).
So, in Tokugawa Japan, the anomaly between the formal rigidity and
the actual fluidity of the social and economic system generated
enquiry and innovation in many areas of political, economic, and
ethical thought.

THE CONFUCIAN HERITAGE

Although economic thought in Tokugawa Japan increasingly involved
questioning of some aspects of philosophical tradition, it never wholly
escaped the influence of that tradition. The newly emerging ideas on
the economy, therefore, cannot be understood without some
knowledge of their philosophical roots, particularly Confucianism,
which constituted the most important of these roots. Howard Smith
defines the essence of Confucius's teaching as being

that the goal for the individual is the development of personality
until the ideal of a perfect man, a true gentleman, a sage, is reached.

11

On the other hand, his goal for society is universal order and harmony under the rule of a perfect sage.

(Smith 1974: 62)

Although the emphasis on these two aspects of morality – the private and the public – varied as new schools of Confucian thought emerged and waned, the concern for 'universal order and harmony' meant that Confucianism could never wholly divorce itself from questions of practical politics and (as we have seen) provided some of the earliest significant contributions to economic thought. The Confucian tradition therefore offered a rich fund of ideas on which Japanese thinkers could draw as they attempted to come to terms with the economic problems of their own age.

It is also worth mentioning that Confucianism had an influence on the development of Western economic thought which has been largely ignored by historians. The French Physiocrats in particular formulated their ideas at a time when Western interest in Chinese culture was at its zenith. The Physiocratic concept of the state, for example, was influenced by the Confucian idea of *li* (in Japanese: *ri*), the principle or natural order inherent in all beings and all social systems. According to this view of the universe, the ideal state is the one which conforms most closely to its natural *li*, or, as the Abbé Baudeau put it,

[The] single supreme will which exercises supreme power is not, strictly speaking, a human will at all. It is just the voice of nature – the will of God. The Chinese are the only people whose philosophy seems to have got hold of this supreme truth, and they regard their Emperor as the eldest son of God.

(Quoted in Gide and Rist 1913: 36)

The idea of a naturally harmonious and self-regulating order, which the ruler symbolizes but does not disturb, was conveyed via Quesnay ('the venerable Confucius of Europe', as a contemporary flatteringly called him) into the economic theorizing of Adam Smith. Thus the points of similarity that sometimes appear between eighteenth-century economic thought in Europe and Japan are more than pure coincidence.

The dominant form of Confucian philosophy in the early Tokugawa period was the Chu Hsi school (*Shushigaku* in Japanese), a complex metaphysical and ethical system that placed less emphasis on the study of the Confucian classics than on training and meditation designed to reveal the pure *ri* concealed within each human individual (Maruyama 1974: Chap. 2). In the eighteenth and early nineteenth centuries, however, this philosophy came to be challenged from a number of directions. On the one hand, Confucian scholars such as Ogyū Sorai and Arai Hakuseki introduced new approaches that placed greater emphasis both on the study of classical Confucian writings and on the application of ethics to practical issues of public policy. On the other, National Learning (*Kokugaku*) attempted to assert the superiority of Japan's indigenous Shintō classics, the *Kojiki* and *Nihon Shoki*, while Dutch Learning (*Rangaku*) propagated the Western knowledge of mathematics, cartography, anatomy, and astronomy, introduced through the Dutch trading post in Nagasaki.

Although the dominance of Chu Hsi Confucianism weakened in the second half of the Tokugawa period, some fundamental Confucian ideas continued to provide the framework for economic thought even into the closing years of the era and beyond. The Confucian influence is particularly evident in the concept of economics itself. The term *keizai* – which in modern Japanese means 'economy' – already existed in Tokugawa Japan, but its meaning bore overtones far removed from twentieth-century notions of economics as the science of efficiently allocating scarce resources amongst alternative uses.

Keizai was an abbreviation of the phrase *keikoku saimin* (or *keisei saimin*), which may be roughly translated as 'administering the nation and relieving the suffering of the people'. Dazai Shundai begins his *Economic Annals (Keizai Roku)*, published in 1729, with the following reflections on the etymology of the term:

To govern the whole nation under heaven is *keizai*. It is the virtue of ruling society and relieving the sufferings of the people. *Kei* is wise statesmanship (*keirin*). . . . *Kei* literally means 'to control a thread'. The warp of a piece of material is called *kei* and the woof, *i*. When a weaving woman makes silk cloth, she first prepares the warp . . . and then she weaves in the woof. *Kei* is also 'management' [or 'construction'] (*keiei*). . . . When you construct a royal palace, you must first make a plan of the whole, and then you carry out the plan. This is *kei*.
Sai means the virtue of salvation (*saidō*). This may also be read *wataru*, and literally means 'to carry someone across a river to the farther bank'. . . . It is also the virtue of bringing relief (*kyūsai*), which may be read *sukuu*, and means 'to relieve people of their sufferings'. Moreover, it may be interpreted as meaning 'accomplishment' or 'bringing to fruition'. Therefore the term

13

[*keizai*] has many meanings, but the essential point of those meanings is simply this: in short, to manage affairs and to bring these affairs to a successful conclusion.

(Dazai 1972: 16)

The idea of *keizai*, in other words, has its origins in the Confucian world of public ethics with its paragon of the virtuous ruler. While economics in Europe, under the influence of Newtonian physics, came to present itself as a detached and objective science, *keizai* was a philosophical system inescapably bound up with questions of justice, law, and morality. It is entirely consistent with this tradition, therefore, that Shundai's *Economic Annals* should contain sections on crime and punishment, geography, and education, for these matters were all integral parts of *keizai*. In the same way, Arai Hakuseki, the leading economic adviser of his day, would have made no distinction between his contributions to currency reform and trade policy and his advice on appropriate epitaphs for a deceased shogun. All of these tasks were equally concerned with *keizai*, the holding together of the social fabric of the nation.

This ethical and political vision of *keizai* remained essentially unchanged throughout the Tokugawa age, but the problems that individual thinkers saw as fundamental to a harmonious economic order altered as Japanese society itself evolved. I shall make no attempt to provide an all-inclusive account of the economic ideas in existence in Tokugawa Japan, but will focus instead on a small number of leading thinkers whose writings clearly reflect the principal currents of change at work within Japanese intellectual life.

AGRICULTURE AS THE BASIS OF THE ECONOMY: KUMAZAWA BANZAN (1619–91)

In a changing world where the dominant social theories are clearly out of kilter with reality, philosophers may take one of two approaches: either they may argue that society should be made to conform to the ideals of existing theory, or they may try to modify theory to encompass existing reality. Kumazawa Banzan was one of those who chose the first approach, and he was in that sense a conservative. This does not mean, though, that we can regard him as a supporter of the political establishment. On the contrary, his impassioned social criticism earned him the profound suspicion of the Shogunal government, and his most famous work, the *Daigaku Wakumon*, was banned from sale.

Banzan's social critique was based on a deep and genuine concern for the poverty of farmers and above all of the lower ranking *samurai*, a concern that sprang from personal experience. With the establishment of the Tokugawa regime, *samurai* who had earned a living as soldiers during the previous century of political turmoil found themselves without occupation. Though many were employed by the shogunate or domains as advisers, administrators, and teachers, a substantial number became *rōnin*, masterless *samurai*, whose existence was at the best of times precarious. Because of the separation of the warrior class from the land, the *rōnin* could no longer support themselves by farming, and, since the Tokugawa status system prohibited them from engaging in trade, were sometimes left without legitimate sources of income.

Kumazawa Banzan was born into a *rōnin* family in 1619. At the age of 16 he was given a minor position in the houshold of the *Daimyō* of Okayama, but four years later, for reasons that remain obscure, he left this post and returned to his family. For the next few years he experienced extreme poverty. Indeed, there was one famine year (he later recalled) 'when it seemed as though, embracing my mother and my sisters and brothers, I might die of starvation' (Kumazawa 1976: 386).

In this unpromising environment Banzan studied Confucian writings, and came particularly under the influence of the Wang Yang-Ming school of thought, a heterodox form of Confucian philosophy that emphasized quietism and meditation. Banzan's own works, however, are distinctly eclectic, and often combine elements of Wang Yang-Ming thought with orthodox Chu Hsi Confucianism and Buddhism. In his late twenties, Banzan was rescued from starvation by the offer of a new appointment in the Domain of Okayama, where he served for ten years, gaining experience of the practical problems of political and economic administration. After retiring from regular employment in 1657 he lived the rest of his life as a wandering scholar. It was in these later years that he wrote his major works, in which reflections on the ethical, religious, and social problems of the day are interspersed with remarkably vivid observations of contemporary Japanese life (Itō 1976).

Through all of Banzan's economic writings there run, like two contrasting but intertwined threads, the themes of luxury and poverty. The rich city, where 'goods are treasured more than good people', is counterposed against the impoverished countryside, where 'the people's food is like the fodder of cows and horses' (Kumazawa 1976: 402, 439). In Banzan's philosophy, however, luxury and poverty are not merely contrasted but are interrelated, the latter being seen as an inescapable consequence of the former.

Rural poverty was a widely recognized problem in seventeenth-century Japan, but the phenomenon was popularly attributed to shortage of agricultural land. A solution was therefore sought in the opening up of new land by clearing forests or converting grasslands to paddy. Banzan decisively rejected this solution, and his reasons for rejecting it are of interest, for they suggest that he had developed an embryonic notion of the law of diminishing returns.

Since Japanese farmers did not raise animals for consumption, they relied heavily on grasslands as a source of fertilizer for their fields. Mountain forests, too, were vital not only as a source of firewood, game, and wild vegetables, but also because they prevented landslides and flooding in the rainy season. Banzan recognized that the destruction of these resources would, in the long run, impoverish the farm populations.

> If the nation consisted only of farmland, and there were no mountain forests or uncultivated areas, the lives of the samurai and common people would be less comfortable. It is better to leave uncultivated land untouched. Moreover, when new lands are opened up old lands sometimes become worse. So it is good to consider the matter carefully.
>
> (Kumazawa 1976: 317)

To Banzan, the solution to the nation's economic woes lay not in extending the area of agriculture, but in a more fundamental reform of the system as a whole. In particular, he identified the sources of luxury and poverty as lying in the spread of the money economy.

> There are many reasons [for the impoverishment of the *samurai* and farmers]. Firstly, in big cities and small alike, on land by the rivers and sea which is convenient for transport, urban areas are being built, and luxury is growing day by day without check. Merchants grow rich while warriors are impoverished. Secondly, the practice of exchanging grain for other goods is steadily disappearing, and gold, silver and copper alone are being used. Prices are becoming high and the nation's gold and silver are flowing into the hands of the merchants. As a result, great and lesser *samurai* are lacking in finances. Thirdly, when proper social customs are abandoned, [economic] affairs become complex. *Samurai* exchange their rice stipends for gold, silver and copper

coins, and so buy goods. If the price of rice is low and the price of goods is high, they are short of money. . . . When the *samurai* are in distress, the amount which they take from the people doubles. . . . The poverty of the *samurai* also means that merchants have no-one with whom they can exchange goods for grain, and only the big merchants, become steadily richer.

(Kumazawa 1971: 249)

Banzan's ideas resemble those of the French Physiocrats in the sense that he, too, saw agriculture as the source of all wealth: sound economic policy, he argued, rested on 'revering grain and despising gold' (*kikoku senkin*). Like the Physiocrats he demanded that the crushing burden of agricultural taxes be lightened so that farmers would have greater incentive to produce, and grain, the source of all true wealth, would be abundant (Kumazawa 1971: 247; 1976: 402). But in Banzan's writings these ideas do not lead (as they do in Quesnay's) towards an analysis of the economy as an interrelated whole. Instead, they lead backward into nostalgia for a world in which 'the five grains' (rice, wheat, Chinese millet, foxtail millet, and beans) rather than gold were truly the measure of all things.

The treasure of the people is grain. Gold, silver, copper and so forth are the servants of grain. They come after grain. . . . The enlightened ruler stores grain plentifully for the people, and, since all buying and selling is performed with grain, the people enjoy abundance. . . . It is difficult to transport large quantities of grain, and therefore, if grain is used [as a means of exchange], trade cannot easily be monopolised. So the price of goods is lowered and luxury does not increase. *Samurai* and farmers are prosperous, while artisans and merchants also have secure fortunes.

(Kumazawa 1976: 437–8)

Banzan, in other words, advocated a retreat from the money economy towards a system in which (as in the past) unhulled rice was the principal measure of value and medium of exchange (Kumazawa 1976: 402). But as we have already seen, he was also acutely aware of the connection between the money economy and the social system in which cities grew, trade flourished, and the ruling class was divorced from the land. He recognized, therefore, that reducing the sphere of monetary exchange must involve a fundamental reshaping of the society, a return to a more self-sufficient way of life. This was to be achieved by recreating the social order of earlier centuries, when

17

the *samurai* lived as farmer-soldiers [*nōhei*] amongst the people, helping in the fields, hunting in the mountains, fishing in the rivers and streams and strengthening their bodies by enduring wind and rain.

(Kumazawa 1976: 448)

If all *samurai* (other than those engaged in essential administrative tasks) returned to the land, the peasantry would no longer have to support a substantial unproductive ruling class, and, Banzan believed, agriculture would flourish.

Kumazawa Banzan's mordant criticism unerringly focused on the fundamental sources of social change in seventeenth-century Japan. He perceived, as few contemporaries did, how the separation of the *samurai* class from the land promoted the monetarization of the economy, and how this in turn led to the expansion and enrichment of the merchant class and to the erosion of the Tokugawa status system. In a sense we might say that within 80 years of the establishment of the Tokugawa regime, Banzan had already identified the factors that would ultimately cause the regime's downfall. But the solutions that he proposed to these problems were anachronistic even at the time in which he was writing. Banzan himself seems reluctantly to have recognized their implausibility, for his comments on the practical implementation of his proposals are, to say the least, half-hearted:

If attempts were made to re-establish the *samurai* on the land under present conditions, the *samurai* would not concur. It might also cause great suffering to the people. Only by entrusting the task to a very talented person and by seizing an opportune moment might it be possible to make the scheme acceptable to *samurai* and people.

(Kumazawa 1976: 458)

INNOVATIONS IN CONFUCIAN ECONOMIC THOUGHT: ARAI HAKUSEKI (1657–1725), OGYU SORAI (1666–1728), AND DAZAI SHUNDAI (1680–1747)

The flowering of that urban culture which Banzan so despised was most brilliantly visible in the closing decades of the seventeenth century. During the Genroku era (1688–1704) the new wealth of the merchants of Edo and Osaka began to find expression in arts and entertainment. The kabuki theatre was refined and popularized; the poems of Matsuo Bashō and the comic tales of Ihara Saikaku reached a wide and enthusiastic readership; and the publishing industry expanded, producing not only literary works but popular instructional texts (often delightfully illustrated) on everything from etiquette to agriculture. But in the splendour of Tokugawa urban culture there is always a certain sense of fragility and unease. Turbulent currents run beneath the surface of the floating world. The social aspect of this brittleness is captured by E.H. Norman when he writes:

> The real and fictional representatives of Genroku culture expend their energy in endless sexual adventures, in continual experiment with luxury and extravagance; this is the only field in which the new *chōnin* class could express its increased power with impunity.
> (Norman 1949: 74–5)

From an economic perspective, the sudden expansion of the commercial economy inevitably generated instability and dislocation. The growth of market transactions created a demand for money which the existing currency system was ill-equipped to meet. The shoguns, in particular, faced a constantly widening gap between rising expenditures and a relatively inflexible source of income. The problem was aggravated by the nature of Japan's foreign trade. The small flow of trade which occurred through the Dutch in Nagasaki consisted almost entirely of imports. Yarn and fabrics, spices and medicinal plants, and a host of miscellaneous items (looking-glasses, eye-glasses, red and black pencils for office use, strange birds) were exchanged for gold and silver, slowly depleting Japan's stocks of precious metals. At the same time, the output of the Japanese gold and silver mines also steadily declined (Takekoshi 1967).

The Tokugawa shoguns responded to declining revenues just as medieval and early modern European monarchs had responded to similar crises. In 1695 they undertook the first of twelve recoinages which were to be carried out before the Meiji Restoration of 1868. Debasement of the coinage yielded substantial short-term profits for the shogunate, but at the same time provoked inflation, disrupted the financial system, and in the long run hastened the erosion of the Tokugawa status system.

The dilemmas that Japanese thinkers faced in their attempts to comprehend these problems are very clearly apparent in the contrasting views of Arai Hakuseki and Ogyū Sorai. Hakuseki and Sorai were unquestionably the most eminent intellectual figures of their day (some would argue, of the Tokugawa period as a whole). Their

19

fundamental philosophies were in many ways very similar, for each brought to Confucianism a practical, rationalistic, historically-based approach that contrasted with the mystical tendencies of the Chu-Hsi school. Yet they served different shoguns, advocated radically different monetary policies, and obliquely criticized one another in their writings. Their ideas on the economy are therefore most easily appreciated by considering them side by side.

Ogyū Sorai is best remembered as the originator of a significant reformation in Confucian thought. In contrast to the dominant Chu Hsi school, with its emphasis on the cultivation of the individual *ri*, Sorai's schools of Ancient Learning (*Kogaku*) placed emphasis on public and political morality. In particular, Sorai argued that ethical guidance was to be sought through rigorous study of the earliest Confucian texts. Since these texts were written in classical Chinese, Sorai also devoted much of his energy to linguistic studies, seeking to recapture the precise content of the original words, which he saw as embodying language in its purest form (Maruyama 1974; Lidin 1973).

Although (as we shall see) he made important contributions to debates on the currency problem, Sorai's fundamental approach to the economy was less original than other aspects of his philosophy. In many respects, he was the intellectual heir to the physiocratic theories of Kumazawa Banzan. Like Banzan, he sought relief from the troubles of his age in a return to the social order which, Sorai believed, was laid down by the earliest Chinese rulers. This order, in which the social role of each class was clearly and immutably defined, was threatened by the spreading canker of monetary exchange and, for Sorai as for Banzan, this canker was as much a social and ethical issue as an economic one.

Throughout Sorai's writings, two evils are repeatedly singled out as sources of political and economic disorder. They are, first, the loss of *reihō* (propriety or etiquette) and, second, the *samurai's* practice of 'living like guests at an inn'. By *reihō*, Sorai means 'knowing one's place': in the well-ordered society each individual has a fixed social status, and conforms to the patterns of behaviour and consumption appropriate to that status. The curiously expressive phrase 'living like guests at an inn' (*ryoshuku no kyokai*) was used by Sorai to describe the urbanization and commercialization of the ruling-class way of life. Rather than living on the land and receiving direct tributes in kind, the *samurai* now lived in the cities and received a rice stipend which they were obliged to convert into money in order to purchase their daily needs. This, Sorai argued, not only made the *samurai* irresponsible and sybaritic but also placed excessive political and economic power into the hands of the merchant class.

> The basis of the social order created by the ancient sages was that all people, both high and low, should live on the land. As a result a system of propriety was established. Nowadays, these two elements are lacking, and consequently both high and low experience distress and all manner of evils are brought into being. . . . Both greater and lesser people are living like guests at an inn, which is directly contrary to the way of the sages, who established them on the land. All manner of propriety has disappeared, and, from clothing to houses and utensils, there is no way of distinguishing the noble from the common people.
>
> (Ogyū 1973: 305)

As this quotation suggests, Sorai agreed with Kumazawa Banzan in advocating a return of the *samurai* population to the countryside. But in one significant respect, Sorai differed from Banzan, for he did not suggest the re-establishment of rice as the medium of exchange, but instead accepted the use of coinage and merely sought to restrict its influence by increasing the use of taxes and tributes paid in kind. This difference in approach represented an important step forward in coming to terms with the realities of the Tokugawa economy, because it allowed Sorai to offer a fairly complex analysis of the workings of the currency system.

But acceptance of the money economy is far more clearly marked in the writings of Sorai's contemporary, Arai Hakuseki. Indeed, in Hakuseki's ideas we find a major departure from Confucian traditions, for, rather than emphasizing agriculture as the source of all wealth, Hakuseki gave primacy to the importance of precious metals. In his most famous statement on the subject, Hakuseki reversed the principle of 'revering grain and despising gold', and instead presented precious metals as the resources which, being non-renewable, must be most carefully husbanded.

> Gold and silver are made by heaven and earth. If we use the metaphor of the human form, we can say that they are like the bones, while all other valuable products are like the blood, muscle, skin and hair. Blood, muscle, skin and hair can be damaged and will grow again. But bones, once they are damaged, cannot be regenerated. Gold and silver are like the bones of heaven and earth.

Once they have been removed, they cannot be re-created.

(Arai 1977: vol. 3, p. 673)

In a sense, the contras between the economic approaches of Sorai and Hakuseki seems to reflect contrasts of personality and social position. Sorai was above all a philosopher and teacher, a man who was only occasionally called on to offer political advice, and therefore who viewed economic problems from a somewhat detached position in which ethical considerations were paramount. Hakuseki was, to a far greater extent, a practical man of affairs, whose career reached its summit in the years (from 1709 to 1716) when he was a leading adviser to the shoguns Ienobu and Ietsugu. Not only was he intimately involved in the formulation of policy, he was also a man with a strongly practical and empirical turn of mind. His method of dealing with the social and economic problems on which he was consulted was not so much to refer to the writings of the Confucian sages, but rather to observe the problem at first hand and to collect detailed information on its causes and implications (see, for example, Ackroyd 1979: 155–6).

One of the most important problems that came under Hakuseki's scrutiny during his years as shogunal adviser was the question of foreign trade. Hakuseki not only visited Nagasaki but also held discussions with Dutch traders stationed in Deshima. These discussions, together with data which Hakuseki gathered from Japanese officials in Nagasaki, left him with a profound concern at the impact of trade on the Japanese economy. Though the yearly level of trade was relatively small, imports constituted a perpetual drain on the nation's limited supplies of precious metals, a drain that was aggravated by widespread smuggling and other irregular practices. According to Hakuseki:

If we calculate the sum of gold and silver that has gone to foreign countries for the 107 years since the Keichō era on the basis of the information given by the Nagasaki *Bugyōsho* [magistracy] and compare it with the amount of gold and silver produced in our country within the same period, we can see that we must have lost a quarter of the gold and three-quarters of the silver. Therefore, in another century we shall have lost half our gold, and all the silver will have gone before that period is out. As for copper, not only is what we have now not enough for foreign trade, but insufficient for internal needs as well.

(Ackroyd 1979: 247)

Hakuseki's immediate response to the problem was to propose that foreign trade should be curtailed still further. In fact, with the possible exception of imports of books and medicines, he regarded foreign trade as entirely unnecessary, a throwing away of 'the time honoured treasures of our produce in exchange for the ephemeral novelties that come from abroad' (Ackroyd 1979: 247). In this sense, as the Japanese historian Honjō Eijirō rightly points out, Hakuseki was very different from the European mercantilist thinkers to whom he has sometimes been compared (Honjō 1966: vol. 2, p. 7). Although mercantilists like Thomas Munn also emphasized the importance of amassing precious metals, they believed that this should be achieved by developing the nation's exports so as to ensure the existence of a favourable balance of trade. Hakuseki, on the contrary, expressed no interest in expanding Japanese exports, and instead wished to isolate the country still further from the evils of foreign commerce.

Hakuseki's interest in the supply of non-renewable precious metals also coloured his views on the relationship between the money supply and prices. The high levels of inflation that had occurred since the debasement of the coinage in 1695 had provoked a lively debate amongst government advisers and officials on the determinants of price. In contrast to the prevailing view, which attributed inflation to the poor quality of the Genroku coinage, Hakuseki adopted a strict quantity theory of money (which he characteristically supported by detailed calculations of the amount of coin in circulation).

> As a rule, when the value of goods is high, the value of currency is low, and the reason for the low value of currency is its great quantity. In this situation, if we use laws to control the currency and reduce its quantity, the value of goods will fall and value of currency will increase. When the value of currency is high, because its quantity is low, we should use laws to increase the amount of coin in circulation. In this way, the value of currency and goods will be kept in balance, and wealth will flow abundantly throughout the nation.
>
> (Arai 1977: vol. 6, p. 191)

In a country whose currency was still largely based on precious metals, however, the problems of quantity and quality were not easily separable. When Hakuseki, as adviser to the shogun Ienobu, had the opportunity to put his theories into practice, the policy that he proposed in fact involved a reminting of the coinage, which would both reduce the quantity of gold in circulation and restore its quality to levels

ALBRIGHT COLLEGE LIBRARY 225825

approaching those of the early Tokugawa period. This rather drastic policy was put into effect in 1714, just after Ienobu's death. Unfortunately for Hakuseki, however, it did not result in a 'balance between the value of currency and of goods', nor did it cause wealth to 'flow abundantly throughout the nation'. The simple truth was that the machinery of Tokugawa financial administration lacked the sophistication necessary to carry out such a complex and far-reaching reform successfully. Poor-quality Genroku coins were allowed to remain in circulation alongside the new, reminted coinage, and attempts to regulate exchange rates between the various types of coin were unsuccessful. The reform therefore added further convolutions to the already complicated Tokugawa monetary system, and opened the way to large-scale speculation by the merchant class.

The failure of Hakuseki's policy of recoinage provided a basis on which his rival, Ogyū Sorai, could build an attack on Hakuseki's quantity theory of money. In his work, the *Seidan*, written some ten years after the currency reform of 1714, Sorai observed:

> If we compare today's gold coins with those issued at the time of the Genroku [1695] and Kenji [1711] debasements, we find that their quality has improved while the amount in circulation has fallen to half its previous level. The number of silver coins in circulation is only a third of what it was at the time of the Yotsuhō issue [1711]. But we cannot therefore say that prices have fallen by half since the Genroku and Kenji recoinages, nor that they have returned to their original level. In fact, most prices are ten to twenty times as high as they were forty or fifty years ago.
>
> (Ogyū 1973: 327)

In Sorai's eyes, the policy of recoinage was mistaken because it failed to grasp the moral and social causes of inflation.

> The reason why prices have risen is not that, during the Genroku recoinage, the currency was debased by mixing silver with gold and copper with silver. Nor have price rises been caused by an increase in the amount of gold and silver in circulation. Rather, the reasons are that people are living like guests in an inn, there is no proper system of etiquette [*reihō*] and the power of the merchants has increased. It is the accumulation of these factors which has caused the cost of goods to rise, and for this reason the amount of coinage expanded in the Genroku period and prices became more expensive.
>
> (Ogyū 1973: 333)

24

In this statement Sorai's views on prices appear more conservative and less original than Hakuseki's monetary theory. And yet Sorai's approach, when expanded in more detail, proves to contain a number of interesting contributions to the price debate. Sorai recognized that prices were not regulated by a single causative factor, but were subject to a variety of influences. While Hakuseki had focused exclusively on monetary influences, Sorai drew attention to the importance of costs of production and of the balance of supply and demand. In particular, he suggested three reasons for the continuation of inflation after the 1714 reform. The first was the increasing integration of a nationwide market centred around the great cities of Osaka and Edo. By the 1720s goods from the most distant provinces were being brought into Edo for sale, and transport costs, transaction costs, and local tariffs all added to the final retail price of these commodities. Sorai also noted that the high costs of land and housing in the capital were affecting the cost of a wide range of consumer goods. Second, with the growth of the exchange economy and the blurring of traditional social distinctions, commoners were coming to buy the higher-quality goods that had once been the preserve of the warrior class, and were therefore bidding up their prices. And last, the growing power of the merchants, and their tendency to collusion, enabled them to fix prices and to reap exorbitant profits (Ogyū 1973: 327–30).

In his search for an explanation of the paradox of rising prices at a time of reduced money supply, Sorai also arrived at a recognition of the importance of credit and of the velocity of circulation:

> In actuality, gold and silver do not remain in one place but move around from place to place and from one direction to another. For this reason, one hundred *ryō* of gold may perform the work of a hundred thousand *ryō*. But even if one hundred thousand *ryō* worth of promissory notes are added together, the amount of genuine coin at work is still only one hundred *ryō*. That is the nature of money.
>
> (Ogyū 1973: 337)

Sorai's ideas on prices were further developed by his disciple Dazai Shundai (1680–1747). In his *Keizai Roku*, Shundai not only discussed the problems of currency and inflation but also took up the issue, already touched on by Sorai, of the fluctuating exchange rates between different denominations of coin. He observed, for example, that the *samurai* obtain gold by selling their rice [stipends]. They they obtain copper coins in exchange for their gold, and with these copper coins they buy all their necessities. Such being the case, they are hard up when the value of gold is low and the value of copper coins high. Not so with tradesmen, who can make profits in either case. The best policy to pursue is to make copper coins plentiful so as to lower their value.

(Quoted in Honjō 1965: 66)

As this quotation suggests, Dazai Shundai, like Kumazawa Banzan and Ogyū Sorai, saw the protection of *samurai* status as a vital aim of economic policy. Where he differed from many of his predecessors and contemporaries, however, was in his willingness to accept that commerce, as well as agriculture, was an essential part of economic activity. Crops must not only be grown, they must also be bought and sold. Japan's rulers, Shundai suggested, should take greater advantage of this fact by extending the practice (already employed by some feudal lords) of establishing domain monopolies on the sale of specialized local products (Dazai 1972: 48–51).

But Shundai's support for the promotion of commerce did not imply support for the profit-making activities of the merchant class. On the contrary, one of the merits of the domain monopoly, in Shundai's eyes, was its ability to limit the power of merchants to build fortunes on the profits of trade. The image of the merchant continued to be that, painted by Ogyū Sorai, of the economic parasite who 'unlike the craftsman or farmer earns money just by sitting there without moving a muscle' (Ogyū 1973: 329). In order to find an intellectual defence of commercial profit-making by the merchant class, we must turn from the thought of *samurai* scholars to the writings of the newly-emerging bourgeois philosophers of eighteenth-century Japan.

THE VALUE OF COMMERCE:
ISHIDA BAIGAN (1685–1744)

The Genroku period not only saw the growth of urban culture and aesthetics, but also marked the beginnings of the emergence of a distinctive mercantile ethos that became increasingly articulate as the eighteenth century progressed. The merchant class of mid-Tokugawa Japan was certainly no group of malcontents or potential revolutionaries. The rice merchants, the cloth merchants, and the money-changers of Edo and Osaka were firmly integrated into the Tokugawa economic system and deeply imbued with the ruling-class Confucian concepts of obedience and service to the temporal authorities. But they combined belief in loyalty, honour, and respect for the social order with a sharp sense of thrift, calculation, and economic pragmatism which, to the modern reader, sometimes offers a refreshing contrast to the pious platitudes of Confucian orthodoxy.

This pragmatic spirit is, for example, vividly illustrated in the family rules of the house of Mitsui, which, by the early eighteenth century, had emerged as one of the most influential merchant families in Japan. The Mitsui code of behaviour, promulgated in 1722, includes the following clauses:

> Persons in public office are not, as a rule, prosperous. This is because they concentrate on discharging their public duties and neglect their own family affairs. Do not forget you are a merchant. You must regard dealings with the government always as a sideline of your business. It is therefore a great mistake to cast the family business aside and give precedence to government service. . . .
>
> It is each man's duty to believe in the gods and Buddha and to follow the teachings of Confucius. Nevertheless, it is not good to go to extremes. Those who are immoderate in religion will never be successful merchants. They are bound to neglect their own business and are likely to lead the House into ruin. Special care should be taken not to donate huge sums of money or treasures to temples or shrines.
>
> The gods and Buddha lie within one's heart. Therefore, you should not offer gold and silver to them and expect some special grace in return. Instead of wasting gold and silver on shrines and temples, you should make appropriate contributions to the poor and the suffering; the return will be ten thousand times as large, and your charitable deeds will be valued greatly.
>
> (Quoted in Roberts 1973: 502–3)

Perhaps the most influential figure in the formation of a coherent merchant ethos was the religious philosopher Ishida Baigan. Baigan was born into a peasant household in 1685, but was apprenticed at an early age to a merchant family in Kyoto. A keen student of Shintō, Confucian, and Buddhist thought, Baigan eventually abandoned commercial employment and, at the age of 45, set up a lecture hall in which he preached his own eclectic form of religious belief, *Shingaku* – the study of the 'heart' or 'soul'. Baigan's audience was largely drawn from the merchant stratum of Kyoto society, and his ethical system was remarkably well adapted to their intellectual and emotional needs. Rather than demanding (as Ogyū Sorai's school of Ancient Learning did) the rigourous study of Confucian classics, Baigan's *Shingaku* offered a path of enlightenment paved by meditation, self-restraint, and devotion to one's everyday tasks (Bellah 1957: 134–51; Yamazaki 1981: 89–93).

But even more importantly, Baigan, in contrast to Sorai and other *samurai* intellectuals, offered his merchant followers a philosophy that dignified, rather than condemned, the activities of trade and profit-making. In doing so, Baigan was not proposing any radical alteration to the Tokugawa status system. Unlike the seventeenth-century anarchist Andō Shōeki, he did not condemn the *samurai* class as 'lunatics indeed, who, while fed by the people and thus their sons, yet call the people their sons' (Norman 1949: 243). Instead, Baigan accepted the existence of the Tokugawa social order, and merely attempted to ensure for the merchant class an honoured place within that order. As he wrote in his collection of dialogues, the *Toi Mondō*:

> Warriors, farmers, artisans and merchants are all of assistance in governing the nation. It would not do for any one class to be missing. . . . The *samurai* are vassals who possess high rank. The farmers are the vassals of the fields, and the merchants and artisans are the vassals of the town. . . . The artisans receive their stipend through the wages which are paid in return for their work. The farmers, receive profit from cultivation, and this, too, is just like the stipend received by the *samurai*. Without the productive work of all people, the nation could not stand. The merchant's profit is also like the stipend allowed to officials. If one says to the merchant, 'Your profit alone is a sign of greed, and therefore a deviation from the right path', one is hating the merchant and wishing for his destruction. Why should the merchant alone be detested as an inferior being?
>
> (Ishida 1972: 226)

The American historian Robert Bellah has argued that Baigan's ethical system contributed to the emergence within Japan of a religious environment which (like European Protestantism) was exceptionally conducive to modernization and rationalization (Bellah 1957; his arguments are somewhat qualified in a more recent essay – see Bellah 1978). This view obviously raises the problem of determining how far philosophies like those of Ishida Baigan were causes of, rather than responses to, the rise of a monetarized market economy. For present purposes, however, a more important point is perhaps to consider the logic by which Baigan attempted to justify the profit-making activities of the merchant class. This logic reveals some interesting parallels with the notion of enlightened self-interest which permeated the writings of the European classical economists.

An important difference between the stipend of the *samurai* and the merchant's profit is the fact that, while the one is fixed by law or custom, the other varies according to market circumstances and the skill or cunning of the merchant. Baigan's ethical system does not offer a justification for boundless and unmitigated profiteering, but rather for profit based on honesty (*shōjiki*). In this context, however, 'honesty' means more than the mere avoidance of deceit. It is, as Yamazaki puts it, 'none other than the "innate heart"', that is, the original spirit with which one was born' (Yamazaki 1981: 94).

The 'Way of the Merchant' involves the cultivation of insight into one's true nature. When this insight is achieved, merchants will understand that their real interests lie not in the instant gratification of avarice, but in diligence and frugality, or (to put it another way) in both offering and demanding the best possible value in all their transactions. If all people, both merchants and their customers, conform to this ethos, they will in the long run ensure the greatest prosperity for all.

> Merchants keep careful day-to-day accounts, and therefore regard every *zeni* [copper coin] as being important. The Way of the Merchant is to amass *zeni* until they accumulate wealth. . . The people's mind is like our mind. If we are sparing of every *zeni*, and pay attention to our buying and selling so as not to waste anything, however small, we should think that our customers will also in the first place be thrifty with their money. We should therefore provide good commodities in order to overcome this frugality. If frugality can be overcome benefit will accrue to the people. Thus, when the wealth of the nation circulates about, all people will experience satisfaction, just as the circling of the seasons causes all things to flourish.
>
> (Ishida 1972: 195–6)

The mechanism that ensures this convergence of interests is the market, whose prices define the parameters of permissible profit. In Baigan's scheme, merchants may obtain profit by buying when market prices are low and selling when they are high, but may not reap a 'double profit' by skimping on the quality or quantity of goods sold, or by paying less than market rates to the farmers or artisans whose products they buy (Ishida 1972: 228).

> Goods which do not conform to the publicly determined price are at odds with the requirements of the moment. Prices should not differ [from the prevailing market price]. . . . If, in spite of this, one merchant should decide to be different from others, and say, 'My investment was so much, and my profit must be so much', matters would become difficult. This is the truth. If we deny this truth there can be no commerce. If there were no commerce customers would face inconvenience, and sellers would have no means of selling. Thus, merchants would be unable to live, and would become farmers or artisans.
>
> (Ishida 1972: 226)

The market mechanism, therefore, ensures that the attempt to gain dishonest profit is ultimately self-defeating, 'like eating a sweet poison, from which you yourself are likely to die' (Ishida 1972: 228). Merchants who have experienced enlightenment (*satori*), on the contrary, enrich the entire society while pursuing their own legitimate profit, and are therefore 'the jewels of heaven and earth' (Ishida 1972: 196).

EXCHANGE AS THE MEASURE OF ALL THINGS: KAIHO SEIRYŌ (1755–1817)

As the new ideas on the value of precious metals and the dignity of trade undermined the old certainties of the natural economy, so space was created for the growth of a wide range of new and challenging economic and political perspectives. The social thought of late Tokugawa Japan, indeed, contains such originality and diversity that it is difficult to divide into clearly defined schools or categories.

The conventional division distinguishes three groups: Confucian scholars, adherents of the school of National Learning (*Kokugaku*), and students of Dutch Learning (*Rangaku*) (see for example Varley 1973: Chap. 8). But from the point of view of the history of economic thought, these divisions must be treated with some caution. It is certainly true that a nationalistic, Shintō-inspired stream of thought (on the one hand) and a growing awareness of Western scientific ideas (on the other) came to exert an influence on the philosophers of late Tokugawa Japan which rivalled that of Confucian and neo-Confucian traditions. But in many of the most interesting economic works of the period these three intellectual currents are not counterposed, but inseparably intermingled. In fact, it sometimes seems that the more Japanese thinkers became aware of the scientific and technological dominance of the West, the more they sought – in Shintō mythology and Confucian ethics – traditions that might enable them to withstand that dominance.

Instead of contrasting National Learning and Dutch Learning with each other or with Confucian thought, I shall instead look at two contemporaries – Kaiho Seiryō and Satō Nobuhiro – who used ideas drawn from these varied traditions in order to develop quite different approaches to the economic problems of late eighteenth- and early nineteenth-century Japan.

Both Seiryō and Nobuhiro were men of wide-ranging interests and enquiring minds who travelled throughout Japan, indefatigably collecting the facts, figures, and anecdotes with which they illustrated their voluminous writings. The world they saw in their travels through the Japanese countryside was in the midst of profound and, in some ways, disturbing change. The influence of the market economy was by now reaching even into remote villages, bringing with it greater specialization, new agricultural technologies, and increased productivity, but also a growing separation of the peasantry into rich and poor.

These paradoxes of economic development emerge in sharp relief from the writings of Seiryō and Nobuhiro. Seiryō's *Keiko Dan* includes admiring accounts of the ingenuity and prosperity of rural *sake* brewers and rice merchants, while Nobuhiro writes in almost lyrical terms of the new crops and farming techniques that he observed working their gradual transformations of Japanese rural life. But Nobuhiro in particular is also acutely conscious of the large number of peasants who, unable to take advantage of the commercial economy, were falling further and further into debt and despair.

> Recently in every region the rich have come to be admired, and poor people are despised. This is a great mistake, for poor people cause little harm to a country, but where there are rich people the troubles of the country are increased. The reason for this is that, when rich farmers prosper, they absorb the property of several dozen families. As a result, troubles and distress push the small farmers deeper into poverty, and they sell their fields and houses to the big farmers and become beggars or vagrants.
>
> (Satō 1926: vol. 1, pp. 682–3)

31

The commercialization of the rural economy therefore created new financial and political frictions within the Tokugawa social order. These frictions were partially expressed in increasingly frequent peasant riots, often directed at wealthy farmers and rice merchants, and culminating in the Ōshio Rebellion of 1837, in which one quarter of the city of Osaka was burnt to the ground.

In the eyes of Kaiho Seiryō, the intractable economic and social problems of late Tokugawa Japan pointed to an inescapable and iconoclastic conclusion: precepts drawn from ancient tradition or from the writings of the early Confucian sages were no longer directly applicable to the circumstances of contemporary Japan. The old ideas were not to be taken at face value, but had to be modified and adapted in the light of practical experience.

> Learning does not only mean a precise knowledge of ancient things. Real learning also means a precise knowledge of present day affairs. Many of the deeds which occur today are not encompassed by the wisdom of the Ancients. In general, we can say that learning is useless if it does not shed light upon the present.
>
> (Kaiho 1970: 247–8)

Thus, although Seiryō was deeply influenced by the writings of Confucian philosophers such as Ogyū Sorai and Dazai Shundai, he took a sceptical approach to many of their economic and political ideas. His scorn was particularly directed at the traditional Confucian notion of the benevolent ruler whose enlightened government would bring peace, abundance, leisure, and prosperity to the whole country. After savagely caricaturing this ideal world where 'both high and low relax and enjoy themselves . . . and every variety of food and drink falls as though from heaven', he concluded sternly that

> [t]he world where the rulers do not work and yet receive the respect of their subjects, and where the subjects do not work and yet the rulers act like great benefactors and provide goods as charity, will never exist in a million years.
>
> (Quoted in Kata 1962: 164)

For Seiryō, then, the key to prosperity lay not in the wisdom and kindness of the ruler, but in the hard work and initiative of the entire population. In this sense, his ideas seem to contain an echo of Ishida Baigan's ethos of diligence. This impression is reinforced by the fact that Seiryō, like Baigan, had a high regard for the virtues of the merchant class. Although he himself came from an Edo *samurai* family, Seiryō's travels brought him into frequent contact with urban and rural merchants, and left him with a deep admiration for their initiative, thrift, and determination. In fact, the merchant's pursuit of profit (*kōri*) is elevated in Seiryō's writings to the status of a vital principle for solving the economic problems of the day (Kaiho 1970: 243–7; see also Najita 1978: 27–9).

The particular importance of *kōri*, from Seiryō's point of view, was its relevance to the economic difficulties of the ruling class. Although in certain domains the *daimyō* had developed monopolies of specialized crops or manufactured products, the rice tax continued to be the cornerstone of domain and shogunal finances. This meant that as commerce expanded and the economy became more complex and diversified, so the government was increasingly failing to tap the new sources of wealth that were being created throughout Japan. Caught between rising expenditure and a relatively fixed source of income, *daimyō* and shogun were repeatedly forced to resort to borrowing from large merchant houses, or to still more drastic measures such as cutting the stipends paid to their *samurai* retinues.

This issue, which deeply concerned Kaiho Seiryō, was in essence merely the steadily worsening problem addressed by Kumazawa Banzan in the mid-seventeenth century: the impoverishment of the warrior class relative to the increasing wealth of the merchant class. By comparing Banzan and Seiryō's solutions to this dilemma, therefore, we can see how far Japanese society and social thought had come since the first century of Tokugawa rule. Far from proposing a retreat from the money economy (as Banzan had done), Seiryō argued that the *samurai* should abandon their distaste for commerce and imitate the profit-making activities of the merchant. Where traditional wisdom prescribed frugality as the cure for the financial crisis of the domains, Seiryō also explored the ways in which income could be expanded to meet expenditure, suggesting, for example, that domain governments should promote the production of crops particularly suited to their regions, and share in the profits obtained from exporting these crops to other parts of Japan.

But the most original aspect of Seiryō's economic thought is the logic which he uses to defend *samurai* participation in commerce. Here, he goes far beyond Ishida Baigan's defence of trade (see p. 28) and develops an approach which interprets all social relationships as being in essence market transactions.

From ancient times, the relationship between lord and retainer has been like the relationship of the market. The retainer is granted a stipend, and gives his service to his lord in return. The lord buys from the retainer, and the retainer sells to the lord. It is a market exchange, and this buying and selling is a good and not an evil thing.

(Kaiho 1970: 222)

The ultimate conclusion of this line of reasoning is the identification of market exchange as the principle (*ri*) which, in Confucian thought, imparts order and harmony to human society. All social relationships, Seiryō argues, are based on exchange, and exchange is motivated by the desire to obtain benefit (i.e. profit). Commerce and profit-making therefore come to be seen as vital forces regulating the natural order of things.

All things between heaven and earth are commodities for exchange [*shiromono*], and it is the law of commodities that they should produce other commodities. Without exception, fields produce rice and money produces profit. It is the law of the universe that mountains produce timber, the sea produces fish and salt, and money and rice produce profit.

(Kaiho 1970: 222)

Thus, in Seiryō's writings the language and imagery of Confucian thought is transformed into the rationality of market exchange, and the virtues of Confucian ethics undergo a metamorphosis to emerge as the values of a nascent capitalist economy. Although there is little evidence that Seiryō's proposals for economic reform were directly implemented by domain governments, it is significant that Seiryō discussed his ideas with middle-ranking *samurai* officials in various regions of Japan (Kuranami 1970: 499–500) and so, perhaps, played a part in preparing the ground for the profound changes in economic and political structure that were to take place half a century after his death.

A VISION OF THE STATE-CONTROLLED ECONOMY: SATŌ NOBUHIRO (1769–1850)

Like Kaiho Seiryō, Satō Nobuhiro was an enthusiastic advocate of the view that the political authorities should be directly involved in wealth-creating activities. But the logic on which Nobuhiro based his arguments was quite different from that of Seiryō. While Seiryō extended the laws of market exchange to cover even the political relationship between ruler and ruled, Satō Nobuhiro's economic analysis worked, as it were, in the opposite direction. Nobuhiro's basic principle is precisely the principle that Seiryō rejected: the notion of the benevolent ruler whose greatest duty is to relieve the sufferings of the people.

> *Keizai* [economy] means managing the nation, developing its products, enriching the country and rescuing all its people from suffering. Thus the person who rules the country must be able to carry out his important task without relaxing his vigilance even for a single day. If this administration of *keizai* is neglected, the country will inevitably become weakened, and both rulers and people will lack the necessities of life.
>
> (Satō 1977c: 522)

In this rather conventional recital of the duties of the virtuous ruler, three words stand out: 'developing its products'. Nobuhiro's wise government is not simply one which practices the traditional virtues of charity and justice, but one which actively intervenes to promote prosperity through the introduction of new techniques and new types of production. Thus as his ideas unfold, we find ourselves confronting concepts that are less and less reminiscent of the benevolent feudal prince, and increasingly suggestive of the centralized, development-oriented nation state.

This aspect of Nobuhiro's thought is most clearly evident in his vision of utopia. His picture of the ideal government recurs in several of his economic writings but is most clearly delineated in his extraordinary work, the *Suitō Hiroku* (Confidential Memorandum on Government), probably written in the early 1830s (Shimazaki 1977: 641). In this work Nobuhiro depicts a nation in which the institutions of the Tokugawa social order have been transformed into the implements of a quite different form of social control. The four status groups – warriors, peasants, artisans, and merchants – are replaced by eight occupational classes: farmers, forestry workers, miners, crafts people, merchants, unskilled workers, mariners, and fishermen. Each class is to live in strict segregation from the others, and is to be assigned to the control of one of the six ministries (*fu*) that play the central role in the operation of Nobuhiro's ideal economy: the Ministries of Basic Affairs (i.e. Agriculture), Development, Manufacturing, Circulation, Army, and Navy. (This ministerial structure was loosely based on the ancient Chinese model of government.)

Each ministry has substantial economic functions (the Ministry of the Navy, for example, is responsible for the shipbuilding and fishing industries), but it is the first four which are of particular interest from an economic point of view. The central emphasis in Nobuhiro's description of the duties of these ministries is on development, which is to be achieved through education, training, and the introduction of new technologies. The Ministry of Basic Affairs is to investigate improved agricultural methods and open up new land for farming. The Ministry of Development (which is responsible for forestry and mining) is to promote plantation projects, survey mineral resources, and train miners in better extractive techniques, while the Ministry of Manufactures is assigned the task of expanding the production of necessities such as farm implements, furniture, and transport vehicles, while discouraging the making of luxury goods (Satō 1977b: 489–500).

Since Nobuhiro's utopia has a state-controlled economy, a particularly crucial function is performed by the Ministry of Circulation, which is responsible for the distribution of goods, and so acquires a distant resemblance to the modern planning agency. All commodities are to be bought and sold by this ministry, which is also empowered to

[s]tandardise the price of goods produced by each region, conduct trade with foreign countries, and apply the profits of this trade within the nation so that posterity may flourish.

(Satō 1977b: 503)

In the light of subsequent Japanese development, it is intriguing to observe the place of education in Nobuhiro's scheme for national economic development. A full chapter of his Memorandum is devoted to the subject, and includes a proposal for a nationwide school system to provide a basic moral education for all children from the age of eight. Male children who display particular intelligence are to be selected for a more rigorous education which culminates in training for public service. The educational authorities of the utopian state are also to be in charge of a comprehensive network of welfare institutions, including hospitals and nurseries for the children of the poor (Satō 1977b: 511–16).

If Nobuhiro's emphasis on education, both as a means to economic development and as a tool for social control, foreshadows the policies of later Japanese governments, so too does his advocacy of foreign trade. Here Nobuhiro was influenced by the ideas of his slightly older contemporary Honda Toshiaki (1744–1821). In works such as the *Keisei Hisaku* (Secret Policy for Governing the Country) and *Seiiki Monogatari* (Tales of the Western Regions), Toshiaki had not only provided a relatively detailed (if second-hand) description of European geography and customs but had also argued forcefully for the expansion of foreign trade and for Japanese colonization of neighbouring islands.

Nobuhiro encountered these ideas in early adulthood, when he spent some years in Edo studying under prominent scholars of Dutch Learning. Although he embraced the notions of foreign trade and colonization with enthusiasm, he combined them with the language and imagery of Shintō revivalism in a way that gives his writings a peculiarly nationalistic flavour. Like Honda Toshiaki and other students of Dutch Learning, Nobuhiro was impressed by the growing evidence from Europe that trade could enhance a nation's wealth and influence.

> In the present-day world the country of England is militarily powerful and prosperous, and has control over a very large number of foreign nations, so that the world trembles at its might. This country may be likened to Japan, but the English homelands lie between fifty degrees and sixty degrees north, and as a northern land it has a cold climate and its natural products are excelled by our Japanese products. However, because they have successfully sent ships out across the oceans and have traded with the nations of the world they have now become a most powerful and thriving people. Thus we can know that shipping and trade are important tasks for the nation.
>
> (Quoted in Kata 1962: 257)

But similar evocations of geographical determinism, when combined with fashionable Shintō terminology, could easily be turned into mystical arguments for expansionism and world domination:

> If we consider the whole nation of Japan in terms of the geography of all other nations, we can see that it lies between thirty degrees and forty-five degrees north of the equator. The climate is mild, the soil is fertile and many natural products grow in great abundance. Our country faces the ocean on four sides and is unsurpassed among the nations for its ease of sea transport to neighbouring countries. Its people are also superior to those of other nations in their courage, and its natural conditions are outstanding

37

amongst all nations, and thus the country is perfectly equipped to control and advance nature and the world. By virtue of its superiority, this Land of the Gods, through conquering insignificant barbarians, would be able without difficulty to unite the world and dominate all the nations.

(Satō 1977a: 426)

It is hardly surprising that Nobuhiro's works found an appreciative readership amongst the nationalists of 1930s Japan, and that, as a consequence, they have been rather neglected by post-war academics. But this neglect is unfortunate, for Nobuhiro's ideas not only form part of a significant tradition in Japanese economic and political thought; with their emphasis on state control, welfare, and nationalism, they also represent a response to the problems and paradoxes of the commercial economy which was by no means unique to Japan.

THE OPENING OF FOREIGN TRADE:
YOKOI SHŌNAN (1809-69)

Although the structures of Tokugawa rule were, little by little, crumbling from within, it was an external force which precipitated their ultimate collapse. In an age when European colonialism was reaching its zenith, Japan could no longer hope to remain enclosed in perpetual isolation. The Opium War of 1840-2 and its disastrous consequences for China were reported and debated in Japan, and from that time on the unwelcome appearance of foreign ships off the Japanese coast became an increasingly common occurrence. A vessel called at Nagasaki in 1846, two American ships visited Uraga in the same year, and a British boat stopped at Shimoda in 1848.

It was, however, the arrival of Commodore Matthew Perry in 1853, with his flotilla of four ships (two of them steam-powered) and his formal message from the president of the United States, which presented the shogunate with a foreign challenge that could not be ignored. The implications of this challenge were enormous, for the policy of seclusion was so closely interwoven with the whole Tokugawa notion of order and stability that the one could not be abandoned without the collapse of the other. Japanese political and moral philosophers were faced not only with an imminent threat to the social system in which their ideas were embedded, but also with a possible influx of relatively unknown foreign beliefs, customs, and mores.

In order to appreciate the impact of this challenge on Japanese economic thought, let us consider the life and writings of one of the most prominent *samurai* scholars who lived through the momentous events of the 1850s and 1860s. Yokoi Shōnan was in many ways an intellectual in the classical Tokugawa mould. The younger son of a middle-ranking *samurai* family in the southern domain of Kumamoto, Shōnan was educated at the domain school (an establishment mainly designed for the training of *samurai* officials), and showed such brilliance that he was selected for the unusual privilege of furthering his education in Edo. During his stay in the capital he came under the influence of both the Ancient Learning propagated by the successors of Ogyū Sorai, and the teachings of the Mito school, a group of nationalist scholars based in the Domain of Mito, north of Edo. In 1840, however, Shōnan fell into disgrace, apparently as a result of an indiscretion committed while he was drunk. Deprived of the prospect of promotion within the Domain establishment, Shōnan then set himself up as an independent scholar and teacher, travelled widely within Japan establishing contacts with other administrators and intellectuals, and acquired a substantial reputation as an educationalist and social philosopher.

The main innovation that Shōnan brought to social thought was a form of pragmatism. His 'Realist' school (*Jitsugaku*) echoed the view of the Chinese philosopher, Wang-Yang-ming, that 'to know and not to act is not yet to know'. Learning, however precise or profound, was not true learning unless it could be applied to improving the practical affairs of society. In his economic writings, Shōnan applied this realist philosophy particularly to the duties of the ruler to 'relieve the sufferings of the people', but until the arrival of Perry, Shōnan's approach to foreign nations was essentially a conservative one. Like the Mito school with which he was closely associated, he believed in the innate moral superiority of the Japanese nation and in the necessity of warding off the intrusions of the foreign 'barbarians' at all costs.

Closer contact with the technological might of the West, however, forced Shōnan to revise his approach to the foreign menace. Shortly after the arrival of Perry, when the Russian admiral Putiatin arrived in Nagasaki to open trade negotiations for his country, Shōnan submitted a memorandum to the Japanese negotiators which marked the beginning of his transformation into an advocate of foreign trade. In this document, Shōnan continued to assert the natural superiority of Japan, 'the most excellent nation in the world' (Yokoi 1971a: 434). But rather than arguing that the Shogunate should reject all approaches from foreign counties, he suggested that Japan should seek to distinguish 'righteous nations' (*yūdō no kuni*) from those that lack 'righteousness' (*mudō no kuni*), and to develop political and economic relations with the former (Yokoi 1971a: 434–7). Within a matter of years, his views on trade had become even more outspoken, and he had emerged as a leading proponent of *kaikoku* – the opening of the country.

Shōnan's changing attitude to foreign trade can, no doubt, partly be attributed to the weaknesses of the nationalist Mito school. For all their brave words about 'expelling the barbarian', the Mito scholars had shown little ability to offer practical solutions to the problems posed by Perry's arrival (Yamaguchi 1971: 693–4). But growing support for foreign trade also reflected an increasing awareness of the realities of the world outside Japan. As the shogunate vacillated between a desire to restrict the intrusions of the foreign powers and fear of provoking their aggression, the cracks in the walls of Japanese isolation gradually widened. In 1859 the Western powers were granted rights to trade in the parts of Yokohama, Nagasaki, and Hakodate, and the following year the first Japanese official mission was dispatched to the United States.

Such channels of contact brought an increasing knowledge of Western social and economic systems, and an increasing appreciation of Western military and technological capabilities. By 1860, Shōnan, who never travelled outside Japan and probably never read any major Western economic, political, or social text, had acquired some surprising, if rather idealized, insights into the nature of Western society. Of the United States he wrote, for example:

In America, since the time of Washington, three major policies have been established. The first is to prevent wars throughout the world, since there is nothing on earth as wretched as killing one another. The second is to gather knowledge from all nations so as to enrich the economy. And the third is that the President's power shall not be hereditary, but is handed on to a wise man who is elected as his successor.

(Yokoi 1971b: 448)

It would be a mistake, however, to see Shōnan as evolving from nationalist to internationalist. Throughout, his fundamental aim remained unaltered and identical with the fundamental aim of those scholars and politicians who continued to call for the 'expulsion of the barbarians': it was, in other words, to ensure the strength and integrity of the Japanese nation. Shōnan's pragmatic political philosophy, however, helped him to appreciate, more rapidly than some of his associates, that new means must be found to achieve this objective.

Shōnan's fully developed answer to the questions raised by the foreign menace was spelled out in his *Three Principles of National Policy* (*Kokuze Sanron*), written in 1860. The three principles in question were the principle of a prosperous country (*fukoku ron*), the principle of a strong army (*kyōhei ron*), and the way of the warrior (*shidō*). The concept of a 'prosperous country and a strong army' (*fukoku kyōhei*) appears recurrently in Tokugawa economic writings, and had been given particular emphasis by Honda Toshiaki and Satō Nobuhiro. The creation of a prosperous country, according to Shōnan, would inescapably involve the opening of Japan to foreign trade. Foreign trade was necessary not only because it would bring a variety of economic benefits but also because, ultimately, it was part of a universal order from which Japan could not remain exempt.

> The fortunes of the universe and the condition of the world cannot be governed by the selfish will of human beings. Thus Japan cannot maintain its policy of isolation just because this suits the convenience of one country.
>
> (Yokoi 1971a: 434)

At the same time, however, Shōnan perceived that opening the country in its present state to unlimited foreign trade would surely result in disaster. Nothing less than a total reconstruction of the economic and political system was necessary if Japan was to enjoy the potential benefits of free interaction with the outside world.

In the economic sphere, Shōnan called for the complete dismantling of the feudal restrictions on occupational mobility and inter-domain trade. He did not, however, espouse a doctrine of *laissez-faire*, but instead saw the state as playing a central role in promoting economic development. In this respect, his views are reminiscent of the ideas of Satō Nobuhiro. Shōnan's proposals for government intervention, however, are much more modest than Nobuhiro's sweeping visions of a controlled economy. The government, states Shōnan (and here he is still thinking in terms of domain rather than national government), should promote new forms of agricultural production by offering loans to farmers. It should also test new agricultural technology and equipment, and train farmers in the best methods of production. These proposals are not confined to the farm sector.

In relation to crafts and commerce the same applies. The government should participate in new forms of production by providing loans of money and provisions, and by teaching skills, and in this way should seek to raise profits.

(Yokoi 1971b: 433)

In order to finance these projects, Shōnan advocated that the government should pursue an expansionary monetary policy. This was justified by a rather naïve vision of an unlimited overseas market for Japanese goods, and a somewhat limited understanding of the effects of monetary expansion on the domestic economy.

Let us explain this with an example. Suppose the government prints 10,000 ryō in paper money and lends it to the people for silk production. The Domain government then collects the silk thread which they produce, takes it to the port, and sells it to western merchants for about 11,000 ryō in gold coin. In this way, in a few months, paper money has been turned into real money at great gain, and in addition 1,000 ryō of pure profit has been made.

(Yokoi 1971b: 445)

Shōnan's proposals may have been at times simplistic, but in their recognition of the need for a radical change of the system they struck at the heart of the problem. Moreover, because of his established position in Japanese intellectual life, Shōnan was able to have a considerable influence on practical politics. He acted as occasional adviser to Matsudaira Yoshinaga, *Daimyō* of Echizen, who was to play a central role in the events leading up to the Meiji Restoration. His closest disciple, Yuri Kimimasa, was to be one of the principal architects of early Meiji administrative and financial reforms.

But Shōnan was far from being the only member of the *samurai* class to recognize the need for a radical reform of the economic and political system. Throughout the outerlying domains in particular, opposition to the shogunate was gathering strength, and in 1867–8 it reached a climax in the swift and successful military action which brought an end to two-and-a-half centuries of Tokugawa rule and created a new national government under the nominal leadership of the Emperor Meiji.

The Meiji Restoration opened the way to a new era of Japanese economic development, in which the concept of a 'prosperous country and a strong army' would become the core of the nation's economic policies. Shōnan himself, however, did not live to see his proposals put into practice. The year after the fall of the shogunate, in revenge for his betrayal of the ideal of 'expelling the barbarian', he was assassinated by a conservative extremist.

CONCLUSIONS

On the eve of its first phase of modern industrial growth, Japanese thought contained no category which corresponded precisely to the twentieth-century notion of economics. Indeed, in Europe itself, the intellectual boundaries that would separate economics from the other social sciences were still being drawn. In Japan, the notion of *keikoku saimin* (administering the nation and relieving the sufferings of the people) placed economic thought firmly within the tradition of Confucian debates on the nature of morality, justice, and social order. But in response to the economic changes of the past two centuries, Japanese thinkers had built on those traditions in a variety of new and inventive ways.

The orthodox notion of the static, rice-based economy had fallen into increasing disrepute, and Japanese philosophers had not only accepted the existence of the money economy but also analysed its workings and debated its consequences for the social order. The growing economic power of the merchant class was reflected in the beginnings of a moral philosophy which legitimized commerce and the pursuit of profit, and even led (in the case of Kaiho Seiryō) to a vision of the market as the measure of all things. During the decades immediately preceding the Meiji Restoration, the advantages and disadvantages of foreign trade had been hotly debated, and the role of the government as an active agent in the promotion of economic development was also emerging as an important topic of controversy. The existence of these ideas and debates within Japan meant that Western economic thought, as it began to be explored, appeared not as something utterly alien and incomprehensible, but as a body of knowledge containing many branches that could be related to and grafted on to the existing stock of Japanese thought.

2

The introduction of Western economic thought: from the Meiji Restoration to the First World War

With the Meiji Restoration of 1868 the flow of Western ideas into Japan turned from an uncertain trickle to a flood. In the famous words of the Charter Oath issued by the Emperor Meiji in 1868, the government resolved that 'knowledge shall be sought throughout the world so as to strengthen the foundations of imperial rule' (Tsunoda *et al.* 1964: vol. 2, p. 137). The study of Western social and economic thought inevitably constituted an important part of that knowledge.

The introduction of Western thought into Asian countries in the nineteenth and twentieth centuries was frequently as much a destructive as a creative process. Where colonialism imposed Western learning on non-European societies, the consequence was often the extinguishing of local traditions of scholarship, rather than the cross-fertilization of European and indigenous thought (Goonatilake 1984). Because Japan retained its independence, however, Japanese scholars seem to have had rather less difficulty in maintaining contact with their country's earlier intellectual traditions. This is not to deny that much Meiji (and later) economic research consisted of the translation and emulation of Western scholarship. But as the historian of ideas, Maruyama Masao, says:

> To divide [modern Japanese thought] into 'traditional' and 'non-traditional' categories is to make a major mistake. Foreign ideas have been absorbed and incorporated in various ways into our consciousness and way of life, and have stamped their indelible mark on our culture. In this sense, European ideas, too, have long since become part of our tradition. . . . If we analyse the numerous elements which compose our processes of thought and expression, and retrace the lineage of each of these elements, we come across fragments of many ideas which have left their traces on our history.

These include Buddhism, Confucianism, Shamanism and Western thought.

(Maruyama 1961: 8)

Maruyama goes on to suggest that Japanese thinkers have tended to combine these elements in a rather random and eclectic way, and therefore that the development of Japanese ideas has been characterized by a lack of continuity and coherence. As far as Japanese economic thought is concerned, however, the haphazard mixing of Western and non-Western ideas is not particularly evident. Instead, it is perhaps more helpful to think of the pre-Meiji traditions of economic philosophy as providing a framework that (together with the peculiarities of Japan's nineteenth- and twentieth-century development) determined the types of Western ideas that were widely accepted, and the ways in which these ideas were understood by Japanese scholars. In this chapter we shall examine the process by which Japanese thinkers, as they became increasingly familiar with Western economics, began to select certain Western ideas as being particularly relevant to their interests, and to give these ideas a specifically Japanese interpretation.

THE MEIJI POLITICAL AND ECONOMIC REFORMS

The Meiji Restoration opened the way for a fundamental reorganization of Japan's political and economic system. In 1869 the independent political and economic powers of the domains were abolished, and Japan became a unitary and centralized state. The status divisions of the Tokugawa system were also removed, giving all Japanese men theoretical equality in the eyes of the law (though the legal rights of men and women remained unequal). These political reforms laid the foundations for an energetic pusuit of that ideal proposed by Yokoi Shōnan and other late Tokugawa thinkers: the ideal of 'a prosperous country and a strong army'.

The views of the Tokugawa proponents of *kaikoku* are also reflected in the methods by which the Meiji government sought to enrich and strengthen the country. The state, particularly in the early Meiji period, played an active part in fostering new industries and in encouraging the import of modern technology from overseas. During the 1870s the creation of railway, postal, and telegraph networks was begun, and a national banking system established. The government also set up a number of textile, engineering, and other factories that were

45

later sold to private industry at extremely favourable prices. These policies, as well as the establishment of a modern conscript army, were financed by means of a new nationwide land tax, paid in money rather than rice and based not on the yield of the annual harvest, but on the value of the agricultural holding.

The attempt to develop a modern industrial economy necessarily demanded a knowledge of modern economic ideas. In Western Europe theories on taxation, the financial system, the division of labour, international trade, and so on had developed gradually in step with the emergence of a capitalist economy. The Japanese government was, however, faced with the task not only of promoting the import of Western economic institutions but also of encouraging the diffusion of the complex body of knowledge needed to run those institutions effectively. For the economists of late nineteenth-century and early twentieth-century Japan, the simultaneous introduction of an industrial capitalist system and of foreign theories about that system was to create formidable intellectual problems.

MEIJI EDUCATION AND ECONOMIC THOUGHT

Even the Tokugawa shogunate in its last years had become increasingly conscious of the need to promote the study of certain aspects of foreign knowledge. In 1855, two years after the arrival of Commodore Perry, the government opened a school in Edo to train translators of foreign languages: initially Dutch, but later also English, French, and German. The school underwent a number of changes of name in the course of its history, but is best known under the name it bore from 1856 to 1862, as the *Bansho Shirabesho* (Institute for the Study of Barbarian Writings). During the 1860s the Institute, which by then had some 200 students, broadened its curriculum to include military science, navigation, mathematics, metallurgy, cartography, and eventually also geography, history, and physics. Economics was not taught, but the *Bansho Shirabesho* was to play an important part in the introduction of Western economic ideas for two reasons. First, its students and staff included a number of scholars such as Kanda Takahira and Tsuda Mamichi who were amongst the first translators and propagators of Western economic knowledge. Second, it was one of several educational institutions that were eventually brought together to form Japan's first university – Tokyo Imperial University (Tamanoi 1971: 8, 27–9).

Tokyo University, founded in 1877 primarily to train administrators

46

and public servants, has been of enormous importance in the development of Japanese economics, and indeed of modern Japanese scholarship as a whole. Economics was included in its curriculum from the start, initially as an area of study within the Faculty of Letters, and ultimately as a Faculty in its own right. In the early stages, understandably enough, the quality of economics teaching seems to have left something to be desired. The first professor of economics, the young American academic Ernest Fenollosa (1853–1909), was unquestionably an outstanding scholar, but his main area of expertise was philosophy, which he taught, together with politics and economics, at Tokyo University. He was to achieve a lasting reputation neither as a philosopher nor an economist, but as a connoisseur of Japanese art. Lectures in the 1870s and 1880s were commonly given in foreign languages, either by American or European teachers or by Japanese teachers working from foreign texts. Interestingly enough, at least one set of notes, compiled by a student who attended Fenollosa's lectures in 1882–3, still survives. The neat jottings, in English interspersed with occasional words or phrases in Japanese, show that Fenollosa's students were offered an introduction to the ideas of W. Roscher, Friedrich List, J.S. Mill (of whom Fenollosa seems to have been somewhat critical), W.S. Jevons, and J.D. Macleod amongst others, but they also suggest some difficulties in the communication and understanding of these ideas. Of Macleod, for example, the student notes enigmatically:

Mr Macleod says Political Economy is the science of Exchange. He tries to find out some of universal which explain every thing. He speaks of exchangeable quantities. . . . Law of Demand and Supply. Law of Cost of Production. Law of Utility. Law of Labour in things. There are many such assertions. But they are valueless and the real use of Pol. Econo. is to find out certain forces which are really acting actually.

(quoted in Sugihara 1980: 52–3)

Despite hesitant beginnings, however, Tokyo University's economics department was by the end of the century nurturing scholars who were to make significant and original contributions to modern Japanese thought.

In addition to the government-financed Imperial Universities of Tokyo and Kyoto (the latter established in 1897), a number of private colleges also played a crucial role in the dissemination of Western economic thought. The earliest of these was Keiō Gijuku, set up on a modest scale in 1858 by the leading proponent of Western liberalism, Fukuzawa Yukichi (1835–1901). Like the *Bansho Shirabesho* Fukuzawa's school initially concentrated on the teaching of foreign languages. In a matter of years, however, it had become a vehicle for the propogation of Fukuzawa's vision of 'civilization and enlightenment' (*bunmei kaika*). During visits to the West in 1860, 1862, and 1867, Fukuzawa collected Western writings on physics, chemistry, mathematics, history, philosophy, and economics – including the American academic Francis Wayland's *Elements of Political Economy* – which he then introduced into the curriculum of Keiō. His college thus became the only educational institution to teach Western economics before the Meiji Restoration (Koizumi 1966: 17–23; Blacker 1969: 9).

Like Keiō, Hitotsubashi University, which was to become one of Japan's most important centres of economic research, owes its origins to the efforts of an individual advocate of 'civilization and enlightenment'. It was founded in 1875 by Mori Arinori (1847–89) – later to become Japan's first Minister of Education – and was intended specifically to train students in commercial and economic skills. Originally called the School for Commercial Law (*Shōhō Kōshūjo*), it was taken over by the government in 1884 and transformed into Tokyo Commercial College (*Tōkyō Shōgyō Gakkō*). (The present name dates from 1949.)

One aspect of the development of university education in Meiji Japan was to have particular significance for the history of Japanese economic thought. Liberal thinkers such as Fukuzawa Yukichi were greatly impressed by the tradition of academic independence which they encountered in the West, and argued forcefully that universities, although they might serve the government's objective of promoting economic development and national prestige, should not be subservient to the ideology of the state. During the 1880s, the cause of university autonomy was taken up by staff at Tokyo University, and in 1893 they were successful in obtaining a constitution that ensured the independence of the university in hiring, firing, and disciplining its own members. Although freedom of thought in the universitites was to be severely curtailed in the 1920s and 1930s, this achievement was nevertheless an important one. It meant that universities in the early twentieth century were relatively free from the pervasive nationalist influence that permeated primary and secondary education. Therefore, even the imperial universities, created to train efficient servants of the state, became arenas for the debate of ideas that were radically opposed to the aims and policies of the government (Tamanoi 1971: 41–3).

WESTERN ECONOMIC TEXTS IN JAPAN

Western economic ideas were introduced into Japan not only by foreign teachers such as Fenollosa, but also, more importantly, by Japanese scholars like Fukuzawa Yukichi, who studied overseas and whose writings and translations made these ideas accessible to Japanese readers. At first, the focus of this foreign learning was Japan's traditional window on the outside world, The Netherlands. In 1872 Nishi Amane (1829–97) and Tsuda Mamichi (1829–1903), two of the *samurai* scholars of Dutch Learning who had lectured at the *Bansho Shirabesho*, were sent by the government to Holland, where they studied law and economics under the tutelage of Simon Vissering (1818–88), professor of economics at Leiden University. On their return they participated with Fukuzawa Yukichi, Mori Arinori, and a small group of other enthusiasts of Western learning in the creation of the '1873 Society' (*Meirokusha*), an association whose journal, the *Meiroku Zasshi*, became a relatively short-lived but extremely influential forum for the discussion of Western ideas. For this reason, the teaching which Vissering imparted to his two Japanese students came to have a quite disproportionate significance for the development of Japanese economics in the early Meiji period (Bell 1960–1: 54–5).

The lectures that Nishi and Tsuda attended at Leiden University would have given them a relatively good introduction to the traditions of nineteenth-century European liberal thought. Vissering was among the most eminent Dutch economists of his day and was a recognized expert on French and British economic theories. An eloquent advocate of *laissez-faire* whose ideas were influenced by Frédéric Bastiat and (particularly in his later life) by J.S. Mill, Vissering had presented his inaugural address at Leiden University on the subject of 'freedom as the basic principle in economics' (Butter 1969: 1221–6). The impact of this approach to economics was (as we shall see) very apparent in the views which Nishi and Tsuda expressed in their writings after their return to Japan.

Holland was also the source of the first economics texts to be translated into Japanese. The last years of the Shogunate had seen the translation of a number of relatively specialized works such as Parve's *History of Money and Banking in the Dutch East Indies* which, one suspects, did not reach a very wide Japanese readership. In

1867, however, the first Japanese translation of a general economics text was completed. The work in question was William Ellis's *Outline of Social Economy*, a best-selling but now largely forgotten popular introduction to economics. Its translator was Kanda Takahira (1830–98), a well-established political and economic thinker who, with Yokoi Shōnan, had been an articulate advocate of the opening of Japan to foreign trade. Kanda was a scholar of Dutch Learning and a language teacher at the *Bansho Shirabesho*, and he translated Ellis's book, not from the original English, but from a Dutch version which had in turn been translated by Simon Vissering (Tamanoi 1971: 2–6; Tsukatani 1980: 92–3).

By the 1870s, however, a growing number of Japanese scholars were acquiring a working knowledge of English, French, or German, and economics texts began to be translated directly from these languages rather than from Dutch. Many of the texts were still popular introductory works like Ellis's, but gradually the classical works of European economics also began to appear in Japanese form. A Japanese edition of Adam Smith's *Wealth of Nations* was published in several parts from 1884 onwards, and John Stuart Mill's *Principles of Political Economy* appeared in translation two years later. One important contributor to this process was the economic journalist Ōshima Sadamasu (1854–1914), who was responsible for the translation of Malthus's *Essay on the Principles of Population* in 1876, Jevon's *Money and Mechanism of Exchange* in 1882, and List's *National System of Political Economy* in 1889 (Tamanoi 1971: 19; Honjō 1965: 274).

When we speak of the translation of Western economic writings, it is important to remember that this meant much more than the simple rendering of words and phrases from one language to another. The translators of Smith, Mill, and Malthus were introducing into Japanese thought a complex and often unfamiliar body of ideas. In many cases, the Japanese language possessed no equivalents to European economic terms, and scholars like Kanda and Ōshima were obliged to develop the vocabulary of economics *de novo* by adapting or combining existing Japanese words. Thus, although the Japanese work *kyōkyū* clearly corresponded to the English 'supply', there was no obvious translation for the word 'demand' when used in an economic context. Kanda's approximation was the neologism *kyūshu*, a combination of the character for 'to request' and 'to take'. (The generally accepted translation for 'demand' came to be *juyō*, combining two characters meaning 'to require' or 'need'.) It was necessary for him to supplement Ellis's comments on the laws of supply and demand with the explanation: 'Supply (*kyōkyū*) means that which I provide to another person. Demand (*kyūshu*) means that which I take from someone else.' Even the word 'society' had no precise Japanese equivalent and was translated in a variety of ways until the modern word '*shakai*' acquired general recognition (Tamanoi 1971: 7–9, 16).

Western economic theories, moreover, could not be understood in isolation. They were deeply imbedded in the interconnected system of scientific, social, and ethical ideas that had emerged from the European enlightenment and developed through the subsequent processes of industrialization, political revolution, and imperial expansion. Many of the earliest interpreters of Western economics, therefore, were not, and could not be, specialist economists, but were rather students of the Western liberal tradition as a whole.

This universalist approach to Western culture was particularly evident in the thought and writings of the *Meirokusha*. The society's journal, the *Meiroku Zasshi*, included a number of articles on economic theory and policy, but also addressed the topics of politics, society, religion, education, language, and culture. An individual member like Tsuda Mamichi might contribute articles on the topic of free trade, but intersperse these with essays on government, Japanese folklore, the use of torture, and the causes of earthquakes.

Certain fundamental features of the Western liberal tradition were particularly novel and controversial, and appear as recurrent themes in the writings of the *Meirokusha*, both on economic and non-economic topics. Perhaps the most important of these features was the concept of immutable laws, accessible to human investigation and understanding, which governed the workings of human society as well as the natural world. Although some Tokugawa writers such as Kaiho Seiryō had begun to give an economic interpretation to the principle (*ri*) that maintained the harmony of the universe, the idea that the whole process of production and distribution was (in Mill's words) 'as much a subject for scientific enquiry as any of the physical laws of nature' was still an unfamiliar one. In their eagerness to convey the idea that the laws of economics were as scientific as those of the physical world, Japanese liberals sometimes blurred the distinctions which even Mill and his followers had maintained between economic and natural phenomena. Thus Tsuda could write, in defence of *laissez-faire*, that imports and exports must always balance each other in the long run, for the principle of trade

is like the principle of the winds and the tides. Now advancing and now receding, sometimes moving from East and sometimes

from the West, the winds and tides ultimately achieve equilibrium.
(Braisted 1976: 326)

Another essential but unfamiliar aspect of nineteenth-century Western thought was the idea of progress. Confucian philosophy had tended to view human history as a process of decline from the golden age of ancient China, in which sages had laid down the principles of morality and wise government. But the economics of Adam Smith and John Stuart Mill, and the positivist history of H.T. Buckle and François Guizot (who also exerted a powerful influence on Japanese liberal thought), demanded a radically different view of the human past (see Blacker 1969: 92–3). As the *Meirokusha* member Nishimura Shigeki explained in his commentary on the meaning of the Western word 'civilization':

Rising one after another . . . [the] great states during their flourishing periods always generated progress by steering the course of civilization in advance of the world. But when their time was up, their power greatly declined, and their progress came to an end. If one country stopped progressing, however, another arose to become the leader of nations and to advance the course of civilization.
(Braisted 1976: 449)

The diffusion of this idea within Japan was, of course, crucial since it was precisely the vision of national and international progress which underpinned the development policies of the Meiji government and of subsequent Japanese governments in the twentieth century.

Undoubtedly the most difficult and controversial of the fundamental concepts of European classical economics, however, was the concept of individual liberty. Another contributor to the *Meiroku Zasshi*, Nakamura Masanao, informed his readers that

Western languages possess the word 'liberty' for which there is no equivalent in either Chinese or Japanese. . . . Today, Europeans have acquired 'liberty' and follow their hearts' desires since they have generally destroyed the customs of trifling with human freedoms. No longer silenced by useless restrictions, individuals may expand their aspirations and plan alike for public benefits.
(Braisted 1976: 162. The *Meirokusha* was, in fact,
influential in popularizing the modern Japanese
word for 'liberty': *jiyū*.)

In the political sphere, the introduction of the notion of liberty inevitably encouraged discussion of such sensitive issues as freedom of speech and freedom of thought; in the economic sphere, it became inseparably connected with the question of *laissez-faire*. *Laissez-faire*, in fact, and particularly the application of this concept to international trade, was the most important topic of economic debate in the *Meiroku Zasshi*. In a sense this debate was purely academic, since the commercial treaties negotiated with the Western powers during the 1850s had committed Japan to maintaining a single non-discriminatory tariff of 5 per cent on all imports. There were many in Japan (even within the liberal *Meirokusha*) who detested this provision, believing that it had been imposed on Japan in a moment of political weakness, and that it deprived Japan of the opportunity to protect its own nascent industries from the onslaught of foreign manufactured imports. But the returned scholars of economics, particularly Tsuda Mamichi, defended free trade in terms that clearly reveal the influence of the extreme *laissez-faire* views of European economists such as Bastiat. Noting that 'it is generally accepted among Western political economists that . . . tarrifs, rather than provide protection, are bad measures injurious to the people generally' (Braisted 1976: 56), Tsuda went on to enumerate reasons why protective tariffs were specifically unsuited to the conditions of contemporary Japan. In particular, he argued that the free import of Western goods would increase Japanese knowledge of foreign culture and technology, and so assist the nation in its pursuit of 'civilization and enlightenment'. In this sense, therefore, he saw a high level of imports as laying the foundations for future economic and social development. Yet at the same time Tsuda seems to have had little confidence in the ability of Japan to achieve such economic development, for elsewhere he argued that the nation's industries were so far behind those of the West that it was futile to attempt to foster their growth through tariff protection (Braisted 1976: 56–9, and 324–7)

A somewhat more subtle and complex approach to free trade was expounded by Kanda Takahira. Kanda acknowledged the fears of the scholars and officials who believed that Japan's import surplus was gradually depleting the country of its precious reserves of metals. He argued, however, that the main cause of this problem was not the existence of free trade but the fact that the Meiji government had attempted to fill its empty treasuries by printing large amounts of unconvertible paper money. The paper notes were not only unacceptable as a means of international payment; they also provoked domestic inflation, making it more difficult for Japan to sell its products overseas. Kanda's solution to the Japanese trade imbalance therefore lay not in protectionism but in a currency reform that would restore the convertibility of paper money and restrain inflation.

Although he supported free trade, Kanda was not an unmitigated advocate of *laissez-faire*. He argued, for example, that the government should provide incentives to assist the development of Japanese iron mining. In the early stages, he agreed, domestically produced iron might be more expensive than imported ore, but the opening of Japanese mines would serve the needs both of industrial development and military security, and would reduce costs in the long run.

> Our situation [wrote Kanda] may be compared to that of a fellow who must buy mortar, pestle and sieve to hull the large quantity of rice in his storehouse. My critic would say that the fellow had best buy only enough polished rice from a dealer to meet his daily needs since the price of his rice will actually become high when he buys the polishing equipment. This might be all right if his needs were limited to one or two *to* [a small measure of volume]. But it would be absurd for the fellow to allow his rice to rot in the storehouse while he purchases unlimited amounts of rice over an indefinite period of time. Even the most ignorant husband and the most foolish wife would never indulge in such an uneconomical practice.
>
> (Braisted 1976: 458)

Government support for iron mining was necessary, Kanda believed, because private capital was insufficiently developed to undertake the task immediately. In this respect, Kanda's views coincide with those of English utilitarians such as Mill who accepted that, although government intervention in the economy was as a rule undesirable, the state might be required 'in the particular circumstances of a given age or nation' to undertake a wide range of entrepreneurial action: 'the public being either too poor to command the necessary resources, or too little advanced in intelligence to appreciate the ends, or not sufficiently practiced in joint action to be capable of the means' (Mill 1973: 978).

Although the last issue of the *Meiroku Zasshi* appeared in 1875, the debate on free trade continued, with the cause of *laissez-faire* receiving particular support in the pages of the Tokyo Economic Journal (*Tōkyō Keizai Zasshi*) which commenced publication four years later, and was to survive until 1923. The *Tōkyō Keizai Zasshi* was founded and run by a passionate opponent of protectionism,

Taguchi Ukichi (1857–1905), whose publishing enterprise was also responsible for bringing out the first Japanese edition of Adam Smith's *Wealth of Nations*. Like the members of the *Meirokusha*, Taguchi had wide-ranging interests: he wrote extensively on Japanese political and cultural development, but also had a thorough knowledge of the theories of the English classical economists and of his protectionist adversaries (Sugihara 1980: 59–64 and 147–58; Tsukatani 1980: 75–80).

For Taguchi, the beauty of classical economics lay in the fact that it was founded on a universal principle which operated beyond the constraints of place or time. He therefore condemned the idea, expressed both by Mill and by the German historical school, that sound economic policies might vary according to the level of national development. The proponents of such views, claimed Taguchi, did not understand the true principle of economics; and it is no coincidence that his word for this principle was *ri*. For Taguchi, although he may not have understood its historical lineage, recognized the thread of ideas which linked the Chinese philosophy of the wise ruler with the European philosophy of *laissez-faire*, and he used this link as a means of relating his own economic liberalism to traditional ethics of pre-Meiji Japan. As he wrote in an early article:

> The ancient sages made inaction the foundation of the way of government. Their words may appear simple, but in fact they contain the true principle of wise economics.
>
> (Quoted in Sugihara 1980: 147)

THE INFLUENCE AND LIMITATIONS OF LIBERAL ECONOMICS

In the context of early Meiji Japan, scholars like Tsuda Mamichi, Kanda Takahira, and Taguchi Ukichi were rare possessors of essential but esoteric knowledge, and it was not surprising that the government should have paid some attention to their views. Several of the *Meirokusha* members had close personal connections with the political world, but none more so than Kanda, whose ideas were to have a profound and lasting impact on Japanese economic and social development.

The Meiji government had inherited from the Tokugawa Shogunate the unwieldy system of a rice tax paid in kind on the basis of a yearly assessment of yield. This taxation system was not only incapable of providing adequate revenue to meet the needs of the new government, but also clearly an unsuitable basis for the finances of a modern industrializing economy. In the early 1870s, therefore, the Finance Ministry sought advice from a handful of prominent politicians and scholars on the subject of the tax reform. Amongst those who submitted memoranda on the topic was Kanda Takahira.

The development of Kanda's ideas on tax reform can be traced back to his first work, the *Nōshōben* (Lecture on Agriculture and Commerce) written in 1860. Here Kanda had contrasted the poverty and stagnation of agrarian nations with the prosperity and dynamism of countries whose economies were founded on trade. The former, he noted, were disadvantaged by the fact that their governments depended for their revenue on taxes extracted from poor peasants, who were likely to grow disaffected and rebellious when the tax burden rose too high. The governments of trading nations, on the contrary, could rely on taxes levied on the prosperous commercial sector of the economy, and so enjoyed far greater latitude in their financial policies. The conclusion which Kanda reached, therefore, was that as the nation developed, agricultural taxes should be gradually reduced and taxes on commerce expanded (Tsukatani 1980: 60–2).

This ideal, however, was not one that could be attained in the circumstances of early Meiji Japan. In the early 1870s Japan was still an overwhelmingly agrarian society in which farming and forestry provided over 70 per cent of employment. Kanda recognized that, under these conditions, the peasantry must continue to play its traditional role of upholding the edifice of state finances, but at the same time he perceived that a reorganization of the agrarian tax system could provide a basis for the transformation of Japan from a feudal to a commercial and capitalist society. The two documents in which Kanda set out his proposals for tax reform – 'Suggestions for Reform of the Land Tax' (*Denso Kaikaku Gi*, 1870) and the more detailed *New Land-Tax Law* (*Denso Shinhō*, 1872) – clearly show the influence of the English liberal economic thought, for by now Kanda had completed his translation of Ellis's economic text. The first objective of Kanda's proposals was to remove the inefficiency and inequity that characterized the Tokugawa tax system, where complex assessments of land area and harvest yields had been necessary to determine the amount of tax to be paid.

The solution to these evils, in Kanda's opinion, lay in the free working of market forces. The government, he argued, should remove restrictions on the sale and purchase of land and institute a monetary land tax based on the market value of farm holdings. This would do much more than merely simplify and streamline the taxation system.

It would also base Japanese agriculture – the core of the early Meiji economy – on the principles of private property and market competition. Kanda was well aware that the injection of market forces into Japanese village society was likely to result in a widening gulf between rich and poor farmers, but he accepted this consequence with a logic that clearly reflects the influence of the more ruthless elements of Western liberal thought:

> Human nature may be wise or foolish, diligent or idle, thrifty or wasteful. It is a natural principle that those who are wise, diligent and thrifty will gradually grow rich, while those who are foolish, idle and wasteful will gradually become poor. If, however, we try to prevent the consolidation [of landholdings], and desire the rich and poor to be made equal, we will surely deprive the wealthy of their vigour without bestowing it upon the poor. This bad practice will suppress wisdom, diligence and thrift, but will not make the foolish, idle and wasteful more hard working.
>
> (Quoted in Tsukatani 1980: 62–3)

Kanda's proposals were not implemented in their entirety, for the new land tax of 1873 was based on the assessed value, rather than the market price, of land. But it was, as Kanda had wished, a uniform monetary tax, and this, together with the removal of traditional restraints on the sale and purchase of land, had precisely the consequences that Kanda anticipated: it hastened the conversion of traditional rural social relationships into commercial relationships and promoted the polarization of wealth within the village economy. The new land tax therefore provided the financial basis for the modernization policies of the Meiji government, but at the same time sowed the seeds of one of the most serious social problems of the early twentieth century.

It is also of interest that Matsukata Masayoshi, the official responsible for the formulation of the new land tax, was later, as Finance Minister, to carry out a number of reforms that were broadly in line with liberal economic theory. Not only did he restore the convertibility of the Japanese currency, as recommended by Kanda in the 1870s; he also initiated the sale of government-owned factories and mines to private enterprise. Although this last policy was probably motivated more by financial necessity than by ideological considerations, Matsukata had clearly assimilated the basic principles of *laissez-faire* (Smith 1955: 92–5). As he wrote in his report on the adoption of the gold standard:

The natural function of government is chiefly to protect the public interest and guarantee peace to the community. The government should never attempt to compete with the people in industry and commerce. It falls within the sphere of government to look after matters of education, armament, and the police, while matters concerning trade and industry fall outside its sphere. In fact in these matters the government can never hope to rival in shrewdness, foresight and enterprise men who are activated by immediate motives of self-interest.

(Quoted in Smith 1955: 95)

In general, however, liberal and utilitarian economic ideas had far less political impact in Japan than they did in Britain. The economic circumstances of early Meiji Japan were, after all, very different from those of Victorian England. There was no extensive industrial capitalist class, whose members might desire to carry on their business unhindered by government interference. On the contrary, the small number of new industrialists were well aware of their fragile position in the world economy, and generally welcomed the guidance and assistance of the state. Most of them, too, were closely integrated into a small but powerful network of personal relationships which linked the political and economic leaders of the day, and for that reason were all the less likely to view the state action with fear or suspicion. The liberal theories of the British classical economists therefore had relatively little appeal to the self-interest of Meiji businessmen, and, from the government's point of view, had the additional disadvantage of being associated with the suspect political ideology of parliamentary democracy. An elected assembly was not to come into being in Japan until 1890, and then only on the basis of a very limited suffrage, while the government regarded with particular disfavour the liberal principles of freedom of speech and of the press. Even the *Meiroku Zasshi* was forced to abandon publication in response to the strict press control laws enforced from mid-1875 onwards (Braisted 1976: xii–xiv).

In this discouraging environment many of the liberal scholars of the 1870s drifted increasingly towards nationalist and conservative philosophies as they grew older, while the generation that followed them tended instead to seek out alternative intellectual traditions which could give meaning to the specific economic and social structures of Meiji Japan.

PROTECTIONISM

One significant alternative was to be found in the writings of the protectionist critics of British classical economics, of whom the most influential, as far as Meiji economic thought was concerned, were the American Henry Charles Carey (1793–1879) and the German Friedrich List (1789–1846).

Carey's populist ideas, which attacked the theory of free trade on moral as well as economic grounds, were introduced to Japanese readers in the *Hogo Zeisetsu* (Theory of Protectionist Tariffs), the very first Japanese work to advocate the principles of protectionism. This brief document was written in 1870 by Wakayama Norikazu, a former English interpreter who was at that time an official of the Ministry of Finance. Wakayama was clearly familiar with Ricardo's concept of comparative advantage, but he attacked it, less on theoretical than on empirical grounds. Japanese trade and industry, he argued, were far too weak to compete with the economic might of the Western powers, and protective tariffs were needed to control the influx of unnecessary foreign products, to preserve Japanese prosperity, and thus to earn the respect of the foreign nations who constituted potential threats to Japan's security. Wakayama's arguments were supported by a substantial appendix in which, quoting from Carey, he listed numerous historical examples of the successful use of protectionist policies by foreign nations (Wakayama 1950: vol. 2, 733–45).

Wakayama's ideas, although they display a familiarity with Western economic thought, are at the same time strongly reminiscent of the pre-Meiji arguments against the opening of foreign trade. The old fears that trade will introduce unnecessary foreign luxuries, diminish domestic supplies of gold and silver, and above all undermine Japan's political independence are very much in evidence. Gradually, however, new arguments began to enter into Japanese protectionist thought. The *Meirokusha* member, Sugi Kōji, for example, opposed Tsuda Mamichi's views on free trade with a demand for the protection of carefully selected infant industries. In an article written in 1874, he quoted the examples not only of western Protectionists from Oliver Cromwell to Henry Charles Carey, but also of that great Japanese protectionist Arai Hakuseki, and went on to observe that

> people of increasingly ripe training and steadily advancing skills welcome free trade and dislike protection because this protection then prevents them from freely carrying on their business. Again, people whose training is not yet ripe and whose skills are not yet

advanced dislike free trade and welcome protection. This is because they must be protected until they are mature, just as children by their parents and students by their teachers.

(Braisted 1976: 305)

A particularly important milestone in the development of Japanese protectionist thought came with the translation in the late 1880s of Friedrich List's *National System of Political Economy*. List and his followers in the German historical school had challenged the British liberal economic tradition at a far more fundamental level than Henry Carey had done. According to List, the essential weakness in the theories of Quesnay, Adam Smith, and their intellectual successors was their failure to recognize the role of the nation in economic life. Instead of basing their theories on the real world, which consisted of separate nations at differing stages of development, they postulated a fictitious 'cosmopolitical' world in which national boundaries were assumed away (List 1928: 97–107).

List's ideas, developed in the environment of German society during its earliest stages of industrialization, had a certain appeal to those concerned with the economic state of Meiji Japan, and were a source of inspiration to many economic scholars around the turn of the century. As List's translator, Ōshima Sadamasu, observed, the historical school's view of society implied an approach to the discipline of economics which was radically different from that of the British classical school (or the 'natural liberty' school, as he called them). While the British classical economists had looked for economic laws that were as universal as the laws of the physical sciences, the historical economists began by accepting that the principles of the social and economic sciences were specific to a given time and place.

If all apples fall towards the ground in England, we can presume that all apples will fall towards the ground in every country of the world. But in the case of politics, law or economics, what is suitable for England may not be applicable to France, for nations may be old or new, large or small, strong or weak, and their position, climate, customs and etiquette are also interconnected. . . . Yet there are those who, having read two or three English economic texts, then want to take these and apply them to our country, whose circumstances, population, wealth and strength are entirely different.

(Quoted in Honjō 1966: vol. 2, 339–40)

The attempt to elevate the principle of comparative advantage to the status of a universal law was, Ōshima argued, merely a device to perpetuate the dominance of the existing economic powers over newly idustrializing nations such as Germany and Japan. In the short term, free trade might indeed appear to maximize the benefits of all, but this perspective ignored the long-run dynamics of the international economic system. As Ōshima wrote, in words that resemble some much more modern critiques of Ricardian comparative advantage, the ultimate implication of the theory of free trade is that 'agricultural nations must remain agricultural, and industrial nations must remain industrial' (quoted in Honjō 1966, vol. 2, 341). Government intervention in industry and commerce was therefore essential if Japan was to alter the pattern of the world economy and claim its place as a modern industrialized nation.

The protectionist views of the historical school were propagated in Japanese not only by the writings and translations of men like Ōshima, but also through the activities of the National Economics Association (*Kokka Keizai Kai*), established in 1890. This association was among the first of many similar societies which, over the past century, have brought together economists from a variety of educational and other institutions. At the same time they have also encouraged the fragmentation of Japanese economic scholarship along distinct factional and ideological lines. The position of the National Economics Association in the major controversies of the day was made absolutely clear in its founding manifesto, to which Ōshima Sadamasu was one of the principal signatories.

Power is created by wealth. It is unheard of that power can exist where there is no wealth. The competition which is occurring at present between nation and nation is nothing but a competition of strength and of productive power. Thus the problem of independence is a problem of wealth. The problem of a country's wealth is of more importance than the system of trade. This is particularly true in the present circumstances of our country. In these circumstances the only approach which we should adopt is that of national economics, i.e. the economic philosophy that each nation must treat its own self-defence and independent development as the most important factors. It is now urgent that we should exert ourselves to investigate the ways of pursuing this economic philosophy. Therefore we establish the National Economics Association and invite the membership of like-minded scholars.

(Quoted in Honjō 1966: 334–5)

The assertive nationalist tone which appears in the pronouncements of the National Economics Association and the writings of the protectionist economists at this time perhaps reflects something more than the influence of the German historical school. By the 1890s, the Meiji policies of industrialization and modernization were beginning to produce substantial results. Between 1875 and 1895, iron and steel production had doubled, machinery production had increased sevenfold, and textile production (which accounted for almost half of Japan's manufactured output) had increased more than eightfold (Andō 1979: 10–11). Japan had also built up a formidable military force whose capabilities were to be demonstrated by its victory in the war with China (1894–5).

As a result of its growing economic and military strength, Japan was now in a position to renegotiate the offending foreign treaties which had restricted the nation's tariff autonomy, and, in a gradual process from 1894 to 1911, national control over trade policy was restored. Protectionist policies therefore became a genuine option for the Japanese government in the late Meiji period and, partly through the influence of organizations like the National Economics Association (whose membership included politicians as well as journalists and academic economists) new tariffs and subsidies were introduced to foster a number of infant industries such as steel and shipbuilding.

As the economy developed, however, so the social problems and dislocations of industrialization also became increasingly evident. By the end of the nineteenth century, these problems had emerged as the central topic of Japanese economic debate, and new theories, borrowed principally from a younger generation of German scholars, were being used to analyse them.

THE ASSOCIATION FOR THE STUDY OF SOCIAL POLICY

In the forty-odd years between the death of Friedrich List and the popularization of his ideas in Japan, the theories of the historical school within Germany itself had undergone considerable development. The dominant figure in the late nineteenth-century German historical school was Gustav von Schmoller (1838–1917), professor of economics at the University of Berlin, a scholar whose views differed in a number of significant ways from those of List and other nationalist economists of the earlier generation.

In the first place, Schmoller took the critique of the abstract, theoretical tendencies of British classical economics further even than List had done, arguing that the collection and analysis of factual economic data, rather than deductive theorising, was the primary task of the economist. Second, Schmoller placed great emphasis on both the ethical and the practical dimensions of economics. The study of the economy was not, in his view, a morally neutral positivist science, but a means to the achievement of a healthy and harmonious society. A central concern of his empirical investigations was to understand the economic causes of social problems such as poverty and class conflict, and to devise policies that would ameliorate these problems. It was this aim which inspired the establishment in 1872 of the influential *Verein für Sozialpolitik* (Association for Social Policy) which provided a forum for debating the ideas of Schmoller and his followers.

The members of the Association came to be popularly and derisively known as the *Kathedersozialisten* – 'socialists of the professorial chair' – but their approach to economic and political problems was in fact quite different from that of most utopian and Marxist socialists. The reforms which the Association for Social Policy proposed were intended not to overthrow, but rather to preserve the existing economic and political system by domesticating the potentially dangerous forces of organized labour and creating a sense of common purpose amongst labour and management.

The views of the German *Kathedersozialisten* exerted a very powerful influence on Japanese economics at the turn of the century. In part, this influence seems to have reflected similarities in the economic and political circumstances of the two countries. Both nations had actively interventionist governments bent on promoting industrial expansion. But the very process of government intervention, by hastening the speed of industrialization, intensified the social dislocation that has accompanied industrial revolutions in all countries and all periods of history. There was therefore a certain logic in demanding that the government should simultaneously devise social policies that would prevent this dislocation from becoming a source of unrest or even revolution.

The approach of the social policy school, moreover, corresponded very well to the pre-Meiji Japanese tradition of *keikoku saimin*: 'administering the nation and relieving the sufferings of the people'. Like the Confucian scholars of Tokugawa Japan, the *Kathedersozialisten* saw economics as inseparably interwoven with moral and political issues, and above all as embodying the duty of the government to show concern for the social welfare of its subjects. It is symbolically appropriate that Kanai Noburu, the first economist to expound the views of the social policy school in Japan, should have named his first four children Kei, Koku, Sai, and Min (Bernstein 1976: 37). (The following four were named Sei, Gi, Shō, and Ri, spelling the words 'justice' and 'victory'.)

The most important instrument in spreading the ideas of the new historical school within Japan was the Association for the Study of Social Policy (*Shakai Seisaku Gakkai*), established in 1896 and modelled on the German *Verein für Sozialpolitik*. In its early stages the *Shakai Seisaku Gakkai* operated on a small scale. Its members – a handful of scholars, most of whom had returned from studying at German universities – met regularly to exchange ideas on the economic and social problems of the day. By the early twentieth century however, the growing interest in the social policy approach to economics encouraged the Association to reach out towards a wider audience, and from 1907 to 1924 it organized major annual conferences, each focusing on a topic of particular interest to members, and often including papers by the leading economists of the late Meiji and early Taishō Japan. The list of conference titles, therefore, provides a very good indication both of the major concerns of the social policy school and of the principal topics of contemporary economic and social debate.

The first conference, held at Tokyo University in December 1907, focused on factory legislation and labour problems, and included papers on workers' compensation, health standards in the factory, and labour problems in an international context. Amongst the topics of subsequent annual meetings were the tariff question and social policy (1908), the problem of migration (1909), labour disputes (1913), the problems of government-run enterprises (1916), small-scale industry (1917), women workers in Japan (1918), and the problems of Japanese tenant farmers (1922) (Sumiya 1967: 174–8).

In its initial manifesto issued in 1900, the Association defined its political standpoint in terms that were entirely faithful to the principles of the German *Kathedersozialisten*:

> We oppose *laisser faire*. The reason for this is that the extreme exercise of self-interest and uncontrolled free competition would result in an excessive gulf between rich and poor. We also oppose socialism. The reason for this is that the destruction of the existing economic structure and the abolition of capitalists would be harmful to the progress of the national destiny. . . .
>
> Our beliefs are as follows: we support the existing economic system of private property and wish, within this system, to

prevent class conflict and promote social harmony by means both of individual action and the authority of the state.

(Quoted in Sumiya 1967: 252)

In practice, however, the economists, journalists, social reformers, and others who gathered at the annual conferences of the Association for the Study of Social Policy represented a wide spectrum of political opinion, from extreme nationalism to Christian Socialism and crypto-anarchism. This diversity of views was to lead to recurrent debates and fissions within the Association, debates that can be best understood by examining the works of the two outstanding representatives of social policy thought in Japan, Kanai Noburu and Fukuda Tokuzō.

THE SOCIAL POLICY THOUGHT OF KANAI NOBURU (1865–1933) AND FUKUDA TOKUZŌ (1874–1930)

Kanai Noburu (his given name is sometimes read as 'En') came from a background typical of many early twentieth-century Japanese academics. His father was a low-ranking *samurai* who acquired a position in the Ministry of Education soon after the Meiji Restoration, and Kanai himself studied at Tokyo University, where he was recognized as one of the most brilliant students of his generation. As an undergraduate Kanai attended courses given by Karl Rathgen, the German professor of statistics at Tokyo University, and by the economics professor Wadagaki Kenzō, both of whom aroused his interest in the ideas of the German historical school. As a result of these influences he chose to take German as his major foreign language. Soon after graduation he travelled to Germany, where he lived from 1886–9, studying at the universities of Heidelberg and Halle and attending lectures by Gustav von Schmoller and Adolf Wagner in Berlin (Sumiya 1967: 255–7).

Kanai seized with great enthusiasm on the new ideas of the social policy school, which he saw as superior not only to the theories of the British classical economists but also to the views of the earlier German historical school. In an article written in 1888, in which he sought to introduce the social policy school to Japanese readers, Kanai listed the features which, in his opinion, distinguished this approach to economics from all others. These included the recognition that economic phenomena were inseparable from social phenomena; the understanding that human wants were complex and could not simply be reduced to the pursuit of profit; the use of inductive as well as

65

deductive methods of research; and the belief that the duty of the state was to protect the weak and restrain the powerful (Tsukatani 1980: 199–200).

So impressed was Kanai by the ideas of the social policy school that, after moving to Britain in 1889, he spent his year in London conducting social research in the East End rather than attending formal economics lectures. On his return to Japan in 1890, he set about propagating his new-found theories through his lectures at Tokyo University, his numerous books and articles, and later his member-ship of the Association for the Study of Social Policy (Sumiya 1967: 257–8).

The ideas that Kanai brought back with him from Germany had particular relevance to the Japanese political debates of the 1890s. The Japanese factory workforce was at that time expanding rapidly, and had reached almost half a million by the end of the century. In the absence of an effective trade union movement or of government regulation of the working environment, industrial labourers endured conditions that were starkly revealed in the surveys undertaken by the social reformer Yokoyama Gennosuke during the later 1890s. In the spinning factories, for example Yokoama found workers (mostly young women) working a twelve-hour day in poorly ventilated rooms where the summer temperature often rose above 100 °F (Yokoyama 1972: 154–68).

By the beginning of the decade, factory reform had become a major political issue. The Meiji government was eager to introduce regula-tions on working hours and conditions – less, perhaps, for humanitarian reasons, than because it saw the reluctance of workers to enter the factories as a potential constraint on industrial growth (Taira 1970: 86–8). Reform was also a means of stemming the tide of working-class discontent which expressed itself in a growing number of spontaneous disputes in the factories and mines. Factory legislation, however, was vehemently opposed not only by most business leaders but also by *laissez-faire* economists such as Taguchi Ukichi, who accused would-be reformers of wishing to transform Japanese factories into 'a paradise for the workers and a hell for managers and shareholders' (quoted in Sumiya 1967: 263–4).

It was at this point that the economists of the social policy school entered the debate. Kanai took a relatively optimistic view of Japanese living and working conditions, which he believed to be far better than those he had witnessed in the East End of London. Nevertheless, he accepted the necessity of factory legislation, not as a cure for existing social problems but as a means of averting conflicts that might arise as industrialization progressed, and particularly as a means of preventing the workers from forming their own union organizations, a prospect which Kanai regarded as 'a poison' (Tsukatani 1980: 207).

This approach to social reform was a natural outcome of Kanai's view of the economic and political system as a whole. In contrast to the liberal economists, who conceived of the state as a legal entity entrusted with protecting the rights of the individual, Kanai saw the state as an organic body in which the interests of the individual were submerged, and whose harmonious growth was the supreme goal:

> The highest objective of social policy is to re-unite the various social classes who, in recent times, have been growing more and more divided from one another. . . . Thus all classes will experience true happiness and will go forward in cooperation with one another, and, for the first time . . . we may create the foundations of a prosperous country and a strong army [fukoku kyōhei] which will bring about harmony, health, progress and development for the entire and united national society.
>
> (Quoted in Tsukatani 1980: 209)

Like the members of the German *Verein für Sozialpolitik*, therefore, Kanai combined a concern for social reform with a profound nationalism that became increasingly pronounced as he grew older. By the end of the Meiji period he was enthusiastically supporting Japan's imperial expansion, which he saw as a panacea for domestic poverty and overpopulation (Tsukatani 1980: 207–9).

It was inevitable that such sentiments should antagonize the left-wing economists and political activists who had gathered under the banner of the Association for the Study of Social Policy. In the early years of the Association's existence, agreement on the need for state intervention in social affairs had obscured but not reconciled profound differences in the philosophical positions of its members. By the second decade of the twentieth century, however, these divisions were beginning to surface in the form of serious political rifts. On the one hand, a part of the social policy school's original platform of objectives had been achieved with the introduction, in 1911, of Japan's first – albeit very limited – factory legislation. On the other (as we shall see in the next chapter), Marxist ideas were beginning to exert an important influence on sections of the Japanese intelligentsia, including some members of the Association for the Study of Social Policy itself.

By this time, the dominant figure within the Association was the Keiō professor of economics, Fukuda Tokuzō. Fukuda, who had previously studied and taught at Tokyo Commercial College, was an outstanding linguist who possessed a profound and extensive knowledge of Western economic ideas. From 1898 to 1901 he had lived in Germany, where he studied with Lujo Brentano (1844–1931), a leading member of the German social policy school. Under Brentano's guidance, Fakuda wrote (in German) the first serious study of Japanese economic development, which was published in 1900 under the title *Gesellschaftliche und Wirtschaftliche Entwicklung in Japan* (Social and Economic Development in Japan).

In his early years, Fukuda's intellectual position was somewhat to the left of centre within the social policy school. Unlike Kanai, who vehemently opposed the development of trade unionism, Fukuda was influenced by the ideas of early socialist economists like the nineteenth-century British writer Thomas Hodgskin, an advocate of trade unionism who had regarded labour as the only source of increases in wealth. Fukuda, however, read and drew inspiration from a wide range of sources. By the time he moved to Keiō University in 1905 he was already lecturing on the newly emerging theories of the European neo-classical school, and in particular on the ideas of Alfred Marshall. At about the same time he also began to study Marxist economic theory, a subject that was still unfamiliar to most Japanese readers. His discussions of Marxism in works such as *A Research Guide to Socialism (Shakaishugi Kenkyū no Shiori)*, published in 1906, were among the first serious analyses of Marxist theory to be written in Japanese.

From the start, however, Fukuda was strongly critical of Marx and particularly of the determinist tendencies which he saw as inherent in Marx's materialist view of history. As time went on, Fukuda's writings and academic activity became increasingly dominated by his desire to combat the growing influence of Marxist thought in Japan: he was, for example, to fight strenuously though unsuccessfully for the exclusion of a number of left-wingers from the Association for the Study of Social Policy (Tamanoi 1971: 82).

The nature of Fukuda's objections to Marxism are most clearly spelled out in his work *Social Policy and Class Conflict (Shakai Seisaku to Kaikyū Tōsō)*, first published in 1922. Here Fukuda argued that it was inconsistent for Marxists to claim support for the policies of social reform, since true followers of Marx should believe that, without such reforms, the capitalist system is in any case destined to collapse and be replaced by a socialist utopia.

[S]ocial policy cannot be based on Marx's materialist conception of history. We must reject such an idea – indeed, it seems to me an extraordinary, inexplicable enigma that Marxists should support the same social policies that we support – and at the same time we must use correct teaching, i.e. social policy, to reveal the errors of the materialist conception of history inherent in socialism. From this standpoint it will be apparent that there is a fundamental difference between the views of state and society expounded in socialism and those expounded in social policy.

(Fukuda 1922: Introduction, 6)

Fukuda also rejected the Marxist view of the economy as (in modern terminology) a zero-sum game, where workers' gains could only be achieved by the expropriation of the capitalists. In order to support these arguments, Fukuda increasingly drew, not upon the theories of the German social policy school, but upon the marginalist approach of the British and Austrian neo-classical economists. A particularly powerful influence on Fukuda's later years came from the neo-classical welfare economics of Arthur Pigou (1877–1959). Pigou emphasized that the welfare of the working classes was dependent on the size and stability of national income, as well as on the way in which that income was distributed. Fukuda used this approach to support his own view that the interests of the working class were best served by seeking compromises within the framework of capitalism, rather than by seeking to destroy the system as a whole (Fukuda 1922: 226–34).

In different ways, therefore, Fukuda was influential in introducing to Japan both the economic ideas of Karl Marx and those of Marx's most determined critics, the economists of the neo-classical school. As these ideas were popularized, the divisions within the Association for the Study of Social Policy, and within Japanese economics as a whole, widened. By the early 1920s the Association had crumbled into opposing factions, and from then onwards the two schools of thought which Fukuda had helped to introduce were to define the boundaries of a deep and irreconcilable dichotomy within the study of economics in Japan.

CONCLUSIONS

In the years from the Meiji Restoration to the First World War the Japanese economy underwent a remarkable transformation, changing from an economically isolated and overwhelmingly agrarian society to a trading nation with a flourishing mechanized textiles industry and a smaller but rapidly growing heavy industrial sector.

The simultaneous transformation that occurred in Japanese economic thought was hardly less remarkable. A wide range of foreign economic, political, and philosophical ideas – including the liberal traditions of the British classical economists, the nationalist views of the German historical school, the theories of social policy, Marxian socialism, and the new marginalist views of neo-classical economics – were imported into Japan, and began to be assimilated to Japanese intellectual traditions and economic circumstances. Although it would be wrong to over-emphasize the direct impact that such ideas had on Japanese economic policy, imported theories did at least provide an intellectual justification for significant political innovations including the new land tax, the financial reforms of the Matsukata era, the use of tariff protection from the 1890s onwards, and the introduction of factory legislation in the early twentieth century. Moreover, the Western ideas imported during the Meiji period created the foundations for the emergence of new and increasingly original Japanese developments in economic thought in the decades that followed.

3

Economic debates in inter-war Japan

The Tokyo University economist Shibagaki Kazuo has identified the period from the last years of Meiji to the 1920s as marking the beginning of 'scientific attempts to apply economic theory to the analysis of the Japanese economy' (Saeki and Shibagaki 1972: 15). Shibagaki's statement may be open to debate, but it is certainly true that the Taishō (1912–26) and early Shōwa (1926–89) periods saw a change of emphasis in Japanese economic research.

During the late nineteenth century, Japanese economists had studied and imported Western theories, and had from time to time used these theories to justify their support of specific economic policies. But there had been little attempt to define the fundamental nature of the Japanese economy, or to relate Japan to Western schemes of economic evolution. From the First World War onwards, however, the analysis of Japan's economic structure, particularly in term of Marx's theory of modes of production, became a central concern of Japanese economic studies. This concern sparked fierce controversies, not only between Marxists and non-Marxists, but also amongst Marxist economists themselves; in so doing it encouraged more thorough research of both historical and contemporary economic conditions within Japan.

INTER-WAR JAPAN: ECONOMIC GROWTH AND POLITICAL REPRESSION

The First World War had a strong stimulative effect on Japanese industrialization. Industrial production grew at an annual average rate of around 9 per cent during the war years, with growth being most rapid in the newly emerging heavy industrial sectors such as steel and shipbuilding. By the end of the 1920s, Japan was an industrialized nation in the sense that mining and manufacturing accounted for a larger share of national income than agriculture.

During the 1920s, however, symptoms of severe instability were also apparent within the Japanese economy (as indeed within the international economy as a whole). A number of industrial and financial enterprises which had over-extended themselves during the war boom collapsed, and the prices of agricultural products, which determined the incomes of half the Japanese workforce, fell sharply. Economic imbalances were reflected in social tensions. The gap between rich and poor appears to have widened overall during the Taishō era, and industrial disputes were common. In the countryside, the sense of crisis was even more acute. Small peasant farmers were at times even faced with the threat of starvation, and rural poverty, together with the breakdown of traditional social relationships in the countryside, resulted in an increasing number of tenancy disputes between landlords and peasants.

In political terms, the years from 1912 to 1926 are often seen as a period in which democratic rights were extended. The old *samurai* oligarchs of the Meiji period were, for the most part, dead or in retirement, and political parties were coming to play a more important role as stepping stones to government office. In 1925, after a lengthy popular campaign, the franchise was extended to give the vote to all men aged 25 and over. But despite these developments numerous restrictions on political freedom remained in force; in particular, the draconian Peace Police Law of 1900, which gave the police sweeping powers to arrest political 'subversives', was further extended in the 1920s with the passing of a new Peace Preservation Law.

From 1929 the onset of the world depression brought fundamental changes to Japan's external relations and domestic economic policies. Japan recovered from the immediate effects of the depression relatively quickly, largely because of increased government expenditures associated with military expansion on the Asian mainland. During the 1930s, indeed, industrial production grew rapidly, but this growth was achieved only at the cost of increasing economic and political conflict overseas and an increasingly repressive regime at home. From 1931, government control of financial and industrial activity expanded rapidly. At the same time, the suppression of political dissent was intensified. The widespread arrests of political activists during the late 1920s and the 1930s, and the censorship of political debate, were to have a particularly great impact on the development of Japanese economic thought. These repressive actions were directed above all against those who were identified as having Marxist leanings, and it was Marxism that had been perhaps the greatest new influence on economic ideas in the period from the First World War to the 1930s depression.

MARXISM AND JAPANESE ECONOMIC THOUGHT

Foreign scholars have often expressed surprise at the extensive influence of Marxism on Japanese intellectual life. E.O. Reischauer, for example has written:

> Japanese Marxism has proved an extremely hardy plant. Its failure to correspond to the facts of twentieth-century history, even as these unfold within Japan itself, have not blighted it. . . . Marxism has flourished even despite a most infertile emotional soil.
>
> (Reischauer 1964: 225)

On reflection, however, the appeal of Marxism to the Japanese intelligentsia is less surprising than it at first appears. Despite Marx's prediction that revolution would occur first in the most developed capitalist nations, it has generally been true that Marxist ideas have had their greatest impact in nations on the periphery of the capitalist world (Russia, China, and more recently the less developed nations of Africa and Latin America).

The parallels between Russia and Japan are particularly interesting. Both were latecomers to industrialization whose governments forced the pace of modernization; both, in the early decades of the twentieth century, had large agrarian sectors in which the remnants of pre-capitalist social relationships were only gradually disappearing. Both also had influential and relatively independent-minded coteries of intellectuals that were much obsessed with the problems of relating Western ideas to indigenous culture. Why Marxism had so much more impact on practical politics in Russia than in Japan is an intriguing question which goes beyond the scope of this book, but it is possible to suggest some specific reasons for the importance that Marxism assumed in the economic thought of interwar Japan.

In the first place, the economic circumstances of Japan in the 1920s and early 1930s, where severe rural depression coexisted with the growing wealth of handful of giant oligopolistic industrial enterprises (the *zaibatsu*), hardly seemed to conform to the optimistic vision of free-enterprise economy presented by Marx's neo-classical critics. Moreover, many Japanese economists (Kawakami Hajime is the outstanding example) were clearly attracted by the moral passion that they encountered in Marx's writings. As we shall see, Kawakami expressly related this view of economics as a crusade against injustice to the pre-Meiji traditions of Japanese ethical and economic thought. Finally, the close link that existed between Japanese and German academic economics made it inevitable that Japanese scholars would be exposed to serious debate of Marx's ideas, for Marxism was a far more important part of academic discourse in continental Europe than it was, for example, in Britain or the United States.

Socialist ideas of various types had begun to enter Japan in the latter part of the nineteenth century. One reference to the subject, indeed, can be dated back as far as 1872, when Nishi Amane, in an address to the emperor on Western political thought, contrasted the 'communalists' (*tsūyūgaku-ha*), who proposed that all wealth should be divided equally, with the 'economists' (*keizaigaku-ha*) who argued that wealth or poverty were the consequences of one's own wisdom or folly (Tamanoi 1971: 12).

The early currents of Japanese socialist thought, however, derived their impetus from sources other than Marxism. One important influence was the popular rights movement of the 1870s and 1880s, a somewhat amorphous political movement initiated by disaffected former *samurai*, but which soon expanded to gain the support of significant sections of the rural population. The principal objective uniting the participants in the popular rights movement was the aim of creating a representative constitutional system of government, but some left-wing activists in the movement also emphasized the need for a more equitable distribution of wealth (Bowen 1980). Amongst those who were deeply influenced by the popular rights movement was the leading early twentieth-century socialist Kōtoku Shūsui, who was executed in 1911 on a fabricated charge of plotting to assassinate the emperor.

A very different source of socialist ideas in Meiji Japan was the activity of Christian missionaries. Restrictions on missionary activity had been lifted in 1883, and by 1888 the missions were claiming some 50,000 Japanese converts to the various Christian denominations (Shaw 1922: 82). Although many missionaries were politically conservative, there were some who brought with them not only bibles but also the works of Christian socialists such as Charles Kingsley.

By the end of the Meiji era the diverse currents of socialist and reformist thought were beginning to be brought together through the emergence of the Japanese labour movement. In the late nineteenth century, such industrial disputes as occurred were for the most part spontaneous and disorganized, the impromptu reactions of employees against intolerable working conditions, but during the late 1890s and early 1900s a number of attempts were made to establish unions of skilled industrial workers in trades like printing and metal working. In 1912 the first national labour organization, the *Yūaikai* (Friendly Society) was established under the guidance of the Christian social reformer Suzuki Bunji (1885–1945). Christian socialists and other radicals, including Kōtoku Shūsui, also participated in the creation of political organizations such as the rapidly suppressed Social Democratic Party (*Shakai Minshūtō*) of 1901 and the slightly longer-lived Socialist Association (*Shakaishugi Kyōkai*) of 1900 (Scalapino 1983: 8–41).

By the outbreak of the First World War, the writings of men like Fukuda Tokuzō and Kōtoku Shūsui (who helped to produce the first Japanese translation of the *Communist Manifesto*) had introduced Japanese scholars at least to certain aspects of Marxist thought. Ōuchi Hyōe, one of the leading members of the Marxist *Rōnō* school, later recalled that during his undergraduate years at Tokyo University from 1907 to 1910 'most new students . . . were quite familiar with Marx and I think that most had at least read *Capital* to some extent' (Ōuchi 1960: 23). But Marxist ideas at that stage remained within the walls of the faculties and had little practical impact on political movements or on the wider intellectual world.

> There was probably no-one among the students who really saw Marxism in practical terms, or who thought of socialism as an ideal for Japanese political movements. In other words, socialism was seen as a foreign academic discipline, a foreign idea, but not as a movement.
>
> (Ōuchi 1960: 28)

After his return from study in the United States during the First World War, however, Ōuchi found a very different atmosphere in Japan. The more democratic mood of Taishō Japan had opened the way to a freer debate of radical ideas, and the Russian Revolution inspired wider interest in Marxism. The outbreak of strikes and rice riots throughout Japan in the final year of the war, provoked by rampant inflation and occurring almost simultaneously with the Russian Revolution, emphasized the possible relevance of foreign political upheavals for Japan itself.

Public debates became more and more left-wing with every month,

75

and the more left-wing they became the greater their popularity grew.

(Ōuchi 1960: 69)

This transition in Japanese thought from the rather academic and utopian socialism of the late Meiji period to the Marxism and political activism of the 1920s is particularly well illustrated in the career and writings of the man who emerged as Japan's first eminent Marxist economist: Kawakami Hajime.

THE MARXIST ECONOMICS OF KAWAKAMI HAJIME (1879–1946) AND KUSHIDA TAMIZŌ (1885–1934)

Kawakami Hajime was the eldest son of a minor local administrator from Yamaguchi Prefecture in western Japan. He entered Tokyo University as a student of politics and economics in 1898, and studied under Matsuzaki Kuranosuke, a protégé of Kanai Noboru, whose lectures seem to have evoked singularly little enthusiasm from the young Kawakami.

Even as a high school student Kawakami had been intensely idealistic and much concerned with problems of morality. These concerns remained with him in adulthood, causing him at one point to abandon a post as a lecturer in agricultural economics at Tokyo University in order to join a commune run by a syncretic religious sect called the Garden of Selflessness. Although his ethical perspectives had initially been derived from Confucian tradition, Kawakami was strongly influenced both by Christianity and by Tolstoyan humanism. In his early writings, while he condemned the political establishment, he also criticized socialism for its neglect of individual morality (Bernstein 1976: Chaps 1–3). This combination of social concern and mistrust of socialism made it easy for Kawakami to find acceptance amongst the members of the Association for the Study of Social Policy (see pp. 62–5). During the early years of the twentieth century he was an active participant in the Association's conferences, at which he presented papers in 1908 and 1912 (Sumiya 1967: 175–6).

In 1908 Kawakami re-entered academic life as a lecturer in the economics faculty of Kyoto University, and five years later he was granted government support for a study visit to France, Germany, and Britain, an event that was to have a formative impact on his economic ideas (Bernstein 1976: 71–83). Rather like Kanai Noboru before him, Kawakami learned less from his formal studies in Europe than from his observation of social conditions. He was in particular deeply disturbed by the poverty that he encountered both in the slums of London and in the backwaters of rural England. Since Britain was still seen as the richest, most powerful, and most technologically advanced nation on earth – the country whose achievements Japanese government and industrialists most desired to emulate – the discovery of widespread poverty in Britain raised profound questions about the nature of the economic system itself.

In 1916, immediately after his return from Europe, Kawakami attempted to address these questions in a series of newspaper articles which were subsequently compiled into a book entitled *A Tale of Poverty* (*Bimbō Monogatari*). The articles contained in *A Tale of Poverty* are popular in style and interspersed with delightful asides on everything from the family of life of Karl Marx to the entomology of the leaf-cutter ant. They are also of real significance both because of the great impact they were to have on Japanese thought and because of the light they shed on Kawakami's intellectual development.

The starting point of *A Tale of Poverty* is the observation that even in the richest countries of the world, large sections of the population are unable to afford the bare necessities of life. In order to substantiate this observation, Kawakami quotes extensively from such works of Western social research as Charles Booth's *Life and Labour of the People of London* and B. Seebohm Rowntree's *Poverty: A Study of Town Life*. He then goes on to confront the question that inevitably follows: why should poverty persist in the midst of the wealth and technological sophistication of the world's richest nations? Kawakami considers, and rejects, two popular answers to this question. The first is the Malthusian answer, that the benefits of expanding productivity are negated by the growth of population. Kawakami refutes this on both empirical and theoretical grounds. Industrial productivity in advanced countries like Britain, he argues, has grown far more rapidly than the size of the population over the past 100 years; furthermore, Malthus's theory fails to explain why some people enrich themselves while others remain poor (Kawakami 1965: 77–8). The second popular explanation that Kawakami considers is the view that poverty is simply the consequence of the unequal distribution of the nation's wealth. This idea, Kawakami claims, is a superficial one which fails to comprehend the real workings of the modern exchange economy (Kawakami 1965: 80).

Kawakami is now ready to present his own analysis of the sources of economic injustice. Production in the capitalist system, he explains, is designed not to fulfil human need, but to meet effective demand.

Business enterprises produce a mass of unnecessary luxuries to serve the whims of the rich because the rich can support their whims with real purchasing power. Meanwhile, the basic needs of the poor are ignored because they are not expressed in terms of monetary demand.

> [T]he reason why insufficient necessities of life are produced is that the world's productive power is squandered on the manufacturing of luxury goods. If the necessities of life were produced in slightly larger quantities than the demand of the impoverished masses could support, the exchange price of these goods would fall and profits would be reduced. Therefore businessmen limit the production of such goods. It seems to me that this is the main structural economic reason why so many people in civilised countries suffer poverty at the present time.
>
> (Kawakami 1965: 87)

What is fascinating about this approach is the way in which Kawakami links modern economic analysis to the moral precepts of such Tokugawa philosophers as Kumazawa Banzan and Ogyū Sorai. This link is particularly evident in proposed solutions to the problem of poverty. His first solution — restraint and frugality on the part of the rich — could be lifted straight from the pages of Banzan's writings, and even his more modern-sounding proposals for the nationalization of industry and for state-run welfare schemes contain echoes of Satō Nobuhiro's egalitarian nationalism (Kawakami 1965: 90). But at the same time Kawakami supports his views with an analysis founded on an extensive knowledge of Western economic theory; his concept of poverty as the inevitable obverse of excessive wealth also in some ways foreshadows the views of modern radical theorists, who have similarly seen the poverty of the underdeveloped world as an inescapable concomitant of the 'overdevelopment' of rich nations (e.g. Mandel 1971; Caldwell 1977).

The links between modern theory and traditional Japanese thought also form the main theme of Kawakami's discussion of Marxism. By the time he wrote *A Tale of Poverty*, Kawakami had already acquired a deep respect for Marx, whom he describes as 'one of the greatest thinkers of the nineteenth century' (Kawakami 1965: 122). But his interpretation of Marx's materialist concept of history is, to say the least, an idiosyncratic one. Kawakami paraphrases Marx's view of the economic structure as the base whose development determines the changing shape of law, politics, ideology, morality, and culture, and then goes on to suggest that this view is in essence identical with the Confucian idea that human beings will only act morally when their material needs are satisfied. In Kumazawa Banzan's words 'when food is scarce . . . contention is rife and crime never ceases' (quoted in Kawakami 1965: 125).

This comparison is, of course, a misleading oversimplification of Marx's dialectical materialism, but it is an interesting simplification because it very clearly reveals the key to Kawakami's concept of economics. For Kawakami, economics is never merely the study of the production and distribution of wealth. Rather, the ultimate object of economics is to make human beings more fully human. In his early work Kawakami presents poverty as an evil because it reduces the poor to a subhuman level of existence. But at the same time he does not believe that wealth by itself brings happiness, and indeed sees excessive wealth as being as much a source of misery as excessive poverty (Kawakami 1965: 42)

Despite its wide popular appeal, *A Tale of Poverty* came under almost immediate attack from younger scholars whose knowledge of Marx's writings was more profound than Kawakami's. The leading critic was Kawakami's former student, Kushida Tamizō, a scholar whose debates with Kawakami were to play a vital role in a development of Japanese Marxist economics. In contrast to the conventional image of the teacher-student relationship, Kushida's relationship with Kawakami was characterized by mutual respect as well as sharp intellectual disputes from which the student repeatedly emerged as victor over the teacher. Kushida's attack on *A Tale of Poverty*, in which he accused Kawakami of being an idealist rather than a materialist, shocked Kawakami into reconsidering his position and embarking on a more thorough study of Marx's writings.

The consequences of this study are clearly apparent in Kawakami's writings during the early 1920s. In 1922, for example, he entered into a debate with the leading Japanese neo-classical economist Koizumi Shinzō (see pp. 88–91), who had launched an attack on Marx's labour theory of value. Kawakami responded with a series of articles in which he criticized the neo-classical school and developed his own defence of the labour theory of value. In these articles he recast Marx's view – that exchange value is determined by the amount of labour required to produce a given commodity – into the statement that the value of any object reflects the amount of human effort and sacrifice involved in its production. This, Kawakami argued, is a clear and irrefutable fact of human society:

Marx's so-called value is none other than the value of the costs incurred in production from a human standpoint. . . . As long as we conceive of the economic value of a particular object from the human standpoint, we cannot fail to accept Marx's labour theory of value.

(Quoted in Sugihara 1980: 382)

By this time Kawakami was far more strongly influenced by Marxism, and far more knowledgeable on the subject, than he had been when he wrote *A Tale of Poverty*. But his interpretation of Marx's labour theory of value was still open to criticism. As Kushida Tamizō was quick to point out, Kawakami had tried to create a universal and immutable theory of value that applied to all things at all times, whereas Marx himself had been emphatic that the laws of value varied with changing economic structures, and that fully developed commodity exchange was specific to capitalism. Once again Kawakami was forced to return to further study of Marx, and once again he eventually bowed to the views of his former student.

The fruits of Kawakami's prolonged intellectual struggles with Marxism included a Japanese translation of *Capital* and a number of other works in which a relatively orthodox Marxian approach to the economy is intermeshed with Kawakami's long-standing concern for humanitarian and moral issues. In his *Introduction to 'Capital'* (*Shihonron Nyūmon*), published in 1932, Kawakami provided a straightforward outline of Marx's labour theory of value and materialist view of history. The lengthy preface to the text, however, reveals Kawakami still battling to reconcile his own conception of individual morality with the Marxist view that human history is ultimately determined by the development of economic structures rather than by the acts of individuals. Kawakami resolves this long-lasting dilemma by emphasizing the importance of class struggle. Changing economic systems may shape the course of history, but new systems can only replace the old if suppressed classes rise up to challenge the entrenched interests of the existing ruling élite. This class struggle itself can only come about through the conscious action of human individuals (Kawakami 1945: 46–8). Marxism, therefore, is not only a philosophy and an economic theory, but also 'consists of practice' and so 'has the most revolutionary conclusions' (Kawakami 1945: 1).

These last words are not merely empty rhetoric. In 1928 Kawakami had been dismissed from Kyoto University for political activities including support for a radical candidate in the general election of that year. Four years later, after prolonged doubt and debate, he joined the underground Japanese Communist Party, and in 1933, at the age of 54, he was arrested for subversion. Although (unlike some other 1930s radicals) Kawakami refused to recant his Marxist beliefs, he did agree, as a condition of his release in 1937, to abandon political activity, and the final years of his life were spent in secluded retirement (Bernstein 1976: 154–64).

THE KŌZA SCHOOL ANALYSIS OF JAPANESE CAPITALISM: NORO EITARŌ (1900–34) AND YAMADA MORITARŌ (1897–1980)

Kawakami Hajime was by no means the only left-wing intellectual to discover that in the Japan of the 1920s and 1930s, the distinction between academic research and political involvement was an impossible one to maintain. It was not simply that the late Taishō and early Shōwa periods were years of great political ferment, in which trade union activity reached its pre-war peak and numerous radical parties were created and suppressed; the very nature of the draconian security laws meant that any scholar whose lectures and writings expressed left-wing views was subject, as Kawakami had been, to dismissal and ultimate arrest.

In this environment it was not surprising that Marxist economic thought soon became inseparably entangled in questions of practical political strategy. A number of Kawakami's fellow academics joined the newly created Japanese Communist Party, which therefore came to have intellectual significance out of all proportion to its very small size. Others supported a miscellany of left-wing political groups formed in the mid-1920s. The central problem which these Japanese Marxists faced was that in order to work towards a socialist revolution, it was necessary to understand how Japan fitted into the Marxian schema of economic and social development. Marx, after all, had envisaged the transition to socialism as occurring only after a long period of capitalist development and decay, whereas Japanese Marxists were confronting a capitalist system whose origins were relatively recent. Did this mean, then, that Japanese Communists must wait for, or even promote, the further development of capitalist institutions before they could attempt to overthrow these institutions?

The problem was not, of course, a new one. In pre-revolutionary Russia a similar debate had occurred over the possibility of 'premature' revolution within a semi-developed capitalist society (Medvedev 1979). The outcome of the debate in Japan, however, was rather different from that in Russia. On its foundation in 1922, the Japanese

Communist Party consisted of a very small group of people whose activities were subject to constant police surveillance and harassment: indeed, most of the founding members were arrested within the first year of the party's existence. Under these circumstances, a number of Japanese Marxists came to the conclusion that a separate Communist Party could play no useful role in Japanese politics. The correct course, they argued, was to create a mass-based organization of workers, peasants, and others which would eventually evolve into a revolutionary movement capable of overthrowing capitalism. By 1927 this group had separated from the Japanese Communist Party and was to form the core of the *Rōnō* school (discussed in the following section) (see Hoston 1986: 48–54). The remaining Communist Party members, meanwhile, came to see their own dilemma as arising from the survival of feudal or absolutist elements in Japanese society, and defined as one of their objectives the achievement of the bourgeois democratic reforms which must precede a future socialist revolution.

This perspective was most clearly expressed in the so-called '1932 Thesis', drawn up by the Japanese Communist Party after consultation with Comintern. The 1932 Thesis stated that while the ultimate objective was the establishment of a dictatorship of the proletariat, the way forward must first be cleared by a bourgeois revolution that would abolish the institution of emperor and redistribute the wealth of the land-owning class (Nihon Kyōsantō 1978: 70; Hoston 1986: 71–4).

The main considerations behind this analysis of the Japanese economic situation were doubtless strategic as much as academic. Japan at that time was becoming increasingly involved in military expansion on the Asian mainland, and the most pressing need, from the perspective of international communism, was for the Japanese Party to combat the rise of Japanese militarism. But the 1932 Thesis also drew inspiration from some serious works of economic scholarship, particularly from the researches of the young Keiō-educated economist and historian, Noro Eitarō, who was himself a leading member of the Japanese Communist Party in the early 1930s (Fujii 1976: 258–63).

Noro had begun to expound his analysis of Japanese capitalism from the mid-1920s onwards, but its most complete statement was presented in his *History of the Development of Japanese Capitalism* (*Nihon Shihonshugi Hattatsushi*) published in 1930. This work shows the imprint not only of Marx's ideas but also of Lenin's theory of imperialism, which has had a particularly great influence on Japanese radical thought. Using the Leninist analytical framework Noro argued that Japan had undergone its first industrial revolution – based on textiles and other light manufacturing – in the last decades of the nineteenth century. From the Russo-Japanese War (1904–5) onwards, Noro wrote, it had entered the imperialist stage of development, in which the heavy industries of the 'second industrial revolution' (steel, armaments, etc.) became increasingly important (Noro 1983: vol. 1, 88–114).

But the feverish pace of Japanese economic development, combined with the peculiarities of the international environment in which Japan industrialized, had resulted (Noro claimed) in distortions in the nature of Japanese capitalism. The semi-feudal ties between landlord and peasant were not dissolved, but were rather incorporated into, and intensified by, the capitalist economic system. Japanese industrial entrepreneurs and large landlords did not emerge as an independent political force as they had done in Europe, but instead remained dependent on the support of the imperial bureaucracy and military. At the same time, in the outside world, the age of *laissez-faire* was giving way to an age of tariffs and imperial rivalries, a situation that reinforced the domestic Japanese tendencies towards cartel-formation and government protection of industry. Consequently, the development of capitalism in Japan had not resulted (as it had elsewhere) in the creation of a liberal democratic system, but rather in the formation of an absolutist or autocratic political order, in which the new industrial and financial elite sheltered under the wing of a repressive militarist government (Noro 1983: vol. 1, 115–32, 252–62).

This interpretation of Japanese capitalism was restated and refined in a multi-volume collection of *Lectures on the Historical Development of Japanese Capitalism* (*Nihon Shihonshugi Hattatsu Shi Kōza*, 1932–3), from which the Kōza school derives its popular name. The *Lectures* were the joint brainchild of a number of leading left-wing thinkers including Noro Eitarō, the historians Hattori Shiso (1901–56) and Hani Gorō (1901–83), and two former Tokyo University economists, Hirano Yoshitarō (1897–1986) and Yamada Moritarō. It is, however, Yamada's contribution, later republished separately under the title *An Analysis of Japanese Capitalism* (*Nihon Shihonshugi Bunseki*, 1934), that was perhaps most influential in developing the distinctive Kōza school approach.

Yamada's analysis opens with an unequivocal statement on Japan's position in the schema of capitalist development:

British capitalism appeared in the birthplace of the struggle for liberalism; German and U.S. capitalism emerged in the home of concentration and monopoly; Russian and Japanese capitalism took shape in countries characterised by militaristic serfdom or semi-serfdom. In terms of world history each of these types is distinct.

(Yamada 1934: 3)

The remainder of the book is largely devoted to elucidating the meaning of the phrase 'militaristic serfdom or semi-serfdom' and to demonstrating its applicability to Japanese conditions. Yamada sees an integral connection between two apparently contradictory facets of Japanese society: on the one hand, the development of relatively advanced heavy industries oriented to military demand (armaments, shipbuilding, coal mining, etc.), and on the other the existence of a large impoverished peasant economy. The relationship he traces between these facets is a circular one: the state requires a strong army to suppress domestic discontent and promote overseas expansion; it therefore supports and protects military-related industries. Finance for these industries is raised principally through heavy taxes on the rural sector; these taxes, combined with exorbitant land rents, aggravate the discontent of the peasantry. The threat of peasant rebellion in turn intensifies the need for military might (Yamada 1934: *passim*; see particularly pp. 67–73).

The role of peasant agriculture in this analysis is a particularly crucial one: Yamada describes it as the 'foundation' (*kitei*) of the economic structure. Like Noro, he argues that the 1873 land tax, designed by economic liberals such as Kanda and Matsukata, had not in fact resulted in the complete penetration of capitalism into Japanese agriculture. Instead, the feudal relationship between peasant and domain lord had merely been transformed into a semi-feudal relationship between peasant and landlord. The landlords passed on to their tenants the burden of land and other taxes, at the same time imposing exorbitant rents which, according to Yamada's researches, often left no more than a third of the meagre harvest in the hands of the peasant producer (Yamada 1934: 189). Japanese land rents, Yamada observes, are largely paid in kind, and are far higher than those of other capitalist countries. This last point he attributes to the fact that Japanese rents do not reflect a commercial exchange. Instead, they are determined by the political ability of landlords, with the support of government and military, to impose their exploitation on the peasantry through 'non-economic force' (Yamada 1934: 193).

The role of 'non-economic force', Yamada argues, is even more apparent in the survival of a system of quasi-serfdom, whereby tenant farmers were obliged to perform labour services in the landlord's field or house. Quoting a number of reported cases from the Taishō and early Shōwa periods, Yamada suggests that this practice is still current throughout 1930s Japan (Yamada 1934: 212–21).

From the *kōza* school perspective, therefore, the problem of applying Marxist analysis to Japanese capitalism could be solved by suggesting the existence of various differing models of capitalist development. In late developing capitalist nations such as Japan, the evolution of social and political structures might follow a rather different path from that depicted by Marx in his analysis of western European capitalism. Both the internal environment, with its 'feudal remnants' and the external environment, with its imperialistic rivalries, helped to create an economy in which advanced heavy industry coexisted with a retarded agricultural sector, and where a small but significant capitalist class flourished without the trappings of liberal democracy. This approach was, of course, a convenient one in that it dovetailed neatly with the strategic interests of the Communist Party leadership. However, it also represented an interesting attempt to adapt the patterns of Marxist and Leninist theory to the circumstances of twentieth-century Japan, even though it continues to present Japan and other late developers essentially as deviants from the 'normal' model of capitalist development represented (above all) by Britain.

THE RŌNŌ SCHOOL'S ALTERNATIVE ANALYSIS: TSUCHIYA TAKAO (1896–) AND SAKISAKA ITSURŌ (1897–1985)

The *Kōza* school's analysis of Japanese capitalism soon became the target of criticism from economists and historians associated with the Marxists who had separated from the Communist Party in 1924–5. In political terms, the leading figure in this group was Yamakawa Hitoshi (Kin) (1880–1958), a former anarchist and a founding member of the Communist Party, who, in 1927, was instrumental in establishing the journal *Worker and Farmer* (*Rōnō*). Although many of the so-called *Rōnō* school academics had little direct connection with the journal, they shared with Yamakawa a disliking for the rigidity and dogmatism that, in their view, characterized the attitudes of the Japanese Communist Party and the *Kōza* school.

In spite of the ascerbic tone which often entered into the *Rōnō* school/*Kōza* school debate, it is worth emphasizing that the views of the two schools had a great deal in common. Both agreed that Japan had progressed rapidly to an imperialist stage of capitalist development, yet both recognized the impossibility of applying European

85

models precisely to Japanese development. However, *Rōnō* school members such as Kushida Tamizō, Ōuchi Hyōe, Tsuchiya Takao, and Sakisaka Itsurō attacked the *Kōza* school on three principal grounds. First, they argued that *Kōza* scholars, having found a theory that suited their political needs, then imposed this theory on reality with insufficient regard for inconvenient facts. As Tsuchiya Takao put it in his critique of Yamada Moritarō, they had 'an attitude which tries, with unreasonable simplification, to force Japanese capitalism into a single mould' (Tsuchiya 1937: 77).

Second, the *Rōnō* school suggested that their opponents failed to appreciate the elements of dynamism and change within the Japanese capitalist system. Third, they argued that the *Kōza* school exaggerated the differences and underestimated the similarities between Japanese capitalism and capitalism in Europe and America. In this sense, as Nagasu Kazuji has rather aptly put it, the issue was whether the object of study was 'the development of *Japanese* capitalism' or 'the development of Japanese *capitalism*' (Nagasu 1965: 97). These points were elaborated in numerous journal articles produced by the main *Rōnō* school theorists during the 1930s. Two collections of these essays, however – Tsuchiya's *Collected Writings on the History of Japanese Capitalism* (*Nihon Shihonshugi Shi Ronshū*, 1937) and Sakisaka's *Problems of Japanese Capitalism* (*Nihon Shihonshugi no Shomondai*, 1937) – will serve to illustrate the main features of the *Rōnō* school perspective.

Tsuchiya's writings reflect their author's background as an economic historian, influenced not only by Marxism but also by the Social Policy School's meticulous regard for historical data (see Aoki 1976: 230). One of his most significant points of dispute with the *Kōza* school relates to its tendency (in Tsuchiya's eyes) to treat historical and economic facts without sufficient care. This criticism is directed specifically at Yamada Moritarō's concept of 'semi-serfdom' in Japanese agriculture. Tsuchiya argues that Yamada's examples of modern 'serfdom' are drawn from outdated documents and presented in a misleading light. Going back to Yamada's own sources, Tsuchiya demonstrates that the cases of unpaid labour-service which he records are derived from a very small number of remote mountain villages – hardly enough to support the idea that 'semi-serfdom' was typical of twentieth-century Japanese agriculture (Tsuchiya 1937: 84–93). More generally, Tsuchiya attacks the whole notion of 'semi-serfdom' or 'semi-feudalism' as being meaningless. In what precise way, he asks, can the Japan of the 1930s be said to resemble the feudal Japan of the seventeenth or eighteenth centuries (Tsuchiya 1937: 80)?

In contrast to Yamada's relatively static picture of the rural economy, Tsuchiya presents a picture of considerable dynamism, in which commercial exchange relations between landlord and tenant are seen as originating in the late Tokugawa age. As rural areas were drawn into the money economy during the eighteenth and early nineteenth centuries, many small farmers lost ownership of their holding, despite official prohibitions on the sale of land. The 'new landlords' who gained control of these holdings were, Tsuchiya suggested, not only large farmers but also often townsmen, who acquired land as a commercial investment, thus injecting a form of proto-capitalism into Japanese agriculture.

> [W]hether in the commercial management of newly-reclaimed fields by townsmen or in the consolidation of holdings by landlords, we cannot but see the corrosive influence of commercial capital and usurer capital, and thus we see also the embryonic development of capitalist landholding and the capitalist management of agriculture.
>
> (Tsuchiya 1934: 4; see also Tsuchiya 1977: 158–60)

This analysis of the pre-Meiji origins of Japanese capitalism was supported by the researches of Hattori Shisō, who suggested that 'manufactures', in Marx's sense of the word, had reached a relatively advanced level of development in Tokugawa Japan, thus laying the foundations for Japan's rapid adoption of Western industrial techniques in the late nineteenth century (Hattori 1955: vol. 1).

A similar emphasis on the dynamism of the Japan economics system is to be found in Sakisaka's essays. Sakisaka is particularly critical of the *Kōza* school's tendency to treat post-Meiji Japan as though it were a static system. This approach, Sakisaka suggests, entirely ignores the profound changes that have occurred, and continue to occur, within the system – above all the gradual transformation of the peasantry into a modern proletariat. While Tsuchiya questions the evidence for the survival of labour services in twentieth-century Japan, Sakisaka casts doubts on Yamada's wage figures, which implied that Japanese workers were employed in 'semi-slave' conditions, earning wages lower even than those of Indian workers. Like Tsuchiya, Sakisaka suggests that the *Kōza* school economist is distorting the evidence to suit his own preconceived model of Japanese capitalism (Sakisaka 1958).

Some interesting parallels can be observed between the *Kōza-Rōnō* controversy and Marxist debates in other times and places. The problems of the relationship between theory and historical evidence, for example, have re-emerged in recent years in the exchanges between Louis Althusser in France and E.P. Thompson in Britain. Thompson's distaste for obscure terminology and his advocacy of a flexible application of theory to reality often echoes the *Rōnō* school's critique of its opponents (see Thompson 1978). More widely, as Germaine Hoston points out, the problems of the application of Marxist theory to less-developed countries has been one of the major issues of political and economic debate in the post-war world (Hoston 1986: ix–xv). Unfortunately, the political antagonisms implicit within the inter-war Japanese controversy hindered the two sides from a constructive development of the many ideas that they shared. The animosity of the debate is also, perhaps, one reason why foreign scholars of Japan have tended until recently to treat both schools with scant respect, failing to see that their polemics concealed much substantial research and original theorizing. (The first major English-language monograph on the debate was not published until 1986.) However, the energy with which the controversy was pursued did have certain beneficial effects. Both sides were forced to address, and to refine their views on, the difficult question of the application of Marxist theory to Japanese capitalism, and both defended their views by unearthing a wealth of historical and economic data. They therefore helped to provide both the theoretical and the empirical bases for countless later studies of the development of Japanese capitalism.

KOIZUMI SHINZŌ (1888–1966) AND THE CRITIQUE OF MARXISM

Although debates amongst Marxist factions often seemed to occupy the centre stage during the 1920s and early 1930s, other schools of economic thought were also extending a growing influence within Japan. Amongst the most important of these was the Austrian school, that rather loosely linked group of scholars who derived inspiration from the work of the leading marginalist economist Carl Menger (1840–1921).

Menger, a fierce critic of the empiricist tendencies of the German social policy school, had independently arrived at a theory which closely resembled that of the British economist W.J. Jevons. Menger's economics, in other words, was founded on the notion that the value of commodities derives not from their cost of production but from their ability to satisfy human needs, needs whose magnitude can be expressed on a graduated scale, so that value rises the more essential and the less abundant the commodity. Of Menger's disciples, the two who attracted the greatest interest in inter-war Japan were Eugen von Böhm-Bawerk (1851–1914), who used marginalist theory as a weapon in a comprehensive attack on Marx's labour theory of value, and Joseph Schumpeter (1883–1950), who developed a much more eclectic economic style, blending neo-classical analysis with quantitative and historical studies.

As we saw in the previous chapter, Fukuda Tokuzō played an important part in introducing the new marginalist ideas into Japan. Fukuda's interest in marginalism and his mistrust of Marxism were transmitted to his most famous disciple, Koizumi Shinzō, who borrowed from the ideas of the Austrian school in his attempt to continue Fukuda's attack on the dominance of Marxism in Japanese economic thought.

Koizumi came from a family with a strong scholarly tradition, his father having succeeded Fukuzawa Yukichi as chairman of Keiō. Koizumi himself graduated from Keiō University and, after a period of overseas study in England and Germany, was appointed professor of economics in 1919, eventually becoming chairman of the university, a post which he held from 1933 to 1947. His significant contributions to the debate on value began to appear in the early 1920s and provoked a heated exchange with several Marxist scholars including Kawakami Hajime, Kushida Tamizō, and Yamakawa Hitoshi (Itoh 1980: 17–18).

Koizumi's critique of Marxist economics focused on its controversial cornerstone, the labour theory of value, and was very strongly influenced by Böhm-Bawerk's classic *Karl Marx and the Close of his System* (1896). Like Böhm-Bawerk, Koizumi pointed to the apparent contradiction between Marx's theory of value, set out in Volume 1 of *Capital*, and his theory of prices of production, introduced in Volume 3. In the earlier volume, Marx had emphasized that the exchange value of a product is equal to the 'labour time socially necessary for its production' (Marx 1976: vol. 1, 129) and that surplus value (i.e. the value produced by workers over and above the cost of their own subsistence) is the source of all profit. He had also assumed that the rate of surplus value will be the same across all branches of industry. But as Marx was well aware, this would imply that the actual rate of profit varied between different industries: industries that used large amounts of labour in relation to the amount of fixed capital would earn relatively higher levels of profit, a situation that would be untenable in a competitive economy.

In Volume 3 of *Capital*, Marx had attempted to resolve this problem by transforming exchange values into prices of production. Here he suggested that surplus value, once created, was redistributed throughout the economy in such a way that an equal rate of profit was obtained. Koizumi, like Böhm-Bawerk, attacked this 'solution' to the problem of profits as being totally inconsistent with Marx's original statements on value. If prices of production prevailed, Koizumi argued, then goods might exchange at values that bore no direct relationship to the number of hours of labour taken to produce them (Koizumi 1967–72: vol. 3, 173, 178–9; see also Böhm-Bawerk 1949: 28–30). Koizumi particularly stressed the apparent inconsistency in Marx's treatment of labour itself. Wages represented the cost of goods needed to sustain the individual worker, but the cost of these goods was expressed in terms of prices and not of labour values. Therefore, labour itself violated the principles set out in Volume 1 of *Capital*: its value was not determined by the amount of work needed to sustain the life of the individual labourer (Koizumi 1967–72: vol. 3, 188; see also Böhm-Bawerk 1949: 57–8).

All in all, Koizumi concludes, Marx's theory consists on the one hand of self-contradictions and on the other of circular arguments. The theory of prices of production merely states that the price of a commodity is determined by the cost of each of the elements (capital and labour power) consumed in its production, and the price of each of these elements is in turn determined by the cost of the capital and labour power consumed in *their* production, and so on *ad infinitum*. Drawing on a metaphor popular with the Austrian school, Koizumi likens this logic to the mythological idea that the world was supported on the shoulders of Atlas: if Atlas were standing on earth, then presumably there must be a second Atlas holding up a second world, and he in turn must be standing on a third globe supported by a third Atlas, and so on (Koizumi 1967–72: vol. 3, 189–90).

These criticisms evoked immediate responses from leading Japanese Marxists including Kawakami Hajime, Kushida Tamizō, and Yamakawa Hitoshi, and the ensuing debate closely mirrored a controversy that had occurred some 20 years earlier between European neoclassical and Marxist economists. Kushida reiterated the argument first put forward by Rudolf Hilferding (1877–1941) in reply to Böhm-Bawerk's critique of Marx. The theory of value set out in Volume 1 of *Capital* was not, according to this argument, contradicted by the theory of prices set out in Volume 3. Rather, the two theories applied to economies in different stages of economic development. While Volume 1 described the state of 'simple commodity production' that existed in pre-capitalist exchange economies, the price theory of Volume 3 described conditions in a fully fledged capitalist economy (Hilferding 1949: 163–7). Kushida supported this view by quoting the opening lines of *Capital*, in which commodity exchange is described as the 'elementary form' of capitalism. The phrase 'elementary form', he claimed, implied a primitive form of exchange which had existed in pre-capitalist phases of economic development (quoted in Koizumi 1966: 306).

Koizumi, however, remained unconvinced. In subsequent articles, he questioned whether the stage of simple commodity exchange described by Hilferding and Kushida could ever have existed. Kushida had suggested that in such a society, labour and capital would not flow freely from one branch of industry to another, and therefore that prices of production would not be equalized throughout the economy. However, Koizumi pointed out that in a society in which guilds or similar social institutions prevented the movement of capital and labour, prices would simply be fixed by monopoly regulation. In that case, Marx's theory of value (which assumed the existence of free competition) would have no relevance to the actual processes of economic exchange (Koizumi 1967–72: vol. 3, 309–10).

In retrospect we can say that the debate between Koizumi and his Marxist critics made only slight contributions to economic knowledge. In general, both sides in the debate were content to restate ideas already developed by their European counterparts, and where they did attempt originality (as in the case of Kushida's interpretation of Marx's 'elementary form') their arguments were often misdirected. The controversy, however, was an important one because it placed the theory of value at the centre of Japanese economic discourse, and so prepared the ground for significant theoretical advances by post-war economists from Uno Kōzō in the 1950s to Morishima Michio in the 1970s (see pp. 116–21, 173–7).

THE INFLUENCE OF NEO-CLASSICAL ECONOMISTS IN INTER-WAR JAPAN:
NAKAYAMA ICHIRŌ (1898–1980) AND
TAKATA YASUMA (1883–1972)

The influence of the Austrian school and of European neo-classicism in general, of course, extended beyond the boundaries of the debate on value theory. During the 1920s and 1930s a number of young Japanese economists (many of them, once again, students of Fukuda

Tokuzō) acquired a working knowledge of newly emerging theories in areas such as general equilibrium theory, imperfect competition, and the analysis of growth cycles.

In this last field of research, a particularly important impetus came from the ideas of Joseph Schumpeter, who made a brief but well-publicized lecture tour of Japan in 1931. Schumpeter's visit came at a time when the Japanese economy was experiencing the full force of the world depression. Inept financial policy (including an ill-timed return to the gold standard) had aggravated the economic downturn, and depression, in combination with prolonged stagnation in the agricultural sector, resulted in rising unemployment and falling wages. In the circumstances it was not surprising that Schumpeter's theories of economic cycles, which explained the world depression as a confluence of the downswings of long-term and short-term cycles, should have attracted considerable interest in Japan (Tamanoi 1971: 159–64).

One of those who was particularly influenced by the Schumpeterian approach to economics was Nakayama Ichirō. Nakayama, like Koizumi Shinzō, was a product of the economic education of Fukuda Tokuzō. Under Fukuda's guidance, he conducted research into the origins of marginalist theory, and had developed an approach to economics founded on the general equilibrium theory of Leon Walras. After studying with Schumpeter at the University of Bonn in the late 1920s, Nakayama returned to teach economics at Tokyo Commercial College and published a number of influential economic texts. His *Pure Economics* (*Junsui Keizaigaku*, 1933) in particular helped to introduce a whole generation of Japanese students to the concepts of marginalism and general equilibrium analysis (Matsuura 1972: 539–40; Tamanoi 1971: 167–71).

Nakayama, however, was not content merely to interpret Walras's ideas to a Japanese audience; he also subjected those ideas to careful critical scrutiny. Like many Japanese neo-classical economists, Nakayama was especially uneasy at the obvious contradiction between the elegance and order of equilibrium theory, and the complex, confused, and perpetually changing realities of the economic world. In order to deal with this dichotomy, Nakayama adopted the distinction between 'economic statics' and 'economic dynamics' which had been suggested by John Stuart Mill and further developed by Schumpeter in his *Theory of Economic Development* (1912). But, where Schumpeter had seen general equilibrium theory as having relevance only to economic statics, Nakayama attempted to use the Walrasian system as a basis for both branches of economic enquiry.

In order to achieve this aim he argued that equilibrium theory was not a description of economic reality but rather a tool to be applied in differing ways to differing areas of analysis. While the concept of equilibrium was directly applicable to the study of economic statics, it was only indirectly applicable to economic dynamics, where the object of investigation was the process by which a new equilibrium emerged out of the destruction of the old (Nakayama 1972a: particularly pp. 8-9).

The problems of reconciling neo-classical theory and reality reappear in the writings of Nakayama's prominent contemporary and rival, Takata Yasuma (1883–1972). Takata, however, approached the problem from a quite different perspective, attempting to incorporate the insights of sociology into the framework of neo-classical analysis. Takata's 'power theory' (*seiryoku setsu*) proposes that the utility of a commodity reflects not only its ability to satisfy physical needs, but also its ability to fulfil the natural human desire for power and social esteem. This concept of extra-economic utility is particularly crucial to Takata's analysis of the wage system. Observing, as John Maynard Keynes did, the 'monetary illusion' which causes workers to resist wage cuts even when prices fall, Takata argues that the nominal value of the wage is as important as its real purchasing power, for it is this nominal value that 'reveals to people how much one is able to earn and so satisfies or fails to satisfy a demand for honour and status' (Takata 1941: 227–8 see also Tsujimura 1984: 88–107).

It will be apparent from the comments in this section that the 'time lag' which had existed between Japanese and European economics in the Meiji period was gradually narrowing. It had taken several decades for the works of John Stuart Mill, Friedrich List, and Karl Marx to reach Japan, but by the 1920s and 1930s, with well-established schools of economics in several universities, Japanese economists were able to debate the ideas of theorists such as Pigou and Schumpeter almost as soon as these were published in Europe.

This speed of interaction was particularly evident in the case of the most celebrated theoretical innovation of the 1930s, J.M. Keynes's general theory of employment, interest, and money. In 1936, the year in which Keynes's *magnum opus* was published, Nakayama Ichirō, together with a handful of other prominent Tokyo-based economists, established a study group to examine Keynes's ideas. The outcome of their discussions was the publication in 1941 of *A Commentary on Keynes' General Theory* (*Keinzu Ippan Riron Kaisetsu*), a collection of essays which at once introduced Japanese readers to Keynes's theories and pointed to a number of possible criticisms of those

93

theories. Nakayama's own contribution to the book, while emphasizing the great importance of Keynes's work, also included some fairly conventional neo-classical criticisms of Keynesian analysis. In particular, Nakayama objected to Keynes's departure from the traditional marginalist interpretation of interest rates, and argued that the macroeconomic approach of the *General Theory* had weaknesses that could only be remedied by microeconomic analysis (Nakayama 1972b).

Although the writings of Japanese economists themselves still received virtually no attention in the West, the growing interaction between Japanese and foreign scholars of economics during the 1920s and 1930s did create a solid foundation for the future development of both Marxian and neo-classical economics in Japan. This foundation was to prove essential to the resurgence of Japanese economic thought after 1945. In the intervening period, however, the dominance of militarism within Japan and the accompanying rise of international political tensions were to result in the temporary isolation of Japan from intellectual contact with the rest of the world, and for a while to the stifling of debate and creativity within Japan itself.

ECONOMICS AND MILITARISM: TAKAHASHI KAMEKICHI (1891–1977) AND KITA IKKI (1883–1937)

The onset of the world depression exacerbated nationalist and expansionist tendencies which had already been apparent in Taishō Japan. From 1931 onwards the domestic economic situation was eased by the policies of the new Finance Minister Takahashi Korekiyo, who took Japan off the gold standard and substantially increased government expenditure. A large share of this budgetary expansion, however, was directly related to Japan's growing military involvement in mainland Asia, and particularly to the 'Manchurian incident', which marked a new stage in the manipulation of government policy by the military. Meanwhile, as one industrialized country after another raised protectionist barriers around its economies, there was growing sympathy within Japan for those who demanded the creation of a Japanese-dominated economic bloc extending into China and Southeast Asia.

Ultranationalism in Japan, as elsewhere, included a strong anti-intellectual element, and particularly a suspicion of imported academic ideas. The policies pursued by the military and the extreme right, however, were not entirely devoid of theoretical foundations, and the relationship between economic theory and nationalist ideology is an intriguing one which deserves more attention than it has received so far. Nationalist writers in inter-war Japan drew their inspiration from a variety of sources, most of which have already been touched on in this study. In part, their ideas reflected the mythologies of Japanese ethnic and moral superiority propagated by the scholars of National Leaning in the late Tokugawa period. On to these indigenous roots, however, they grafted a variety of concepts drawn from Western political and economic theory. The emphasis on the organic nature of the state, so prominent in the writings of the German historical school and of its nineteenth-century Japanese admirers, is repeated in the writings of twentieth-century nationalists such as Kita Ikki. So too is that mistrust both of capitalism and of communism which had been the hallmark of the Social Policy school. (It is no coincidence that some members of the German Social Policy school, such as Werner Sombart, went on to become advocates of German National Socialism). Many of the ideologues of Japanese ultranationalism had also been strongly influenced by aspects of Marxist thought, though they used these ideas in ways quite alien to Marx's own internationalist and materialist philosophy.

The emphasis placed on these diverse influences varied from one nationalist writer to another. Here we shall consider the ideas of two particularly influential theorists whose nationalism was combined with a relatively strong element of social radicalism. Both Takahashi Kamekichi and Kita Ikki had links in their early life with the political left, Kita having been an associate of Kōtoku Shūsui and Takahashi a founding member of the left-wing Political Studies Association (*Seiji Kenkyū Kai*). By the second half of the 1920s, however, Takahashi's views were increasingly coming into conflict with those of socialist theorists, and in 1927 he published an article which provoked a fierce debate with Noro Eitarō and other Marxists (Takahashi 1927; Hoston 1986: Chap. 4).

The thesis that Takahashi put forward in this article centred on the concept of 'petty imperialism'. As the phrase suggests, the thesis borrowed much of its terminology from Lenin and Hilferding, but the conclusions to which it pointed were diametrically opposed to those of the Marxist theory of imperialism, for Takahashi sought to vindicate, rather than to condemn, Japan's overseas military expansion. Takahashi began by arguing that Lenin's notion of imperialism could not be applied to Japan, because Japan lacked the fundamental features ascribed by Lenin to imperialist nations. Japan had not reached the 'highest stage of capitalism' and its industries were not (according to Takahashi) characterized by concentration and monopoly. The forces driving Japanese outward expansionism were thus quite different from those that propelled the colonial activities of the Western powers. The most important of these forces in Japan's case was the pressure of a large and expanding population on limited domestic resources.

> Japan is not so much 'inevitably' forced to fight for a market for the products of its capitalism or for raw materials. It is rather much more true to say that Japan is 'inevitably' forced to fight for an 'outlet for its surplus population'.
>
> (Takahashi 1927: 32)

This view, of course, contains echoes of the German National Socialists' demand for *lebensraum*, but Takahashi gave it a somewhat different perspective by relating Japan's population problems to the country's status in the world economic system. Japan, he suggested, was unable to find a peaceful solution to the problems because it was denied fair access to world markets, which were dominated by the major Western powers. In this way, Japan could be presented as a victim of the international imperialist system, and her fight for *lebensraum* as having 'much in common with a proletarian war of liberation' (Takahashi 1927: 32).

Here Takahashi is in essence taking the Marxian concept of conflict between bourgeoisie and proletariat and recasting it in national rather than class terms. The world is seen as being divided between bourgeois and proletarian nations, and Japan is identified as a revolutionary force within the proletarian group (Takahashi 1927: 91). This analysis, however, poses logical problems that Takahashi's writings fail to resolve. On the one hand, he argues that Japanese military expansion is necessary in order to open the way for the further development of Japanese capitalism; on the other, he presents Japan as the liberator of other Asian nations from the yoke of Western colonialism. It is perhaps unfortunate that critics of Takahashi such as Noro Eitarō spent less time examining these implicit contradictions than they did attempting to prove that every aspect of Lenin's analysis of imperialism was literally applicable to Japan (Noro 1983: 143–82).

The concept of bourgeois and proletarian nations also appears in the writings of the most famous political theorist of ultranationalism, Kita Ikki. Like Takahashi, Kita had by the 1920s exchanged earlier left-wing sympathies for an eclectic mixture of nationalist and radical sentiments, but the idea of internal revolution, which Takahashi had abandoned, continued to play an important role in Kita's writings. Kita described his political objective as the establishment of 'pure socialism' (*junsei shakaishugi*), and his analysis in places resembled that of Marxist theorists but for Kita's idiosyncratic use of terminology drawn from Japanese history. Kita, for example, saw the sources of poverty as lying in the exploitative role of landlords and capitalists who, in the process of industrialization, had gradually deprived small farmers and artisans of their means of livelihood. Out of this had emerged, first, a competitive phase of capitalism, which Kita described as the age of 'economic warring states' (*keizaiteki sengoku jidai*), and later a period of monopoly capital, whose controlling families Kita likened to 'feudal lords' (*daimyō*) (see Naniwada 1973: 202–3).

In his *Outline Plan for the Reconstruction of Japan* (*Nihon Kaizō Hōan Taikō*), published in 1923, Kita proposed a 'revolution from above', initiated by the emperor and the military, which would overthrow this capitalist order, nationalize the property of big business and landlords and improve the welfare and working conditions of ordinary Japanese people. The post-revolutionary utopia he envisaged was a socialist one in the sense that it would be based on equal work and equal rewards for all, but the essential objective of this utopia was not so much the freeing of the human individual from exploitation as the welding together of individuals into an organic state – a state whose evolution transcended the rights and interests of its constituent members (Kita 1971). Kita's revolution also has had international dimension. Indeed, Kita argued that the Marxist-Leninist revolution achieved in Russia was merely a partial revolution, since it addressed only class inequalities within one country, and left unresolved the inequalities between nations.

Justice is that which demarcates the line between the interest of one and the interest of another. Class struggle occurs within countries because this dividing line is unfairly drawn. Likewise, international war is justified when it aims to transform the present unjust dividing line into a just one. Britain is a millionaire who sits astride the world, and Russia is a landowner who owns half the northern hemisphere. Does not Japan, to whom the international division of wealth has allotted the part of a proletarian with a tiny archipelago of islands, have the right to declare war on these countries and destroy their monopoly in the name of justice?

(Kita 1971: 90)

97

The vision of oppressed and oppressor nations put forward by Japanese ultranationalists has been likened by some historians to the more recent concept of conflict between the First and Third Worlds (Hoston 1984: 29–30). But although there are interesting parallels between inter-war Japanese nationalism and later radical nationalist movements in countries such as Argentina and Iran, this comparison needs to be made with some caution. The link between nationalism and social revolution in post-war less-developed countries was strengthened by the fact that the domestic capitalist class was often dependent on foreign multinational investment, a situation that did not exist in interwar Japan. Japan in the 1920s and 1930s, moreover, was in a peculiarly ambivalent position. In a country that was neither underdeveloped nor a fully accepted equal of the major industrialized nations, the nationalist challenge to the existing colonial powers quickly became inextricably associated with the suppression of nationalist aspirations in other Asian countries such as China and Korea.

The ideas of Kita Ikki in particular had a profound impact on the lower-ranking 'young turks' of the Japanese army. But after the abortive military coup of 26 February 1936, and the subsequent execution of Kita for subversion, it was a somewhat different form of nationalist philosophy that came to dominate Japanese political life. While the radical and utopian elements of ultranationalist thought were suppressed, the justifications of overseas expansion and of government intervention in the economy were enthusiastically embraced by military leaders and right-wing politicians. By 1937, Japan was involved in full-scale war in China, but the wartime constraints that were imposed on finance, industry, and labour served to strengthen rather than weaken the power of the *zaibatsu* and so to intensify the economic inequalities within the Japanese system.

ECONOMIC RESEARCH IN WARTIME JAPAN

War rarely creates a congenial atmosphere for intellectual endeavour, and in Japan the negative effects of war were compounded by the intensification of political repression during the late 1930s and early 1940s. The persecution of the political left had begun in earnest as early as 1923, when leading figures associated with the Japanese Communist Party were rounded up by police under the provisions of the Peace Police Law. During the 1930s the witch hunt gradually extended to catch those who had escaped arrest in the 1920s, as well as those who merely taught subversive ideas. Some recanted their views; others either remained in prison or were forced to withdraw from public life. A few were killed, among them Noro Eitarō, who died, aged 34, at the hands of the police.

From the point of view of economic research a particularly·notorious case was the 'professors incident' of 1938, in which several of Tokyo University's leading economists – including Ōuchi Hyōe and Arisawa Hiromi – were arrested. Although they were released without being brought to trial, the arrests forced these scholars out of academic life and signalled a silencing of Marxian economics in Tokyo University that lasted until the end of the Pacific War (Ōuchi 1960: 247–50). Though the left was the main target of political repression, it was by no means the only target. Liberals like the social and economic theorist Kawai Eijirō (1891–1944), who had written a critical study of fascism, were also dismissed from their teaching positions.

The resulting intellectual vacuum was rather inadequately filled by attempts to adapt the state-centred ideas of fascism to the economic circumstances of Japan. In practice, militarism in Japan lacked strong ideological roots, and the economic policies pursued by the government in the war years more often reflected expediency than deeply held political ideals. There were some, however, who attempted to provide the policies of the 1930s and early 1940s with a degree of intellectual respectability. A major influence in this endeavour came from the work of Hijikata Narumi, whose writings had helped to introduce and interpret the ideas of European fascism to a Japanese audience. One of the chief difficulties faced by Hijikata was, of course, the fact that fascism, as an ideology which emphasized the uniqueness and superiority of certain forms of European culture, could not easily be extended to embrace the economic and social circumstances of Japan. Hijikata tried to overcome this problem by arguing that Japan needed to develop its own system reflecting its own unique 'Japanese spirit', but that the 'Japanese spirit' contained many points of similarity to the Italian and German spirit, thus making it possible for the new Japanese order to be closely comparable to European fascism (see Naniwada 1973: 177–8).

The nature of the Japanese spirit, according to Hijikata, was one that was incompatible with capitalism. In his critique of capitalism, however, Hijikata focused not so much on its tendency to create those social injustices so vividly described by Kita Ikki, but rather on its anarchic structure and its competitive and individualistic character. The form of 'controlled economy' envisaged by Hijikata therefore

99

left ample scope for the private ownership of enterprises, while at the same time proposing a much more active role for the state in the planning of the economic order. In particular, Hijikata argued that the parliamentary system, whose influence on the economic system was essentially a 'passive' one, should be supplemented by an 'economic general headquarters', which would play an active role in influencing levels of supply and prices. This general headquarters would be staffed by economic experts, but would also take advice from a council of elected delegates representing the various economic interest groups (see Naniwada 1973: 182–6).

Hijikata's corporalist ideas were never fully put into effect, but they did achieve a partial realization with the creation, in 1937, of the Cabinet Planning Board, an organization staffed by bureaucrats and other economic experts, and possessing substantial power to control the wartime economy. His ideas also exerted a considerable influence on other economists who achieved a fleeting fame during the war years, most notably Tokyo University's Naniwada Haruo, whose three-volume *Nation and Economy* (*Kokka to Keizai*) became something of a best-seller in the 1940s (Naniwada 1938–41).

Relatively few Japanese economists, however, shared the enthusiasm of Hijikata and Naniwada for European fascism. Their reactions to the rise of militarism were therefore complex and often ambivalent. Some chose to abandon original research during these troubled years, and focused their energies instead on the less hazardous task of translating the works of others. Ōuchi Hyōe, for example, spent much of the Pacific War translating Adam Smith's *Wealth of Nations*. Others were recruited into organizations such as the Bank of Japan or the Cabinet Planning Board, or into the numerous research bodies set up to investigate the economies of the Japanese-occupied areas of East and Southeast Asia.

Within these organizations there was some limited scope for liberal and left-wing economists to express their views in covert ways. Indeed, the wartime Japanese government never achieved a simple, totalitarian control of minds, and as a result its persecution of Marxists and others coexisted with a surprising ability to absorb and make use of certain aspects of Marxian and liberal thought. The contradictory nature of the Japanese system in the late 1930s and early 1940s is particularly well illustrated by the case of the Shōwa Research Association (*Shōwa Kenkyukai*), established in 1936 to

create an adequate exchange of opinions between public servants, the military, businessmen, academics, social commentators etc.,

to pool their experience and knowledge, and by mutual cooperation to create a sound basis for policy formation.

(Quoted in Naniwada 1973: 213–14)

The Institute included among its members several prominent left-
wing and liberal economists (e.g. Ōkōchi Kazuo and Tōhata Seiichi
of Tokyo University) as well as ultranationalists and the alleged
Comintern spy Ozaki Hotsumi (Johnson 1965: 114–16). Its reports,
though couched in the language of nationalism and wholehearted
support for the war in Asia, therefore represented an attempt by certain
intellectuals to moderate the influence of the extreme right in Japan.
The result of this curious mixing of ideas and objectives is evident
in the Institute's advocacy of 'communitarianism' (*kyōdōshugi*), a
concept that it presented as the synthesis emerging from the antitheses
of individualism on the one hand and totalitarianism on the other. The
basis of communitarianism, it suggested, would be the pursuit of
'the public good' rather than individual profit. This would lead to
the replacement of class relationships with 'relationships based on
efficiency of labour (*shokunōteki kankei*) and would ultimately
strengthen the national economy in such a way that the war on
mainland Asia could be brought to a successful conclusion (Naniwada
1973: 223–33).

It may be objected, with some justice, that this sounds very similar
to the corporatism advocated by Hijikata. The difference essentially
is one of nuance, as the more liberal-leaning members of the Association attempted to counterpose the evils of totalitarianism against the
officially condemned evils of individualism, and to secure some
protection for the interests of labour in the economic system of wartime Japan. In Johnson's words, the dilemma of academics who joined
such bodies was that 'they could work only as apparent converts to
ultra-nationalism, as Japanese who seemed to differ with the militarists
and fascist societies only over the best means to achieve common ends'
(Johnson 1965: 117).

Although political repression and the pressures of war temporarily
stifled and distorted Japanese economic thought, the war years saw
the germination of ideas that were to have a great impact on Japanese
economics in later years. On the one hand, the experiences of wartime economic planning provided lessons that were to be of use to
the development economists of post-war Japan. On the other, many
intellectuals who had been excluded from public life continued
privately to read, contemplate, and refine the theoretical bases of their
knowledge. This second group included such economists as Uno

101

Kōzō, who was to emerge as a leading force in the intellectual life of the late 1940s and 1950s. In this way, the foundations were laid for a renaissance of economic thought in the years following Japan's defeat in 1945.

4

Post-war Marxian economics

The influence of Marxism on Japanese intellectual life reached a highwater mark in the years immediately following the Second World War. The left-wing academics who had been dismissed from their posts or imprisoned during the war returned to their universities with reputations enhanced by their history of opposition to militarism. At the same time the leading right-wing ideologues of the war period were purged.

The experiences of war and defeat, and the economic chaos and deprivation which followed, made socialism intellectually and politically appealing to many Japanese people. As Uzawa Hirofumi, one of the leading Japanese economists of the 1970s and 1980s recalls,

> About forty years ago, when I was a student, there was no word which had such an attractive sound as 'socialism'. To be free from the many internal contradictions of capitalism – exploitation, inequity, cultural decadence, etc. – one felt that socialism, characterised as it was by co-operation, equality and the enhancement of culture, indeed represented the direction in which Japan should advance.
>
> (Uzawa 1986: 315)

During the Allied occupation of Japan, which lasted from 1945 until 1952, many of those who had played prominent parts in the Marxist debates of the inter-war years re-emerged as dominant figures in the economics faculties of Japanese universities: among them Yamada Moritarō and Ōuchi Hyōe at Tokyo University, and Sakisaka Itsurō at Kyūshū University. The old debates of the 1920s and 1930s, however, could not simply be resumed at the point at which they had been abandoned, for the changing structure of Japanese economy and

103

society in the immediate post-war years was shifting the very foundations on which the pre-war analysis of Japanese capitalism had been
based.

The onset of rapid economic growth in the late 1950s created
further analytical problems for Japanese Marxists, who were forced
to devise theories and strategies applicable to a country in which
increasing real incomes were promoting the rapid rise of consumer
materialism. In confronting these problems, moreover, Japanese
Marxists found themselves relatively isolated from the international
academic community. Throughout the years of the long post-war
boom, Marxist economics in much of the English-speaking world
experienced what can only be called a period of recession. Although
the works of the small number of leading English-speaking Marxists
– Paul Sweezy and Maurice Dobb, for example – were translated and
eagerly debated in Japan, the opportunities for exchanges of ideas
between Japanese and Western Marxists were therefore limited. It
is true that post-war Japanese Marxism derived some significant
inspiration from theorists in eastern and southern Europe, but even
here ideological divisions (including divisions within Japanese
Marxism itself) restricted the opportunities for dialogue. Unlike their
neo-classical compatriots, therefore, Japanese Marxist economists
were not readily integrated into international academic networks, and
(rather like some fragment of a biological species which is cut off
from others by geographical circumstances) their theories began to
evolve in a number of distinctive directions. It is those directions that
we shall explore in the following pages.

THE OCCUPATION AND THE JAPANESE ECONOMY

The central problem that faced Marxist analysts in the late 1940s and
early 1950s was the interpretation of the post-war democratization
of Japan. Under the control of the Supreme Command Allied Powers
(SCAP), dominated by General Douglas MacArthur and his US
advisers, Japan had become the focus of an extraordinary experiment
in reform and restructuring. Although a Japanese cabinet remained
in existence during the Occupation, the circumstances of Japan's defeat
placed into the hands of the occupying authorities unique powers to
imprint their political and economic ideals on the nation.

From the start, however, the objectives of SCAP were complex
and in some respects contradictory. They incorporated, unquestionably, a strong measure of idealism: a desire that the miseries of war

should be redeemed by the remoulding of Japan according to the classical ideals of Western liberal democracy. But they also involved a desire to make Japan a stable partner in post-war US strategies for the Pacific and the world, and a profound fear that reform might unleash indigenous and uncontrollable forces or revolution.

The most significant of the Occupation reforms, from the perspective of Marxist analysis, was the restructuring of the agrarian system. After an earlier proposal had been rejected by the Allies as too conservative, the Japanese government produced in October 1946 a plan for relatively radical land reform. Under this 'second land reform', absentee landlords were forced to sell all their farm lands, while other landlords' holdings were reduced to an average of one hectare (with slightly larger holdings being permitted in Hokkaidō). Tenant farmers were given substantial assistance to purchase land at prices far lower than market value, and where fields continued to be leased, rents were substantially reduced and the practice of payment in kind was abolished. The effect of this reform, which was carried out in stages over a period of three years, was to convert the majority of tenant farmers into small land-owning peasants. By 1949 the percentage of farmers who rented some or all of their land had fallen to 43 per cent, as compared with 70 per cent before the war.

Industry, though not as profoundly affected, also experienced the reformist zeal of the early Occupation period. Trade union activity was legalized, enabling union membership to swell to a peak of 55 per cent of the workforce by 1949 (*Nihon Rōdō Nenkan*, 1985). New labour standards laws provided a certain minimum level of protection for workers' rights, while the power of the pre-war plutocracy was weakened by the dissolution of the *zaibatsu*. It was in the areas of labour and *zaibatsu* reform, however, that the retreat from democratization – the so-called 'reverse course' – first became apparent. The emergence of radical unionism frightened the authorities into outlawing strikes by public employees and by 1947 SCAP, one of whose first actions had been to remove wartime bans on strike activity, was intervening to prohibit a proposed general strike by Japanese workers.

Measures to weaken the dominance of the giant corporations and reform the structure of Japanese business underwent a similar process of dilution. Laws against monopoly and the excessive concentration of economic power were introduced during the Occupation, but their scope and powers were limited. Even these measures were soon to undergo further neutralization when the Japanese government regained full control of the country's destiny in 1952.

Politically, the utopian vision of a democratic Japan received its clearest expression in the new constitution promulgated in 1947. While (controversially) retaining the emperor as a symbol of 'the will of the people', the postwar constitution enshrined the principles of freedom of speech and thought, universal suffrage, parliamentary government, and demilitarization. Yet within four years of its composition, the US government was already encouraging the establishment of a police reserve – the first step on the road to Japan's rearmament – and two years later Japan's position in the fractured world of the Cold War was cemented by the signing of the Mutual Security Agreement with the United States.

As the Cold War deepened, the Occupation authorities turned their attentions increasingly to the dangers of 'subversion' within Japan. In 1950, under pressure from SCAP, a number of newspapers, broadcasting companies, industrial enterprises, and public corporations were purged of employees suspected of communist sympathies (Kanda 1983: 321-2). Partly in response to this development, the Japanese Communist Party, which had operated openly since Japan's defeat and had offered guarded support for the early occupation reforms, chose to recreate its underground structure and adopt a strategy of armed struggle against the existing political order, a strategy that it maintained until 1955. This approach deepened the ideological divisions between Communist Party members and those Marxists who were affiliated to the Japan Socialist Party or other political groups.

No 'reverse course', however, could return Japan to the *status quo ante*. The nature of the Japanese political, agrarian, and industrial systems in the 1950s was clearly very different from that of the 1930s, and the occupation reforms proved unwittingly to have laid the basis for the phenomenal economic expansion of the 1960s. These changed and continuously changing circumstances demanded new approaches to the analysis of Japanese capitalism, and provided the setting for the emergence of new debates within Japanese Marxist economics.

POST-WAR DEBATES ON JAPANESE CAPITALISM

The division between those economists identified with the *Kōza* school and those identified with the *Rōnō* school did not entirely disappear after 1945. However, the difficulties of interpreting Japan's post-war economic structure and development created an increasingly complex pattern of debate and dialogue, in which the fiercest disagreements often occurred within, rather than between the two pre-war factions.

In the early post-war period much of this debate centred, predictably, on the issue of land reform. Since a central issue in the pre-war *Kōza–Rōnō* controversy had been the extent to which Japanese agriculture could be described as 'feudal', it was hardly surprising that the key issue after 1945 was the extent to which feudalism had been destroyed by land reform. The most unequivocal statement on this subject came, rather surprisingly, from the leading figure of the pre-war *Kōza* school, Yamada Moritarō. Yamada suggested that the occupation reforms had brought about Japan's long-delayed bourgeois democratic revolution and so opened the way to a new phase in the development of Japanese capitalism.

> The historical life of the militaristic, semi-feudal stage of Japanese capitalism, which existed for almost three-quarters of a century from the Meiji Restoration to the defeat [of 1945] has here been brought to a close. One stage has ended, and a new, higher stage may be defined.
>
> (Yamada 1949: 13)

The land reform, according to Yamada, constituted 'the most important issue to Japan's period of democratic revolution', since it removed at a stroke those feudal remnants which the *Kōza* economists had so painstakingly researched and enumerated in the 1920s and 1930s – above all, exorbitantly high non-monetary rents (Yamada 1949).

Yamada himself was later to retreat from this positive assessment of land reform, but his analysis, with its emphasis on the break-up of the 'semi-feudal' landlord system and the exposure of small farmers to direct exploitation by capitalism, was pursued further by the *Kōza* scholar Kurihara Hyakuju in his *Theory of Contemporary Japanese Agriculture (Gendai Nihon Nōgyō Ron)* (Kurihara 1951).

Although this view of the revolutionary role of land reform was accepted by some Marxists, there were many members of the *Kōza* school who were more sceptical. As the proposals for land reform began to take shape, a number of Marxist economists sought inspiration and guidance in Lenin's analysis of agricultural reform in Russia. Lenin had observed that the transition from feudalism to capitalism in agriculture could take two forms. One, which he described as the 'Prussian path', occurred where feudal landlords converted their landholdings into capitalist agricultural enterprises. The second, which he termed the 'American path', took place where there is no landlord economy, or else it is broken up by revolution, which confiscates and splits up the feudal estates. In that case the peasant predominates, becomes the sole agent of agriculture, and evolves into a capitalist farmer.

(Lenin 1962: 239)

Although both forms of development implied an end to feudalism, the 'Prussian path' was likely to retard the development of capitalism and impose a heavy burden of misery on the peasantry.

During the prolonged and somewhat tedious debate on the relevance of Lenin's two paths to post-war Japan, the suggestion was put forward that the Japanese land reform, imposed from above at a time when the peasantry was economically prostrate, followed the Prussian rather than the American model of agricultural development, and therefore represented a strengthening rather than a weakening of the position of the old landlord class (see, for example, Inoue 1947). As the land reform was put into effect and the number of small independent farmers increased, this view became an increasingly difficult one to defend. However, the response of its main proponent, Inoue Harumaru, was to shift towards an even more sweeping denial of the significance of land reform. In the major post-war *Kōza* school publication, *Lectures on Japanese Capitalism* (*Nihon Shihonshugi Kōza*, 1953–5), Inoue and others argued that the land reform had done little to alter the semi-feudal nature of the Japanese system. On the contrary, they stated:

The inherited semi-feudal system of landholding is now being preserved with the utmost energy not only by power of the Japanese forces of reaction, but also by the controlling authority of the American imperialists.

(Inoue 1957: 113)

This proposition was defended in a number of ways. In the first place, it was argued that the old landlord families retained considerable social and political authority in their home villages, and that land reform had enabled them to win the support of a widened segment of richer peasant farmers (Kondō *et al.* 1953: 66–74). More importantly, the authors of *Lectures on Japanese Capitalism* emphasized that the reform had only redistributed arable land, leaving the uncultivated mountain forests in the hands of their pre-war owners. Small land-owning peasants, they claimed, remained dependent on the landlords because the latter controlled essential forest resources

108

and water supplies (Kondō *et al.* 1953: 82–92). This analysis was accepted by the Japanese Communist Party and became a crucial basis for its strategy during the years of underground activity from 1950 to 1955. By the late 1950s, however, the growth of Japanese industry was beginning to raise new issues for debate, and attempts to base analysis of the post-war economy on notions of a 'semi-feudal' agrarian sector gradually faded into obscurity.

For the economists of the pre-war *Rōnō* school, the problems of analysing the consequences of land reform were somewhat different. Since the *Rōnō* scholars saw the emergence of capitalist relations in agriculture as a gradual process stretching back more than a century, they were less vexed by such issues as whether the post-war reforms constituted a bourgeois revolution, or how they related to Lenin's two-path theory. Most welcomed land reform as removing the last vestiges of feudalism from agriculture, but at the same time, many had reservations about the benefits that the reform would bring to small farmers. Ōuchi Hyōe, for example, in articles published in 1946, observed that land reform in itself could do nothing to alter the 'oriental' nature of Japanese agriculture, with its miniscule land holdings and low labour productivity (Ōuchi 1975a). Besides, Ōuchi pointed out, although the exploitation of peasant by landlord might have ended, small farmers remained vulnerable to exploitation by industrial capital, which could charge oligopolistic prices for agriculture machinery and chemicals while simultaneously using the farm sector as a source of cheap casual and temporary labour (Ōuchi 1975b; for discussion of the debates on land reform see Saeki and Shibagaki 1972: 247–53; Keiō Gijuku Daigaku Keizai Gakkai 1959: vol. 2, pp. 208–22; Kurihara 1947; Itoh 1980: 30–1 and 36).

The debate over land reform was very closely linked to a second major post-war controversy which centred on the so-called 'subordination thesis' (*jūzoku-ron*). There was widespread agreement on the political left that the Mutual Security Agreement had incorporated Japan into a *strategic* system dominated by the United States, but a far more contentious question concerned the extent to which the Japanese *economy* was US-controlled.

As far as the authors of *Lectures on Japanese Capitalism* were concerned, economic subordination to the United States was the key feature of the post-war Japanese system. Inoue's analysis of the land reform rested on the proposition that the power of the pre-war landlord class had been deliberately preserved by the occupation authorities not only for political reasons, but also because the United States wished to undermine Japanese agricultural production and to convert Japan into a market for surplus US farm produce (Inoue 1957: 126–7). In his analysis of Japanese industry and finance, Usami Seijirō similarly argued that Japan's strategic relationship with the United States inevitably involved the 'plundering' of the Japanese economy by US capital (Usami 1957: 83). This process of plundering, Usami stated, was carried out with the enthusiastic cooperation of Japanese big business, who accepted their own subordination to US interests in the belief that this would ensure high rates of profit. The statistics that Usami used to support his thesis are, to say the least, somewhat suspect. His analysis of the largest 174 financial and industrial companies in Japan, for example, purported to show that 79 per cent of their capital was 'foreign-controlled' (Usami 1957: 89). These figures were clearly at odds with the common perception that there was relatively little direct foreign investment in post-war Japan, and it was not long before Usami's data came under critical scrutiny from other Marxist scholars.

The most vehement and articulate of these critics was Ono Yoshihiko (1914–), professor of Osaka City University, whose writings attacked both the substance and the methodology of the subordination thesis. Ono pointed out, for example, that Usami had arrived at his figures by counting as 'foreign-controlled' the total capital of every company that had *any* overseas equity participation, overseas loans, or even licencing agreements with foreign firms (Ono 1963: 78). Ono's own research yielded detailed data to support his contrary proposition that although US aid had had a considerable impact on the post-war Japanese economy, US direct and indirect investment was insignificant from the perspectives both of the US and Japanese economies (Ono 1963: 87–91). The essence of Ono's critique, therefore, was that too much emphasis had been placed on Japan's 'subordination' to the United States, and too little upon the re-emergence of Japan's own economic domination of its Asian neighbours (Ono 1963: 153–66).

In spite of this criticism, however, the notion of Japan's subordination to the United States continued to be of importance to Communist Party strategies during the 1960s. This notion enabled the Party, as it had done before the war, to propose a two-step revolutionary process. In the pre-war years it had been the 'feudal survivals' in Japanese society which had to be removed before a socialist revolution was possible; now it was American imperialism. This situation implied that the Communist movement must begin by pursuing a policy of *han-Bei aikoku* – anti-American patriotism.

The post-war debates on the changing nature of Japanese capitalism yielded some interesting empirical research. But many of the contributions to the debate (and this was true particularly of the essays contained in *Lectures on Japanese Capitalism*) were characterized by a degree of theoretical rigidity and stagnation. Imported and outdated models of capitalist development were often applied with little imagination to contemporary Japanese circumstances. What was needed to rescue the debate from paralysis was the development of fresh theoretical insights into the analysis of capitalism. Fortunately, the freeing of academic activity in the years immediately after the Pacific War created a fertile environment for such theoretical developments. In the following sections we shall look at some of the more innovative Japanese contributions to Marxist economic theory that arose from the intellectual environment of post-war Japan.

MATHEMATICS AND MARXISM: KOSHIMURA SHINZABURŌ (1907–) AND OKISHIO NOBUO (1927–)

Ironically, one important source of inspiration for post-war innovations in Marxist theory was neo-classical economic analysis. More precisely, one might say that the desire of Marxists to counter the increasing influence of marginalism led them to borrow some of the marginalists' clothes. In spite of the ideological factionalism which still existed (with economics faculties and academic associations often being clearly identified as 'Marxist' or 'neo-classical'), Japanese students of economics often received a fairly thorough grounding in both theoretical traditions, and this training provided the basis for some fruitful cross-fertilization of ideas. In fact, as we shall see, a number of the most interesting developments in post-war Japanese economic thought have emerged precisely from this integration of insights drawn from Marxian and neo-classical theory.

Amongst these developments was the application of mathematics to Marxian value theory. Of course, the use of mathematics by Marxists was not in itself new. Marx's own work contains a certain amount of mathematical exposition, and other writers (such as Bortkiewicz in the early twentieth century) subsequently attempted to place Marx's economic theories on a more rigorous mathematical foundation. In general, however, early twentieth-century Marxists had been much less active than neo-classical economists in developing mathematical formulations of their theories. The particular contribution of economists such as Koshimura and Okishio, therefore, was to demonstrate the ways in which mathematical techniques developed by the neo-classical school could be used to clarify and sharpen the precision of Marxian debate.

The context of this integration of mathematics and Marxism is very clearly revealed in the introduction to Koshimura's *Theory of Capital Reproduction and Accumulation*, first published in Japanese in 1956 and translated into English in 1975.

> Modern bourgeois economics uses mathematical methods abundantly to impart an appearance of seeming rigour. Much of this high theory rests on a morass of such subjective, individual and consequently incalculable things as 'marginal utility'. It is not the use of the language of mathematics but its assumptive structure to which we object.
>
> (Koshimura 1975: 10; see also Koshimura 1951)

Koshimura then goes on to illustrate how mathematical methods may be made to serve a very different 'assumptive structure'. For example, matrix algebra, used to such effect by Wasily Leontief in his input-ouput system, becomes in Koshimura's hands a means of translating Marx's theory into formal mathematical models. Koshimura's interpretation of the Marxian transformation problem, for all its logical elegance, loses some of its force because of Koshimura's quite deliberate decision to express the inputs to his system as values rather than prices of production (thus avoiding the issue which Tugan-Baranowsky, Bortkiewicz, and others had debated at such length). Nevertheless, his analysis convincingly demonstrates the power of mathematics to illuminate (if not to solve) crucial problems of Marxist economic theory, among them the problems of monopoly pricing and of the declining trend of profit rates.

Similar techniques are used in even more creative ways by Okishio Nobuo. Okishio borrows some of his analytical tools from the mathematical economist Morishima Michio, who in turn has subsequently responded to and developed ideas suggested by Okishio (see pp. 173–7). Another significant influence on Okishio's work, however, is the so-called 'neo-Ricardianism' of the Cambridge economist Piero Sraffa. But unlike other neo-Ricardians, who have used Sraffa's concepts to refute the labour theory of value, Okishio uses them to defend and refine that theory.

Perhaps the best known of Okishio's contributions to value theory is his mathematical exposition of the 'fundamental Marxian theorem', according to which the equilibrium rate of profit will be positive only where there is positive exploitation of labour. (An exposition of the same theorem was developed almost simultaneously by Morishima and the British economist F. Seton; see Okishio 1963; Morishima and Seton 1961.) But although his economics are founded on Marxist theory, Okishio is not afraid to contradict those aspects of Marx's economic analysis that fail to conform to his rigorous mathematical reasoning. For example, he takes issue with Marx's prediction that the rate of profit in capitalist economies will tend to fall as the organic composition of capital rises. On the contrary, Okishio's model of the economy suggests that where real wages are constant, the introduction of new technologies in the production of capital or consumer goods will always increase the average profit rate. At the same time, however, technological progress will be hampered by the microeconomic perspective of individual capitalists, who are only prepared to introduce new techniques where these reduce their costs at existing prices. In an economic system in which labour is always undervalued, this perspective sets limits on the willingness of business managers to substitute machines for workers (Okishio 1965: 119–48).

It is interesting that the mathematical analyses of Koshimura, Okishio, and Morishima were the first Japanese contribution to Marxian economics to receive widespread recognition in the West. In part this surely reflects the relatively advanced state of this branch of economics in post-war Japan. But it also seems likely that it was the very abstractness of mathematical value analysis – its lack of direct connection to the contemporary Japanese economic and political environment – that made it readily accessible and meaningful to English-speaking economists. Mathematics may not entirely transcend culture, but in the academic world of the late twentieth century, it certainly speaks an international language. Koshimura's *Theory of Capital Reproduction and Accumulation*, for example, was translated into English because a Western academic, skimming through the original without a knowledge of Japanese language,

> noticed that the exposition was formal and algebraic and wished that I could somehow decipher the swift thought sprinting through thickets of algebra interspersed by tantalising diagrams.
>
> (Koshimura 1975: x)

Few other Japanese Marxian texts would have conveyed such an immediate meaning and sense of fascination to a non-Japanese reader.

Even in the area of mathematical economics, however, the flow of ideas from Japan to the West has often been restricted, and potentially important contributions to Marxian debates have failed to reach an international audience. To give just one example, Okishio's mathematical approach to the problem of skilled labour in Marxian analysis predates by many years similar approaches developed by Western economists such as Robert Rowthorn (Okishio 1965: 19–24; Rowthorn 1980: 231–49).

UNEQUAL EXCHANGE:
NAWA TŌICHI (1906–)

The most striking example of the failure of international communication, however, is perhaps provided by the case of debates on unequal exchange. Although the theories of unequal exchange (*futōka kōkan*) developed in Japan in the 1940s and 1950s were not identical to those expounded by European and US political economists in the 1970s, there can be little doubt that the Western debate would have followed a rather different course if its participants had had access to the existing Japanese literature.

In the Japanese context, discussion of the concept of unequal exchange in fact dates back to the 1930s, when the Osaka-based economist Nawa Tōichi raised the issue in an article entitled 'Value problems in international trade' (*Kokusai Boeki ni okeru Kachi Mondai*). It was not until after the Pacific War, however, that Nawa's ideas became a significant topic of controversy amongst Japanese economists, both Marxian and non-Marxian.

The basis of Nawa's arguments was the idea that the labour theory of value, extended to the international economy, could help to explain why certain nations grow rich while others grow poor. According to Ricardo's theory of comparative advantage, differences in productivity provided the basis for international trade, and ensured that all countries gained from participation in the international exchange of goods. But as Nawa pointed out, from the perspective of the labour theory of value, international differences in productivity implied that in the process of trade, an unequal exchange of values would occur between more industrially advanced and less advanced nations. Because the average worker in developed countries is more productive than the average worker in underdeveloped countries, exports from the former contain less labour than exports from the latter, and an invisible transfer of value from the poorer to the richer nations takes place.

114

Nawa illustrated this process of unseen exploitation with the example of trade between an industrialized nation (A) and an agricultural nation (B). The industrialized nation is assumed to be the more efficient producer both of manufactured goods (P) and of agricultural goods (Q), but whereas it is twelve times more efficient than its trading partner in producing manufactured goods, it is only twice as efficient in producing agricultural goods. According to Ricardian theory, country A should specialize in industrial production and country B in agricultural production. But, Nawa argues, if A and B trade along the lines of comparative advantage, A will be exchanging an item that required only a single day's labour for an item that required six days of B's labour: hence exchange is unequal (Nawa 1948: 20-1).

One of those who criticised this view was the trade theorist Akamatsu Kaname, whose well-known 'flying geese' theory is discussed below (see p. 151). Akamatsu accepted that international exchange could be exploitative, but such exploitation would only occur if distortions in the terms of trade artificially undervalued one nation's products in relation to those of other nations. If no such distortion existed, then the higher price commanded by the labour of developed countries must be seen merely as reflecting the greater complexity and intensity of that labour, and could not be termed 'exploitation' in the Marxian sense (Akamatsu 1950: Chap. 5).

Nawa's response to this criticism was to emphasize the difference between 'genuinely complex labour' and 'artificially complex labour'. Marx, it was true, had recognized that the products of complex (that is, highly skilled or trained) workers should be worth more than the products of simple labour. But Nawa claimed that the gap in productivity between developed and less developed countries did not, in general, reflect an inequality in the skills of their workers; rather, it was the result of the more advanced technology embodied in the machinery of industrialized countries. As a result, labour in these countries was artificially valued as being more complex than the labour of less developed nations (Nawa 1950).

Here we can readily observe similarities between the 1950s debate in Japan and the European debate on unequal exchange which occurred in the early 1970s. Nawa's view is close to that of the Belgian Marxist Ernest Mandel, who argued that unequal exchange arises from international differences in productivity and technology (Mandel 1971: 353-70). Akamatsu, however, is nearer to the position taken by Arghiri Emmanuel, who suggested that international differences in productivity are in fact slight, and who based his theory of unequal exchange rather on international variations in the real wage rate. According to Emmanuel, wages in the industrialized nations of the northern hemisphere, and in regions of new settlement such as Australia and New Zealand, have tended to rise much more rapidly than wages in other parts of the world. These wage rises have come about for a variety of political and social reasons, and have persisted because, while capital is internationally mobile, labour for the most part is not (Emmanuel 1972: 105–59). The high remuneration of richer nations' labour biases the terms of trade against less developed countries, thus creating the type of international trade structure that Akamatsu also recognized as exploitative.

The relevance of Nawa's ideas to Japan is obvious. At the time of his writing, from the 1930s to the 1950s, both wages and productivity were substantially lower in Japan than they were in industrially more advanced nations such as the United States. The Japanese theorists of unequal exchange, therefore, were not only concerned with the problems of the poorer Asian and African nations, but also with the effects of the international trading system on Japan itself. In this economic environment the theory of unequal exchange attracted widespread interest amongst Japanese economists, and was used by theorists such as Ikuzawa Kenzō as the basis for a Marxian analysis of the international economic system (Ikuzawa 1957). During the 1960s, however, with rapid economic growth and the narrowing of wage and productivity gaps between Japan and the rest of the industrialized world, the debate on unequal exchange lost much of its original vigour, and attention shifted to other aspects of international economics, such as the rise of the multinational corporation. (For further details on the unequal exchange debate, see Keiō Gijuku Daigaku Keizai Gakkai 1959: 412–20).

THE ECONOMIC THOUGHT OF UNO KŌZŌ (1897–1970)

The most important and controversial new element to enter Japanese Marxist economics in the 1950s, however, was Uno Kōzō's theory of levels of analysis. From the late 1950s onwards Uno's ideas exerted an immense influence, particularly on Marxists associated with the *Rōnō* school – an influence which was magnified by the declining authority of the *Kōza* school in the years of 'de-Stalinization'. More recently, Uno's best-known work, *Keizai Genron* (*Principles of Political Economy*) has been translated into English, and his theories have acquired a small but devoted following amongst Western scholars (see Uno 1980; Allbritton 1986).

Uno's career until the 1950s had been in many ways typical of the early twentieth-century Japanese Marxist scholars. After graduating from Tokyo University in 1921 and studying for two years in Germany, he was appointed to a post on the economics faculty of Tōhoku Imperial University in the northern city of Sendai. In 1938 he was arrested for 'subversive' political views, and, although acquitted, remained outside academia until 1947, when he was appointed to a professorship at Tokyo University (Sekine 1975: 848). It was not until the late 1940s, therefore, that Uno began to make a significant mark on Japanese economic debate, and not until 1950 that the publication of the first of two volumes of *Principles of Political Economy* established his reputation as an original economic thinker. (A revised and abridged version of this book was issued in 1964. It is this abridged version which is now available in English translation; see Uno 1950 and 1952; Uno 1964.)

Uno's contributions to economic thought must be seen in the context of the Marxist debates of the inter-war and early post-war periods. As we have seen, these debates often involved acrimonious disagreements over the relevance of concepts such as feudalism, capitalism, bourgeois revolution, imperialism, and so on to the Japanese economy. The main aim of Uno's theory was to free Marxist thought from the logical and semantic traps in which it had become enmeshed. In this respect, his work bears a slight similarity to Althusser's structuralism, which also sought to resolve the intellectual confusions inherent in Marxist debates over the relationship of 'base' and 'superstructre' (Althusser 1977: particularly Chap. 6). A striking difference between Althusser and Uno, however, lies in the considerable sfylistic clarity of Uno's writing.

In Uno's view, the main cause of confusion in analyses of Japanese capitalism (both by *Kōza* school and *Rōnō* school economists) was the failure of Marxist theorists to distinguish between pure theory, the study of historical development, and the study of contemporary economic conditions. An adequate theory of capitalism – in Japan or elsewhere – had, Uno argued, to operate at a number of distinct levels of analysis. At the deepest and most abstract level, there is 'pure theory' (*genriron*) which generates the concept of 'pure capitalism'. Such an economic system has, of course, never existed in reality, since all historical societies inevitably contain a mass of non-capitalist economic, political, and cultural features that distort or obscure the underlying motions of capital. It is, however, possible for us to construct a mental image of pure capitalism, and such a construction

117

constitutes an essential basis for our understanding of the diverse forms that capitalism takes in the real world.

The second, and somewhat more concrete, level of analysis is what Uno termed 'stage theory' (*dankairon*). At this level it is recognized that the development of capitalism in practice involves a number of successive historical stages, within which societies approximate more or less closely to pure capitalism. Whereas the concept of pure capitalism involves focusing in a highly abstract way on the law of value, and excluding such institutional factors as the joint-stock company or the nation-state, stage theory allows the economist to readmit these factors to consideration, although discourse still remains at a fairly high level of generalization. Last, there is the 'analysis of contemporary conditions' (*genjō bunseki*): the understanding of economic systems past and present, with all their wealth of complexity and contradictions. Such understanding is, of course, the ultimate object of economics, but Uno argued that it must necessarily be built on the firm foundations of pure theory and stage theory (Uno 1964: 12–13).

Uno did not merely accuse his contemporaries of confusing these levels of analysis. To the horror of the more orthodox, he also criticized Marx himself for his logical inconsistencies. The fact that Marx's theories were 'scientific', claimed Uno, did not make them infallible, and it was the duty of later Marxists to correct their mistakes (Uno 1969: 72–3). Uno saw *Capital* as an attempt to extract from the complex realities of mid-nineteenth century Britain, a theory of pure capitalism, but an attempt that was flawed because of Marx's perpetual tendency to slip from abstract analysis to discussion of the economic minutiae of the real world.

In his *Principles of Political Economy*, Uno sought to recitify these faults by reconstructing the analysis of pure capitalism contained in Marx's magnum opus. As well as extracting the essential theoretical elements of Marx's analysis of capitalism, Uno also rearranged these elements to give the analysis greater logical coherence. Having divided his text into three sections – the doctrines of circulation, production, and distribution – Uno went on to propose that the labour theory of value should be discussed not in the context of circulation (where Marx introduces it), but in the context of production. The law of value, Uno emphasized, is not universal and unchanging, but finds its full expression only in capitalist society. It is not until we understand the production processes of capitalism that we can grasp the substance of the theory that labour alone creates value. For it is only under capitalism that labour becomes a uniform commodity, interchangeable between one branch of production and another, and that surplus labour emerges as the heart of the economic system, vital to its perpetual drive toards self-expansion (Uno 1964: 53–65).

Uno's analysis of pure capitalism also differs from Marx's in the emphasis which it gives to the cyclical, fluctuating nature of capitalism. Although he accepts Marx's prediction that profit rates will tend to fall as the organic composition of capital rises, Uno observes that this process is an uneven one, characterized by alternate phases of capital widening and deepening. During the widening phases, the pool of underemployed labour is gradually absored into production until labour shortages, rising wages, and falling profits trigger a financial panic and a period of recession. During the recession unemployment rises, wages fall, and businesses try to revive their profit levels by introducing new productive techniques. Because of the uneven nature of capital investment, the introduction of new technologies may be a prolonged process, but eventually the reduced wages and increased levels of exploitation made possible by new technology will offset the fall in profits and enable the cycle to begin again (Uno 1964: 164–71).

By stripping *Capital* of its rich profusion of historical data, Uno certainly achieves a very succinct statement of the nature of pure capitalism. (The 1964 edition of his *Principles of Political Economy* runs to a mere 227 pages in the original.) But what relationship does this abstract model of capitalism bear to any real historical society? Uno himself argues that his (and Marx's) image of pure capitalism is firmly rooted in historical materialism.

> This pure capitalist society which Marx hypothesised is indicated by the development of seventeenth and eighteenth century capitalism, and is not hypothesised by meditating on various dominant ideas. In this sense, it is quite different from Weber's 'ideal types', which are often misunderstood. Rather it is objectively founded on two hundred years of capitalist development, and on the economic researches which have accompanied that development.
>
> (Uno 1969: 59)

In other words, Uno suggests that by observing certain fundamental tendencies of historical development, and then extrapolating these tendencies to their logical conclusion, we can arrive at a pure theory of the underlying nature of the economic system. As Uno's main English-language apologist Thomas Sekine puts it:

119

> [T]he concept of pure capitalism can be justified on the ground that actual capitalism in its liberal stage of development demonstrated a tendency toward self-perfection, divesting itself more and more of pre-capitalist ecomomic relations.
>
> (Sekine 1975: 857)

The force of this statement becomes clearer when we examine Uno's stage theory, which proposes that capitalism has developed through three major phases: a phase of commercial capitalism (characterized by the dominance of mercantilist thought), a phase of industrial capitalism (characterized by the dominance of liberalism), and a phase of finance capitalism (accompanied by the rise of imperialism) (Uno 1964: 13). As Sekine's statement implies, it was the industrial capitalism of nineteenth-century Britain which Uno saw as conforming most closely to the contours of pure theory. Up to that point, capitalism had become increasingly pure, as pre-capitalist survivals gradually succumbed to the invasive influence of the capitalist system. But during the latter part of the nineteenth century this tendency was reversed. The emergence of very large-scale heavy-industrial production, the rise of the corporation, and the increasingly central role of finance capital created new interferences in the free working of the laws of value. The system became further and further removed from the principles of pure capitalism, until ultimately it entered a period of decay and collapse.

For Uno, the onset of this collapse was signalled by the Russian Revolution of 1917. In the period since the First World War, capitalism must be regarded as being in a phase of decadence, and the laws of pure capitalism as having relatively little hold on reality. In order to understand the workings of the modern system, it was therefore necessary to rely on the 'analysis of contemporary conditions' (Uno 1963: 42). Uno's own contributions to this analysis were more sketchy than his writings on pure theory. His methodological approach, however, provided inspiration to other economists who offered their own analyses of 'contemporary conditions' in Japan (see pp. 121–6).

Ultimately, Uno argued, with the total collapse of capitalism, the laws of value would cease to operate altogether, and economics itself (in our present understanding of the term) would wither away. For, as Uno emphasized, the idea of economics as a sphere of study arose in response to the emergence of the exchange economy in general, and the capitalist exchange economy in particular. 'Economic life', in the sense of the production and consumption of human necessities, exists in all societies. But economics as a discipline exists specifically to study the laws of capitalism, and its objective is to free human beings from the workings of those laws, and so bring about its own demise (Uno 1969: 7–8, 52–3).

Both the strengths and the weaknesses of Uno's theory are most clearly evident when we come to consider its applicability to political practice. By distinguishing between pure theory, stage theory, and the analysis of contemporary conditions, Uno showed that it was possible to escape from the trap of rigidly imposing Marx's and Lenin's views on present-day political circumstances. At the level of stage theory, Uno recognized that the configuration of class antagonisms will take different forms in different phases of capitalist development. Through the analysis of contemporary conditions it becomes clear that practical political campaigns must also pay attention to a host of temporary and local circumstances (Uno 1969: 141–92).

However, Uno's approach to Marxism opened a dangerously wide gulf between the analysis of pure capitalism on the one hand, and the understanding of the existing, present-day economic system on the other. His insistence on a 'pure-theory' derived exclusively from the liberal stage of capitalist development made it increasingly difficult to relate this theory to the dynamics of late twentieth-century capitalism, and threatened to create a situation where the exegesis of pure theory became an intellectual exercise divorced from contemporary issues of political and economic change. As one recent commentator observes:

> Uno's mistake was to give special status to nineteenth century British industrial capitalism and to *Capital*, which elucidated the principles of that industrial capitalism. By endowing this period with special status, he gave rise to the view of a single pure form of capitalism and to the view that the fundamental theory of capitalism could only be established once and for all time.
>
> (Shiozawa 1986: 29)

THE ANALYSIS OF CONTEMPORARY CONDITIONS: ŌUCHI TSUTOMU (1918–) AND ŌSHIMA KIYOSHI (1913–)

Several of Uno's leading followers were to some extent conscious of lacunae in his theories, and attempted to rectify them by stengthening Uno's own rather sketchy analysis of 'contemporary conditions'. In the process, they were also forced to confront the problem of

121

finding Marxian explanations for the rapid growth of Japanese capitalism that was beginning to occur from the late 1950s onwards.

To follow the evolution of Uno-style analysis in the period of high economic growth we must begin with a brief detour into the subject of state monopoly capitalism. This is a concept which has been rather rarely debated by British and US Marxists, but is quite crucial to an understanding of the controversies of the post-war Japanese left. The origins of the term can be traced to Lenin, who used it to describe the German economic system at the time of the First World War. In the 1950s, however, the phrase was given new meaning by the East German Marxist Kurt Zieschang, according to whom state monopoly capitalism constituted a new and distinct stage in the evolution of the capitalist system. Like the earlier imperialist phase identified by Lenin, this new stage was characterized by the concentration of economic power in the hands of a small number of giant corporations. Unlike the earlier imperialist era, however, it was also characterized by the increasingly central role of the state in ensuring the survival of the economic system – through demand management, welfare policies, various forms of assistance to industry, and so on. This growth of state intervention, Zieschang argued, had become vital to the continuation of capitalism because the ever-expanding forces of production had greatly intensified the contradictions between the social nature of the productive system and the private nature of property relations.

The relatively interventionist character of the Japanese state perhaps helps to explain the enthusiasm with which this concept was taken up by economists in Japan. The theory of state monopoly capitalism was introduced into Japan in the late 1950s by a number of dissident *Kōza* school theorists, of whom the most prominent was Igumi Takuichi. In the early stages, however, Igumi and his supporters were criticized by more orthodox Marxists who denied the existence of a distinct state monopoly stage of capitalism, and argued, along more conventional Leninist lines, that the growth of state intervention was merely a transient reaction to the crises of war and economic recession. (For an excellent summary of state monopoly capital theory in Japan see Masamura 1965.)

But the debate on state monopoly capitalism was not confined to members or former members of the *Kōza* school. By the 1960s the concept was also being adopted and developed by the followers of Uno Kōzō – most notably by the Tokyo University economist Ōuchi Tsutomu, whose rather complex and subtle approach to the issue enabled him to integrate the idea of state monpoly capitalism with

Uno's concept of the 'analysis of contemporary conditions'. This integration was by no means simple to achieve. As we have seen, Uno had defined three stages of capitalist development (mercantilist, liberal, and imperialist), but had insisted that the period since 1917 was one of capitalist collapse and could not be analysed in terms of stage theory. How then could one apply the notion of a new 'state monopoly capitalist' stage within the framework of Uno's analysis? Ōuchi approached this problem by distinguishing between stages of capitalist evolution, on the one hand, and phases of human history, on the other. State monopoly capitalism, he suggested, was not a stage of capitalism comparable to the three stages identified by Uno, but it was the *form* that capitalism assumed in the period of human history which encompassed capitalism's demise. In this sense, the study of state monopoly capitalism and Uno's analysis of contemporary conditions could be seen as one and the same thing.

Uno had identified the onset of the collapse of capitalism with the Russian Revolution and the emergence of the first socialist state. In Ōuchi's analysis, however, this external crisis was only one symptom of collapse. Equally important were the internal crises revealed by the growing inability of the capitalist system to recover from economic recession. Thus, for Ōuchi, a crucial moment in the emergence of state monopoly capitalism was the world depression of the 1930s, for it was the experience of this depression that had given birth to new forms of state intervention in the economy, ranging from the economic policies of Nazi Germany to Roosevelt's New Deal (see Ōuchi 1970: 179–80; Kajinishi, Katō, Oshima, and Ōuchi 1960–70: vol. 4, pp. 1175–1207).

Basing his theories on the concept of state monopoly capitalism, Ōuchi was able to propose a new solution to one of the most passionately debated problems of post-war Japanese Marxist analysis: the problem of interpreting the economic and social implications of the Occupation reforms. On this issue, as we have already seen, Marxist theorists had expressed views ranging from Yamada's vision of the reforms as a 'bourgeois revolution' to Inoue's notion that very little had been reformed at all. Ōuchi, rejecting both these perspectives, instead placed the reforms in the context of the emergence of state monopoly capitalism in Japan. This development had begun, he argued, in the 1930s, but at that stage various social and political aspects of the Japanese system had hindered its mature development. The essential function of the occupation reforms, then, had been to remove these inconsonant features and so to 'create a system more appropriate to and compatible with state monopoly capitalism' (Ōuchi 1970: 180).

This was not, of course, meant to imply that the Occupation authorities had consciously set about creating the conditions for state monopoly capitalism in Japan, but rather that by importing the spirit of the New Deal, they had been unwitting agents in the restructuring and strengthening of Japanese state monopoly capitalism. Ōuchi went on to illustrate this process by examining the implications of *zaibatsu* dissolution and land reform. The reform of the *zaibatsu*, he suggested, had hastened the transformation of Japanese big business from family-controlled to managerially controlled enterprise (the latter being an essential element in the state monopoly capitalist structure). Land reform, on the other hand, created the basis for the protectionist agricultural policies that all advanced capitalist countries were forced to pursue in this age of chronic overproduction (Ōuchi 1970: 183–9).

Although parts of this argument – particularly the attempts to link land reform to state monopoly capitalism – seem rather tenuous, Ōuchi's theoretical framework does offer a means of comprehending the elements of continuity and of disjunction in the post-war Occupation reforms. The notion that state monopoly capitalism begins to emerge, in a restricted form, from the early 1930s allows Ōuchi to provide an explanation for the strong threads of similarity linking pre-war and post-war economic and political structures. These threads have also been delineated by Western writers on Japan such as Chalmers Johnson (see Johnson 1982). At the same time, by suggesting that post-war reforms removed existing barriers to the full maturing of state monopoly capitalism, Ōuchi is able to highlight those areas in which significant structural change did occur, and to associate this change with the upsurge in economic growth that occurred during the 1950s and 1960s.

According to Ōuchi's analysis, state monopoly capitalism is generally characterized by stagflation rather than by rapid growth. In Japan's case, however, the sudden dismantling of structures such as the *zaibatsu* and the landlord system, which had restricted the emergence of modern corporations and mass markets, opened the way for the 'economic miracle' of the late 1950s and 1960s. High growth, therefore, was partly a result of the 'post-war factor' (*sengosei*), a phenomenon evident not only in Japan and the other defeated Axis powers, but also in countries such as France which had experienced wartime occupation. At the same time, Japan's economic dynamism was also partly attributable to the country's relative economic backwardness (*kōshinsei*). It was this backwardness that gave rise to large supplies of low-cost labour, the dualistic division between large and small enterprises and the unusually high savings ratio (a feature Ōuchi attributed to the underdeveloped state of the Japanese welfare system). *Kōshinsei* also referred to the technological gap between Japan and other industrialized countries, and to the consequent ability of Japan to import new technologies rather than developing them *de novo* (Ōuchi 1963: vol. 1; Ōuchi 1971: 1–44; Kajinishi, Ōshima, Kato, and Ōuchi 1960–70: vol. 8, 2076–81).

What is remarkable about this analysis of Japanese growth is the similarity of its conclusions to those reached by the neo-classical development economists whose work we shall consider in the next chapter. Despite their very different approach to the economy as a whole, Ohkawa Kazushi also attributed Japan's high growth to flexible, low-cost labour supplies and to the technology gap between Japan and the West, while Shinohara Miyohei emphasized the importance of dualism as a source of growth (Ohkawa and Rosovsky 1973; Shinohara 1962). Some Marxist writers, indeed, have criticized Ōuchi's apparent inconsistency in failing to relate his analysis of Japanese growth more closely to his theory of state monopoly capitalism (see Masamura 1965: 371–2).

Even those who co-operated with Ōuchi in developing the 'analysis of contemporary conditions' did not necessarily accept his interpretation of rapid growth. Ōshima Kiyoshi, who collaborated with Ōuchi and others on the monumental thirteen-volume *Development of Capitalism in Japan (Nihon ni Okeru Shihonshugi no Hattatsu)*, regarded Ōuchi's 'post-war factor' and 'backwardness factor' as secondary, rather than principal, causes of growth (Ōshima and Enomoto 1968: 152). Ōshima himself, in a book written jointly with Enomoto Masatoshi (1933–   ), identified the 'secret of high growth' with the role of the Japanese state in promoting rapid capital accumulation.

Although he recognized that direct government assistance to basic manufacturing had declined in importance since the immediate post-war years, Ōshima saw more indirect forms of government intervention as playing a crucial role in the supply of capital to the newly expanding industries of the 1960s. These included various forms of tax concessions, import controls, and government expenditure on industrial infrastructure. Most important of all, however, was the monetary policy pursued by the government through the intermediary of the Bank of Japan. This policy, which he termed the 'pre-emption of income' (*shotoku no sakidori*), was seen by Ōshima as being a 'form of capital supply characteristic of state monopoly capitalism' (Ōshima and Enomoto 1968: 173).

125

Ōshima's theory of the pre-emption of income is closely related to the condition of 'overloan', which has been recognized by many economists as an important factor in Japan's post-war growth. 'Overloan' refers to the situation whereby manufacturers raise a large part of their capital through loans from the major city banks, and the city banks in turn depend on loans from the Bank of Japan (see for example Uchino 1983: 78–80; Noguchi 1977). Before the mid-1950s this had simply been a mechanism by which idle savings were channelled into productive investment. During the years of high growth, however, it was transformed into an engine of monetary expansion. In Ōshima and Enomoto's words, 'capital was created to fill shortfalls in supply, and, through the resultant expansion of social production, incomes and savings were in turn increased' (Ōshima and Enomoto 1968: 172). It is in this sense, as Ōshima saw it, that the Bank of Japan was 'pre-empting' savings from future incomes – incomes that were to be created by the investment of those savings themselves.

The relative importance of post-war recovery factors, the late development effect, and the role of the government in Japan's economic growth is, of course, a topic of continuing debate among non-Marxist as well as Marxist economists. An important characteristic of Uno-style analysts such as Ōuchi and Ōshima, however, was their ability to conduct this debate with relatively little use of jargon and with meticulous attention to statistical data. This approach may have divorced them somewhat from the revolutionary origins of Marxism, but it did enable them to obtain considerable authority amongst their fellow economists, and therefore to exert a wide-reaching influence on Japanese economic analysis in the 1960s and early 1970s.

THE ECONOMICS OF STRUCTURAL REFORM: NAGASU KAZUJI (1919–)

By the mid-1960s, conditions in Japan were beginning to create a number of difficulties for Marxist theory. The trade union movement, which had flourished in the immediate post-war years, had subsequently become the target of fierce and often successful counter-attacks from management, and particularly since the defeat of the Miike miners' strike of 1960, was in a debilitated state. Worker militancy was also discouraged by the fluidity of the Japanese class system, where peasant farmers were rapidly moving into industrial

126

employment, or, in some cases, combining agricultural and industrial jobs. At the same time, the rising real incomes which accompanied rapid growth helped to undermine support for political radicialism.

It was perhaps not surprising, then, that academic Marxism often seemed far removed from practical politics. There was a constant danger for left-wing economists of, on the one hand, repeating stale dogmas that had little relevance to Japanese reality or, on the other, engaging in detailed empirical studies whose connections to Marxist theory were obscure. What was needed, clearly, was a profound rethinking of traditional Marxian theory itself.

One response to this dilemma, in Japan as elsewhere, was the emergence of a host of new left movements operating outside the bounds of the older-established left-wing parties. Although we shall not examine these movements in detail, their importance should not be forgotten, for they helped to foster a new generation of radical intellectuals who were to be as impatient with the policies of the old left as they were with the policies of conservatism. At the same time, some groups within the existing left-wing parties were also attempting to rethink accepted theories and define new directions. An interesting and particularly influential example of this trend was the 'theory of structural reform' (*kōzō kaikaku ron*) supported by some communist dissidents and adopted by the Socialist Party in the 1960s. This theory received its most eloquent exposition from Nagasu Kazuji, professor of economics at Yokohama University and later Socialist Governor of Kanagawa Prefecture.

The notion of structural reform in fact originates with the Italian Communist Party in the years of de-Stalinization. Like the Uno school's 'analysis of contemporary conditions', it relies heavily on the concept of state monopoly capitalism, but its interpretation of the concept is rather different from the interpretations put forward by Ōuchi and Ōshima. For Nagasu, as for the Uno school theorists, state monopoly capitalism manifests in its most extreme form the contradiction between the private ownership of the means of production and the increasingly social nature of the productive process.

In present-day capitalism the social nature of production and labour is developed to its highest level. In order to maintain private control of this production and labour, and to monopolise its fruits, it becomes necessary for the existing form and reproductive structure of capital to rely upon the highest 'social organ', i.e. the state. Massive state economic functions – large-scale fiscal policies, public credit, monetary controls, controls on trade and foreign change, government-owned and government-run enterprises, etc. – are integrated into the processes of economic reproduction. The very existence of capitalism would now be unthinkable without the intervention of such state functions. This newest stage of capitalist development is none other than 'state monopoly capitalism'.

(Nagasu 1973: 87)

Nagasu, however, differs from Ōuchi and Ōshima not only in treating state monopoly capitalism as a distinct stage of capitalist development, but also in the practical implications that he derives from his analysis. What is crucially important about state monopoly capitalism is, according to the structural reform theorists, that it demands a quite new approach to left-wing political action. For, ironically, the emergence of state monopoly capitalism, with its increasingly socialized production system and its growing reliance on state intervention, has created the very structures that will be required by socialism. Nationalized enterprises, government control of trade and exchange, large-scale managerially-run enterprises – all of these will be necessary elements in the socialist future. The task of the left is therefore not to destroy the system but to redirect its structures from the service of capital to the service of the workers. The outward forms of state monopoly capitalism and socialism are thus identical, but

the content and direction are diametrically opposed. Or, in other words, the economic structure is the same but the class content is reversed. State monopoly capitalism implies the synthesis of productive relations by the state on the initiative of capital, while structural reform implies the same synthesis on the initiative of labour. Thus the former brings a strengthening of social exploitation, while the latter limits it.

(Nagasu 1973: 88-9)

Nagasu's writings represent a new stage in the process of coming to terms with Japan's changing economic circumstances. The emphasis here is no longer on 'feudal remnants' in agriculture, or on miserable wages and working conditions. Instead, the problems on which Nagasu focuses are those of the age of high economic growth: rising inflation levels, for example, and the continuing gap in wages and productivity between the modern, big business sector and the mass of small firms that still employ the major share of the industrial workforce (Nagasu 1965: 103–9, 226–32). Rather than anticipating a revolution by the impoverished proletariat, the structural reform theorists sought to harness the growing disenchantment, amongst workers and amongst the middle classes, with the policies of high growth. For by the mid-1960s, a wide section of the Japanese population was beginning to be aware that the unfettered pursuit of GNP (gross national product) growth was resulting in a neglect of the quality of life, and was indeed creating the new social problems of inflation and pollution.

In the midst of the 'crisis of Marxism' which assailed Japan during the later 1960s and early 1970s, structural reform theory presented a profoundly optimistic view of the future. The growth of goverment planning and the development of a welfare state were, according to this theory, not only in the best interests of the workers but also in the best interests of capital itself. But state intervention, once initiated, would acquire a momentum of its own, gradually and surely moving society in the direction of a peaceful transition to socialism (Nagasu 1965: 204–18). Not surprisingly, this view was roundly attacked as 'reformism' by more traditional Marxists within both the socialist and communist parties. It can also be criticized on the ground that it points towards a highly centralized, state-controlled system. Nagasu, indeed, recognized the possibility of this criticism, and attempted to counter it by emphasizing the importance of government not only 'for the people', but also 'by the people' (Nagasu 1965: 225–6). The exact meaning of this phrase, however, remains obscure, and structural reform theory certainly appears to present a stark contrast to the anarchist tendencies evident in much of the new political theory of the late 1960s. At the same time, however, structural reform theory also represents an important attempt to reassess the connection between Marxian theory and the realities of the late twentieth-century economy. In this sense it can be seen as a precursor to the new Marxist revisionism which was to become increasingly important from the early 1970s onwards.

JAPANESE MARXIAN ECONOMICS REASSESSED

Generally speaking, Japanese Marxian economics has received a very poor press in the West. Martin Bronfenbrenner in the 1950s described it as 'partisan propaganda', riddled with slogans and clichés and devoid of theoretical subtlety (Bronfenbrenner 1956: 391–2). The assessment had scarcely improved by the 1980s, when the left-wing critic John

129

Lie suggested that most Japanese Marxists, under the baleful influence of Uno's theory, had neglected the analysis of contemporary capitalism and become 'severed from any political movement, ignorant of wider intellectual currents, and cocooned in the hermetic world of pure theory' (Lie 1987: 48).

As assessments of the broad range of post-war Marxist economics, these statements seem rather less than fair. Even within the Uno school, as we have seen, economists such as Ōuchi Tsutomu and Ōshima Kiyoshi devoted much time and energy to analysing the dynamics of the contemporary Japanese economy. Despite Uno's own aloofness from political activism, a number of his followers, including Ōuchi, sought to apply their economic theories to political practice (see Hoston 1986: 282). Other Marxists, from the Communist Party faithful of the early post-war period to the structural reform theorists of the 1960s, have also attempted to maintain the connection between economic theory and political action. The dogmatism and jargon which Bronfenbrenner justly criticized in some 1950s Marxian writings becomes less evident in the works of 1960s theorists such as Ōuchi, Ōshima, and Nagasu. Marxism, despite its isolation from international and post-war Japanese intellectual currents, unquestionably generated significant theoretical contributions both to relatively abstract problems, such as the mathematical interpretation of value theory, and to more empirical issues such as the analysis of Japanese economic growth.

Having said this, one must also acknowledge the limitations of Marxian economics in Japan. Perhaps the most telling sign of these limitations is the very slight impact which Marxism, for all its academic influence, has had on post-war Japanese politics. In a climate of economic growth and social fluidity, it proved extremely difficult to relate Marxian theory to contemporary reality in a way that was both theoretically convincing and politically persuasive. The strength of the Marxian economists lay in their readiness to recognize, more quickly than their neo-classical counterparts, the social problems which burgeoned in the shadow of high GNP growth. Yet the popular reaction to inflation, urban congestion and environmental pollution which began to emerge in the late 1960s was generally based not on Marxist theory, but on a spontaneous and intuitive reaction to the stresses of daily life. By the 1970s, therefore, Marxism was losing some of its pre-eminence in Japanese academia, and loss of faith in its fundamental propositions was contributing to the emerging crisis of economic thought.

5

Economic theory and the 'economic miracle'

While left-wing economists were contending with the problems of applying Marxian theory to the circumstances of post-war Japan, neo-classical and Keynesian theorists were acquiring a new position of authority and influence, both in academic and in administrative life. The reasons for the flowering of non-Marxian economics in Japan are not hard to discern. On the one hand, rapid industrial growth from the mid-1950s onwards sustained faith in the ability of capitalism to generate economic prosperity. On the other, the new political alignments of the post-war world brought Japan into the cultural orbit of the United States and ensured that US economic thought would have a particularly great role in shaping the ideas of a new generation of Japanese economists.

ECONOMISTS AND THE GROWTH PROCESS

The relationship between economists and economic growth was a two-sided one. The developments of the late 1950s and 1960s created new challenges to economic theory, and so stimulated the creation and appliction of new economic ideas. But it was also true that the theories introduced and refined by post-war economists helped to inspire the policies of the high growth era. Economists might therefore be not only the analysts, but also the prophets and (to a degree at least) the authors of economic growth.

In purely statistical terms, rapid growth in Japan commenced during the years of the US Occupation. Between 1946 and 1951, real GNP growth (according to later estimates by the Economic Planning Agency) was running at a rate of over 9 per cent per annum. There was little mystery, however, about the reasons for this phenomenon.

After the massive destruction and disruption of the closing phases of the Second World War, Japan's levels of economic activity in 1946 and 1947 were no real reflection of the nation's capacity to produce, and it was inevitable that as reconstruction occurred, high rates of economic growth would be attained. Even when rapid growth continued into the early years of the 1950s, Japan's economic performance did not evoke great surprise. Japan was, after all, particularly well placed to meet the demand for goods and services generated by the war in Korea, and the international boom that accompanied the war was therefore exceptionally strongly marked in Japan.

It was only when growth continued at an unprecedently high speed after the mid-1950s that it became the central topic of Japanese economic debate. Between 1956 and 1973 real GNP grew by an average of some 10 per cent per year (although with sharp cyclical fluctuations). This quantitative expansion was accompanied by profound qualitative changes in the structure of the economy. The process of *jūkagaku kōgyōka* (heavy and chemical industrialization) – as it is termed in Japan – involved a shift of the labour force away from agriculture and light manufacturing and into such industries as metals, machinery, and petrochemicals. Between 1955 and 1965, while industrial output as a whole increased by a factor of 3.7, production of chemicals increased by a factor of 5.3, and production of machinery increased sevenfold (Andō 1979: 10).

The so-called 'economic miracle' not only provided the setting for major economic controversies within Japan, but also attracted the interest of many overseas economists. In the early stages, the principal issue was to find explanations for Japan's remarkable rate of industrial expansion. The explanations put forward would in turn determine the position taken by various economists on the long-term prospects for high growth, and on the policies that were necessary to sustain it. Much less attention was initially paid to the consequences of growth, which, it seems, were often assumed to be positive.

In order to assess the role that Japanese economic thought itself played in promoting the process of high growth, it is necessary to answer two questions, both of which have been the subject of considerable debate within and outside Japan. First, to what extent was growth the result of conscious policy decisions rather than fortuitous economic circumstances? And second, how great was the influence of economists on practical policy? Many writers have emphasized the fact that Japan's post-war pattern of industrialization, which ran contrary to conventional notions of comparative advantage, was achieved with strong government support and guidance, exercised principally through the Ministry of International Trade and Industry (MITI), the Ministry of Finanace, and the Bank of Japan. The instruments of government intervention included tariff protection, tax concessions, preferential allocation of loans and foreign currency to selected industries and the much-discussed process of 'administrative guidance' (*gyōsei shidō*) (see Johnson 1982: Noguchi 1977). More recently, however, there has been a tendency for some economists to cast doubt on the importance and efficacy of the government's role. Kosai and Ogino, for example, argue that the significance of bodies like MITI has been exaggerated, and that

> far from being the outcome of the planning of a small elite, Japan's high growth rate was achieved only as the result of the high rate of saving by the people, by their will to work, and by the vigorous efforts of Japan's entrepreneurs.
>
> (Kosai and Ogino 1984: 120; see also Komiya 1975a,b)

It is important to observe, though, that the question is mainly one of emphasis. Not even writers like Kosai and Ogino, however much they may focus on free market factors, are likely to reject Nakamura Takafusa's assessment of the issue:

> It was primarily the efforts of the people, mainly in the industrial world, which produced economic growth. However, this is not to say that the economic policy played no role in the process. It is a fact that the economic policy making authorities at first underestimated growth capacity, and it is also a fact that once growth had begun, they made every effort to sustain it and strove to remove obstacles to it.
>
> (Nakamura 1981: 80)

If we accept that government policy was a factor that helped to determine the speed and nature of growth, how important were economists in shaping that policy? One relatively cautious assessment of the political role of economists comes from Komiya Ryūtarō, who has stated that

> many academic economists are either too theoretical to be effective in government or are reluctant to leave their university posts, and there are no professional economists outside the academic community.
>
> (Komiya and Yamamoto 1981: 228)

133

Although Komiya mentions the phenomenon of the *kanchō ekonomisuto* (government economist), he bases his negative assessment of the impact of economists on the fact that public service posts in Japan are mostly staffed by career bureaucrats with a general, rather than a specialist training. This system, Komiya implies, leaves few opportunities for government officials to become economists, or, conversely, for economists to become government officials.

The problem with Komiya's analysis is that it says little about the most important way in which economists have influenced policy: through their participation in a wide range of advisory committees, research bodies and quasi-governmental agencies. As we saw in Chapter 3, this tradition dates back to the pre-war years, when organizations such as the Shōwa Research Association at times provided political refuge for economists of liberal or left-wing views.

In the atmosphere of post-war Japan it was, naturally enough, precisely the economic liberals, and particularly those with overseas training, whose counsel was most keenly sought by politicians and officials. The archetypical case was that of Nakayama Ichirō (see pp. 92–4) whose grasp of neo-classical and Keynesian theory was put to use on an extensive range of government committees from the US Occupation period onwards. Nakayama is particuarly remembered for his ten-year chairmanship of the Central Labour Council (*Chūō Rōdō Iinkai*), the industrial arbitration body that helped to mould the shape of labour relations in post-war Japan. Of his work on the Council, Nakayama later recalled:

> the difficulty was that, sandwiched between the powerful unions and the managers with their financial might, I had no power at all, and could use nothing but knowledge to solve the problems. The thing which reversed this sense of powerlessness and opened the way to new solutions was none other than academic scholarship [*gakumon*].
>
> (Quoted in Tsujimura 1984: 37)

The most important arena for interaction between economists and policy-makers, however, was undoubtedly the economic planning process. This will be discussed in more detail when we look at the particularly intriguing role of Ōkita Saburō in harnessing the ideas of economists to policy-making (see pp. 145–9). Here it will be sufficient to observe that several of the economists whose ideas are discussed in this chapter – including Shimomura Osamu, Ōkita Saburō, Kanamori Hisao, and Tsuru Shigeto – were in one way or another involved in the activities of the Economic Planning Agency or its various predecessors. These organizations, as has often been emphasized, were merely advisory and forecasting bodies, and it was left to ministries and private enterprise to implement (or, as the case might be, ignore) their recommendations. There can be little doubt, however, that the Economic White Papers and plans produced by the planning bodies often had a considerable effect in shaping both government action and public expectations of economic growth. This is particularly true of the famous National Income Doubling Plan, composed for the Ikeda administration in 1960, which Nakamura Takafusa describes as having been 'preeminent in its far-reaching effects' (Nakamura 1981: 90)

A further point of contact between economists and policy-makers is provided by the many private or semi-governmental economic research bodies which are from time to time commissioned to provide reports and advice to government on policy issues. These range from large organizations like the Institute of Developing Economies (*Ajia Keizai Kenkyūjo*) – established by special act of parliament and audited by MITI – to smaller research groups such as the Japan Economic Research Centre (*Nihon Keizai Kenkyū Sentā*) and the International Development Centre of Japan (*Kokusai Kaihatsu Sentā*). Once again, many of the economists whose work will be considered here have been active in establishing or presiding over these research bodies: Ōkita Saburo as founder of the International Development Centre; Ohkawa Kazushi, Shinohara Miyohei, and Kanamori Hisao as board members of the Japan Economic Research Centre; and Shinohara, more recently, as chairman of the Institute of Developing Economies.

What emerges from these observations is not that Japan's leading non-Marxian economists had great influence over the details of economic policy-making – nor that they have invariably agreed with the policy directions taken by government – but rather that their theoretical perspectives and empirical research helped to shape the environment in which post-war policy was created. On the one hand, the White Papers, economic plans, and reports for which they were responsible frequently provided the economic analysis on which future decisions were based; on the other, their writings influenced public opinion, serving to strengthen widespread popular support for rapid economic growth during the 1950s and early 1960s. In this sense, the adoption and diffusion of neo-classical and Keynesian economic ideas formed an important element in the emergence on the new 'high-growth culture' of post-war Japan.

135

MODERN ECONOMICS AND THE AMERICAN INFLUENCE

This culture in turn was part of the wider intellectual climate of the 1950s and 1960s, a climate over which US academia had a particularly great influence. Until the Second World War, as we have seen, the overseas connections fostered by Japanese economists lay, for the most part, in Europe. One after another, the outstanding graduates of Tokyo University or Tokyo Commercial College had followed the route to Germany, France, or Britain where they absorbed the ideas of Marx, Schmoller, Schumpeter, Cournot, Marshall, Pigou and others. After 1945, however, Japan's political ties with the United States, together with the growing prestige of American economics, dictated a change of direction. Now the typical itinerary for ambitious young economists (provided that their interests did not lie in Marxism) would involve a stay at Harvard, Stanford, or Chicago University and was likely to be funded, from the 1950s onward, by a Fulbright scholarship.

The ideas that Japan absorbed from this contact came to be inseparably associated in Japanese discourse with the phrase 'modern economics' (*kindai keizaigaku*). The term itself originates in the pre-war period when it was used, somewhat smugly, by some non-Marxian European economists to differentiate their own ideas from the 'outdated' theories of Marxism. But 'modern economics' is a phrase which is useful not only because it provides a shorthand label for non-Marxian economic thought in post-war Japan, but also because it conveys something of the character of that thought. In the first place, Japanese 'modern economics' in the years of high growth was not (as it was later to become) deeply riven by divisions between neo-classicals and Keynesians. Though some economists, particularly by the late 1960s, were beginning to use both neo-classical and Keynesian ideas in a more critical manner, for much of the high-growth era the dominating force was Paul Samuelson's 'neo-classical synthesis', within which Keynesian theory was to be applied to situations of high unemployment while neo-classical theory served to explain the workings of the economy in a state of full employment.

The influence of Samuelson and his colleagues not only gave a degree of intellectual unity to Japanese modern economics, but also helped to give it its specifically modern (as opposed to pre- or post-modern) nature. Modern economics, in other words, came to be characterized in the 1950s and 1960s by faith in notions of growth and progress, and by a vision of the economic world as a mechanical system whose workings could be simulated by mathematical models. At the same time, however, it lacked the grand social visions of nineteenth-century political economy. As a science that claimed to be concerned with fact rather than ideology, modern economics defined its role in terms of the accumulation of empirical, quantifiable evidence and the analysis of that evidence by means of systems of equations. In Tamanoi's words, there was

> a shift from the nineteenth century style of theory which sought laws of motion, to 'operational' theories: i.e. theories which could be handled by means of statistics.
>
> (Tamanoi 1971: 224).

The concepts of continuous progress and statistical measurability were interwoven in that quintessential element in post-war Japanese economic analysis: the GNP growth rate. Indeed, the notion of GNP growth has become so central to our image of the modern Japanese economy that it is rather surprising to recall that the concept of GNP was little known in Japan before 1945. A particularly important influence in the emergence of GNP as the measure of all things came from the work of the American Nobel Laureate Simon Kuznets, who not only participated in compiling official estimates of the United States GNP, but also undertook painstaking comparative analyses of growth factors in a wide range of developed and less-developed nations. Kuznets, together with other American development economists like Gustav Ranis, forged close links with a group of Japanese economists including Ohkawa Kazushi, Shinohara Miyohei, Ōkita Saburō, and Kanamori Hisao, co-operating with them in joint studies of Japanese growth. These contacts were supported on the US side by the Social Science Research Council's Committee on Economic Growth, of which Kuznets was chairman, and on the Japanese side by private research groups such as the Japan Economic Research Centre.

Kuznets expressed some reservations over the use of GNP as a measurement of national wealth and welfare. Unfortunately, however, these reservations were not strongly reflected in Japanese modern economics during the 1950s and early 1960s, and were almost entirely lost when economic theory was translated into the language of policy-makers and popular journalism. So it was that a statistical tool originally developed for quite specific purposes of Keynesian demand management was transformed into the central symbol of post-war Japanese economic and political ideology.

PRIVATE INVESTMENT AND HIGH GROWTH:
SHIMOMURA OSAMU (1910–   )

The first and most enthusiastic prophet of Japanese high growth was the *kanchō ekonomisuto* Shimomura Osamu. The 'Shimomura thesis', put forward as early as 1958, argued that Japan's high growth was not a temporary and fortuitous phenomenon, but could be sustained over a prolonged period of time (Shimomura 1958; see also Saeki and Shibagaki 1972: 60–1). Two years later Shimomura was to employ this same thesis in wholehearted support of Ikeda's National Income Doubling Plan.

Unlike many of his colleagues, Shimomura derived his approach to modern economics less from American economists like Samuelson than from the prominent British Keynesian J.R. Hicks (Saitō and Shimomura 1984). The chief characteristic of Shimomura's own writings, however, was their extremely empirical and practical nature, for Shimomura relied far less on abstract model-building than on observation and calculation of trends in the Japanese economy. This helped to make his work straightforward and readily comprehensible, and to ensure that it reached a wide audience both amongst policy-makers and the general public. The fact that Japan's growth rate did indeed conform to Shimomura's expectations naturally enhanced his reputation as an economist.

The 'Shimomura thesis' is in essence simplicity itself. Its central, often repeated, assertion is that 'in the final analysis, the growth rate will more or less parallel the size of private fixed investment as a percentage of G.N.P.' (Shimomura 1962: 110). Since Japan devoted a particularly large share of its wealth to private fixed investment, it therefore followed that Japan had a high growth potential.

In order to ensure that demand was sufficient to convert this potential into growth, however, Shimomura argued that it was necessary for the government to pursue stimulatory economic policies, and it was this aspect of his analysis that sparked such heated debate with other economists both in academia and in the bureaucracy. The debate focused in particular on two possible bottlenecks to growth. The first was the constraint imposed by domestic supply, and the likelihood that growth-oriented policies, by encouraging demand to outstrip supply, would fuel inflation. The second was the foreign exchange constraint. High growth, it was argued, would raise the level of imports and so place intolerable pressures on Japan's external balance of payments.

In Shimomura's view, however, neither of these problems was

relevant to Japan's economic situation in the late 1950s. Since about 1956, Shimomura argued, the Japanese economy had entered a phase of excess capacity rather than excess demand. This assertion was based on his analysis of the production coefficient of private capital investment, that is, the relationship between one year's increase in the private fixed investment and the following year's increase in GNP. (Shimomura's figures in fact included producers' durable equipment and non-residential housing, but excluded residential housing.) Until 1956, Shimomura calculated, the relationship between these two variables had been of the order of 1:1 but thereafter it had fallen to about 1:0.6. This indicated that the economy was suffering from deficient demand, and that more active growth-stimulating policies were desirable (Shimomura 1959a).

In later works Shimomura developed this argument by comparing price trends with trends in the investment production coefficient. These comparisons demonstrated that prices had generally been stable when the coefficient was in the region of 1:1.1. Juxtaposition of Japanese and the US data, moreover, suggested that the non-inflationary coefficient was unlikely to fall, and might even rise as industrial development proceeded (Shimomura 1962: 32–6). Shimomura, in short, perceived that capital investment embodied new technology and thus increased productivity. As a result, its effects in expanding supply tended to offset its contribution to increased demand. Relatively high levels of investment could thus be sustained without imposing severe upward pressure on prices.

Shimomura also took an optimistic view on the balance of payments issue. Here again, his empirical studies came up with a totemic figure which (like the 1:1 production coefficient) provoked prolonged controversy with other economists. In the case of foreign trade, the figure in question was 9 per cent, which, according to Shimomura, represented Japan's 'marginal import dependence': in other words, every \$100 increase in GNP included on average \$9 worth of imports. Shimomura argued that this level of marginal import dependence was unlikely to rise if high growth were encouraged, because growth-stimulating policies would increase the share of private and government consumption and reduce the share of inventories in GNP. Private and government consumption was less 'import-dependent' than inventory growth, and imports as a percentage of GNP were therefore more likely to fall than to rise. At the same time, high growth (including, as it did, the import and application of more up-to-date technology) would increase the competitiveness of Japanese goods on the world market. Growth promotion, according to this theory, would increase the level of exports more rapidly than it increased the level of imports, and would therefore have a positive, rather than a negative, effect on the balance of payments (see for example Shimomura 1962: 47–53).

The conclusions to be drawn were clear. Japan, Shimomura estimated, was capable of sustaining an economic growth rate of around 9 per cent per year from 1960. All that was needed was the abandonment of financial timidity, and the adoption of bold expansionary policies, especially in the monetary sphere:

> The next ten years . . . will be an epoch of great historical significance. However, our fate ten years from now will be determined by our own choices and decisions and by the level of our creative efforts at the present time. Future possibilities will be opened up and realised, not by a conservative, negative policy of 'safety first', but by resolute and creative vigour. This is a time when we need to go forward with self-confidence and with faith in the creative ability of the Japanese people.
>
> (Shimomura 1962: 5).

Shimomura's ideas thus provided essential theoretical underpinnings for the Ikeda government's ambitious and controversial high-growth policies. (Ikeda indeed accepted Shimomura's 9 per cent growth figure as a target for the first three years of his administration.) But the 'Shimomura thesis' also had an important impact in a quite different sense: by stirring up debate in the world of modern economics, it stimulated the publication of a range of books and articles aimed at refuting aspects of Shimomura's calculations, and in this way was indirectly responsible for some of the more significant advances in the development of post-war Japanese modern economics (see Ōkita 1959a,b; Tsuru 1959; Shinohara 1962: Chap. 5).

FROM CRITIQUE OF THE SHIMOMURA THESIS TO INTERPRETATION OF THE ECONOMIC MIRACLE: SHINOHARA MIYOHEI (1919–)

At first glance it might seem that history has vindicated the Shimomura thesis, for the Japanese economy did indeed maintain high levels of growth (higher even than Shimomura had predicted) for over a decade. On reflection, however, the issue proves a little more complex. Although this growth was achieved, as Shimomura foresaw, without a general deterioration in Japan's balance of payments, it was not achieved without inflation. Consumer prices rose at a rate of 7.2 per cent a year from 1960 to 1965 and 6.3 per cent a year from 1966 to 1973 (Andō 1979: 191). Moreover, during the late 1950s and early 1960s growth was achieved without strongly stimulatory government policy, and indeed government intervention was at times needed to restrain excess demand. As Saeki and Shibagaki observe, the fact that Shimomura's predictions proved historically accurate does not necessarily mean that their theoretical basis was sound (Saeki and Shibagaki 1972: 61).

One of Shimomura's most searching critics was the Hitotsubashi academic, Shinohara Miyohei, who, through his collaboration with US economists and with the economic historian Ohkawa Kazushi (1908–), was to become a particularly influential interpreter of Japan's development to English-speaking audiences. Shinohara, drawing in part on the work of Ōkita Saburō and Tsuru Shigeto, focused his attack on Shimomura's notion that the productive coefficient of private investment was likely to remain stable at around 1:1 under circumstances of high growth. In the first place, as Shinohara pointed out, the statistical evidence from which the 1:1 ration was calculated was in itself suspect. For example, the Shimomura thesis was based on the assumption that in the period 1951–6, the economy was operating at or close to full capacity, whereas in fact, during that period, capacity utilization was rising gradually from relatively low levels (Shinohara 1962: 125–6).

Like many other economists, Shinohara also pointed to the fact that the 1:1 ratio was initially calculated in terms of the gross increase in private fixed investment, including replacement of, as well as additions to, the capital stock. He then went on to demonstrate that far from being stable over time, the ratio of gross fixed investment go GNP growth (I_f / Δ GNP) appears to be inversely related to the speed of growth (Shinohara 1962: 126–33). Later versions of the Shimomura thesis attempted to take account of this criticism by making use of net, rather than gross, investment figures, but even then the optimistic forecasts of high growth did not escape Shinohara Miyohei's censure. Predictions of a 9 per cent growth rate during the 1960s, he argued, failed to take account of potential bottlenecks in the supply of labour, and assumed an unrealistically rapid flow of workers from agriculture to industry (Shinohara 1962: 138–47). In order to appreciate the force of this criticism, we need to relate it to Shinohara's overall vision of the dynamics of Japanese growth.

The debates over issues like the 1:1 ratio, pursued with such passion in the late 1950s and early 1960s, may strike the contemporary reader as somewhat arid and technical. Shinohara Miyohei's writings, however, gave these debates a wider significance by incorporating them into a more general analysis of the sources of rapid growth in Japan. As we have already observed, modern ecomomists like Shinohara, in pursuing this analysis, generated ideas that sometimes converged quite closely with those of certain Marxian theories (e.g. Ōuchi Tsutomu and Ōshima Kiyoshi). In Shinohara's interpretation of the causes of Japanese growth we can define five principal themes, all of which have subsequently been echoed by many other scholars of Japan's industrial development.

The first of these is the theme of post-war recovery, which, according to Shinohara, affected the growth rate of the Japanese economy at least until 1951, and perhaps as late as the mid-1950s (Shinohara 1968: 287). Using comparisons with other countries that had suffered severe war damage, Shinohara demonstrated that the greater the destruction, the faster was the rate of recovery. This inverse relationship helped to explain the particularly high levels of growth achieved by nations such as Japan and West Germany in the immediate post-war years, and the comparatively sluggish economic performance of countries like the United States and Canada (Shinohara 1961: Chap. 2; Shinohara 1962: 7–10).

Post-war recovery, however, was clearly no more than an explanation for one short phase of Japan's industrial development. In analysing the long-term process of growth since the Meiji period, Shinohara placed emphasis on other factors, of which the most important was the deterioration of Japan's terms of trade. From about 1900 onwards, Shinohara argued, the price of exports relative to imports had fallen, making Japanese goods increasingly competitive on world markets, and so enabling Japan to expand its export trade even during the years of the 1930s depression. The low cost of Japanese exports during the 1930s was partly a result of the devaluation of the yen, but another particularly important element in the deteriorating terms of trade was the combination of relatively low wages and rapidly rising productivity. The import of new technology had enabled Japan to achieve levels of productivity which, in some industries, were close to those of Western countries. But wage rises had failed to keep pace with improvements in productivity, thus ensuring that Japanese goods were able to undercut the products of other developed nations in terms of price (Shinohara 1962: 63–75). This analysis could be extended to the post-war period, when the combination of a fixed exchange rate, an abundance of labour, and rapid technological progress again resulted in worsening terms of trade and increasing exports (Shinohara 1961: Chap. 4; Shinohara 1962: 28–37; Shinohara 1964: Chap. 5).

Japan's success as a trading nation was intimately connected to a third component of the Shinohara analysis of growth: the dual industrial structure. Industrial dualism – that is, the symbiotic coexistence of large, modern factories paying relatively high wages and small, unsophisticated workshops paying low wages – had become an important topic of economic debate from 1957 onwards. In that year, the government's Economic White Paper drew attention to the continuing wage gap between large and small firms, and the Tokyo University economist Arisawa Hiromi coined the phrase *nijū kōzō* as the Japanese equivalent of the English term 'dualism' (Masamura 1968: 37–41). A heated controversy on the nature, origins, and implications of industrial dualism ensued, and soon came to embroil many of those economists who were simultaneously engaged in the debate on the Shimomura thesis.

Shinohara Miyohei's theory in general emphasized the functional aspects of industrial dualism. The concentration of capital in the hands of a few firms resulted, he argued, in the significant productivity gaps that existed even within individual industries in Japan. Large firms, having easier access to bank loans and to new technology, achieved high levels of efficiency and were able to pay relatively high wages. The Japanese labour market, however, was not homogeneous, but was rather divided into two sectors – a large-firm sector and a small-firm sector. This dichotomy prevented the wage levels of the more efficient large enterprises from placing upward pressures on wages in their smaller, less productive counterparts (Shinohara 1961: Chap. 5; Shinohara 1962: 17–21).

It was this dual structure that had enabled the Japanese economy to combine increasingly advanced industrial technology with comparatively cheap labour, and had thus contributed to the growing competitiveness of Japan's manufactured exports. At the same time industrial dualism allowed for high levels of saving and capital investment, while incidentally permitting rapid technological change to be achieved without sharply rising unemployment.

> The combination of cheap labour and high-level technology tends to reduce costs and raise profits, thus leading to greater capital financing from internal funds, on the one hand, and a lowering of product prices, on the other, which in turn helps to expand the foreign market.
> (Shinohara 1962: 21; for a discussion of the debate on dualism, see Minami 1986: 317–20).

143

In later writings, Shinohara supplemented this analysis with a fourth factor which, he suggested, had been an important determinant of Japan's economic dynamism in the twentieth century. This factor was Japan's adaptability to new technology and to the needs of a changing industrial environment. Although he gives no elucidation of the reasons for this adaptability, Shinohara hypothesizes that the contrast between British economic stagnation in the 1920s and 1930s and Japanese economic growth in the post-war years may be explained partly in terms of Britain's 'extremely low willingness to transform its industrial structure' and Japan's 'aggressive propensity to introduce foreign technology and to change its industrial structure in a flexible way' (Shinohara 1968: 293; on the comparison between Japan and Britain, see also Shinohara 1964: appendix 2).

Industrial dualism, technological adaptability, and increasing export competitiveness help to explain the generally high rates of growth achieved by Japan in the twentieth century. But as the long-term statistical data indicate, this growth was by no means smooth and continuous. Instead, Shinohara's analysis exposed a pattern of so-called 'Kuznets cycles' – waves of growth each lasting approximately 20 years. (A similar cyclical pattern was simultaneously but independently described by Ohkawa Kazushi.) A final element in Shinohara's analysis of post-war Japanese growth was therefore the assertion that since the late 1940s, the Japanese economy had entered the upswing of a new Kuznets cycle, a cycle that might be expected to peak in the first half of the 1960s (Shinohara 1962: 76–109).

This brief outline of Shinohara's theories helps to shed some light on his cautious approach to Japanese growth in the 1960s. Not only did he foresee the imminent onset of a downswing in the cyclical growth pattern, but more importantly, he predicted that this downswing might be triggered by the shortage of a factor crucial to his entire analysis of Japanese development: labour. It was the relative abundance of labour that accounted both for the persistence of industrial dualism and for Japan's ability to compete effectively in world markets. Rapid growth, however, would exhaust the supply of underemployed labour, narrow the wage gap between large and small firms, and so cut into profits and growth. At the same time, the technological lag between Japan and more highly industrialized nations would also decrease, forcing Japan to become more independent in the development of new technology (Shinohara 1962: 109).

As the events were to prove, Shinohara was unduly pessimistic in believing that these trends would cause declining rates of growth in the 1960s. The error, however, was more one of timing than of substance, for the restraints on growth which he indicated did indeed become crucial problems for the Japanese economy in the following decade. In the meanwhile, Shinohara's writings not only contributed to the debates on the Shimomura thesis and on industrial dualism, but also added to the rapidly growing volume of economic literature on the 'secrets' of Japanese growth.

PLANNING AND ECONOMIC DEVELOPMENT:
ŌKITA SABURŌ (1914–)

One of those who borrowed elements of Shinohara Miyohei's analysis to construct his own theory of Japan's high growth was Ōkita Saburō, perhaps the most influential of all post-war *kanchō ekonomisuto*. During an active administrative and political career which culminated in a period of service as Foreign Minister, Ōkita has written widely on many aspects of the Japanese economy. He participated in the debate on the Shimomura thesis, criticizing Shimomura's use of gross rather than net investment data, and has also demonstrated a particular interest in Japan's economic relations with less-developed Asian nations and in exploring the lessons of Japan's industrialization for those nations (see Ōkita 1970; Ōkita 1980a). His most important role, however, was his involvement in creating both the theoretical and the practical foundations of the post-war economic planning system. This aspect of Ōkita's career, which involved repeated efforts to bridge the gap between academic economics and policy-making, is sufficiently fascinating to be worth delineating in some detail.

Originally trained as an engineer, Ōkita joined the pre-war Ministry of Communications and later became a research and planning officer in the Greater East Asia Ministry during the Pacific War. Here his work was mainly concerned with the supply of raw materials from the Asian mainland to Japanese industry (Ōkita 1961a: 16). The experience of wartime economic management gave Ōkita an appreciation of both the possibilities and the limitations of economic planning. As a government official, he rapidly became aware of the fact that the war had placed intolerable pressures on the Japanese economic system, and even before Japan's defeat, he was already conscious of the need to define directions for post-war recovery and growth.

In the summer of 1945, some weeks before the surrender, Ōkita approached a number of leading economists and technocrats with a proposal to create an informal study group to consider Japan's economic future. Interestingly enough, this study group included not only liberal academics like Nakayama Ichirō but also Marxian economists, among them Ōuchi Hyōe and Inoue Harumaru. With ironically appropriate timing, their first meeting was pre-arranged for 16 August 1945 – the day after the emperor announced the surrender of Japan to the Allied powers.

Soon afterwards, Ōkita was transferred to the Ministry of Foreign Affairs and his research group became officially constituted as the Foreign Affairs Special Research Council (*Gaimushō Tokubetsu Chōsa Iinkai*), with an expanded membership including Arisawa Hiromi, Uno Kōzō, Yamada Moritarō, and Tsuru Shigeto. This group met regularly during the latter part of 1945 and the early months of 1946, and produced two reports: *Measures towards Japan's Economic Reconstruction* (*Nihon Keizai Saiken no Hōto*, October 1945) and *Basic Problems of Japan's Economic Reconstruction* (*Nihon Keizai Saiken no Kihon Mondai*, first issued in March 1946 and reprinted in revised form in September of that year) (Ōkita 1961a: 18–19).

The scope of these reports was a broad one: they attempted to define the peculiarities of the Japanese economic structure, and to consider the problems that Japan's economic and social system was likely to face in the immediate post-war years. The influence of some of the Marxian economists on the committee is evident from the final form of the 1946 report, which emphasized the survival of feudal elements in Japanese agriculture, and spoke of the contradiction between the financial might of the *zaibatsu* on the one hand and the underdeveloped nature of Japan's social infrastructure on the other. The 1946 report also related Japan's pre-war economic and political crisis to the low level of wages, which had restricted domestic demand and forced Japan to become increasingly aggressive in pursuit of new overseas markets. (For a summary of the report's analysis of the Japanese economy, see Ōkita 1961a: 21–4).

The work of the Special Research Council therefore helped to prepare a favourable environment for the social and economic reforms carried out under the US occupation. Ōuchi Hyōe later likened the role of the Council's economists to that of the young Meiji reformers, who had debated the future of Japan with such imagination and passion. However, he went on to observe that 'sadly, similar general debates did not take place on the subsequent state of the Japanese economy' – a pertinent comment, for the deepening tensions of the Cold War were soon to preclude such co-operation between modern and Marxian economists in shaping the future of the nation (Ōuchi 1960: 328).

The wartime economic planning bodies had been abolished on Japan's defeat, but in 1947 some of their functions were revived and incorporated into a new organization, the Economic Stabilization Board (*Keizai Antei Honbu*), of which Ōkita became chief research officer. In this capacity he was involved, with Tsuru Shigeto and Shimomura Osamu, in the composition of Japan's first Economic White Paper and also went on to take responsibility for the composition of the following four White Papers from 1948 to 1951. The Economic Stabilization Board was renamed the Economic Delibera-tion Board in 1952, and in 1954 was transformed into the Economic Planning Agency (*Keizai Kikakuchō*). Ōkita was thereupon appointed to the key position of head of the general planning section within the Agency and in this capacity he became the chief architect of the 1960 National Income Doubling Plan (Ōkita 1961a: Chaps 2–4; Uchino 1980: 98–102).

Ōkita's concept of economic planning was founded on a firm belief in the power of Keynesian intervention to mitigate the self-destructive tendencies inherent in capitalism. Japan's experience before and during the war had given him some sympathy with the Marxian view that, left to its own devices, capitalism would be likely to plunge from boom into crisis, thus triggering imperialist rivalries and wars. However, as he wrote in the 1960s,

the capitalist economy has also learnt much from the experience of economic depression. The development of modern economics, in which Keynesianism plays a central role, has provided theoretical support for the policy measures which must be taken by govern-ments to overcome recession and achieve full employment. At the same time, the refinement of national accounts statistics, which has come with modern economics, has given us a comprehensive picture of movements in the national economy and has clarified . . . both the mechanisms of recession and the nature of necessary anti-recessionary policy.

(Ōkita 1961b: 128)

Despite this optimism, however, Ōkita perceived an inherent risk in Keynesian 'fine-tuning'. The danger was that in reacting to immediate problems of deficient or excessive demand, governments would fail to consider the longer-term implications of their policies for economic development. The object of the national plan, therefore, was to provide 'a guidepost for making current decisions with a long-term perspective' (Ōkita 1980b: 197; see also Ōkita 1961b: 96–108).

Here we can see the roots of Ōkita's difference of opinion with Shimomura Osamu, whose overall approach to the economy in many ways so much resembled his own. Shimomura, discerning signs of deficient demand in late 1950s Japan, argued for radically stimulatory and growth-inducing policies. Ōkita, on the other hand, placing greater emphasis on the need for caution and responsibility in economic planning, questioned the accuracy of Shimomura's forecasting techniques, and supported a somewhat more modest growth target of 7–8 per cent for the 1960s (see Ōkita 1959a,b; Keizai Kikakuchō 1961).

In fact, as we have seen, growth was to exceed even Shimomura's predictions, and the Economic Planning Agency (EPA) was soon forced to produce a revised medium-term plan to take account of the overfulfilment of earlier targets. There are those, indeed, who have suggested that the Agency deliberately erred on the side of caution in order to ensure the maintenance of budget surpluses (see Tresize and Suzuki 1976: 791–2). Whatever the truth of this assertion, it is also clear that the Income Doubling Plan generated sufficient optimism to create an 'announcement effect'. In other words, its formulation and publication generated heightened expectations of change, and so influenced the behaviour of crucial participants in the economic system. This type of announcement effect has increasingly been recognized as an important function of economic plans, and has been consciously used by planning economists as a means of exerting influence on the workings of the free market. As Ōkita puts it, 'the preparation of economic plans itself has had an educative effect upon the various ministries, or business, and on the general public' (Ōkita 1980b: 197).

Against this background, it is not surprising to discover that Ōkita, while analysing the causes of Japanese growth in terms very similar to those used by Shinohara Miyohei, also points to certain additional stimuli to growth, one of which is the role of economic planning and policy. Like Shinohara (and also Ōuchi Tsutomu), Ōkita's analysis of high growth underlines the importance of post-war recovery and of such aspects of economic 'backwardness' as surplus labour and the dual industrial structure. Ōkita, however, also places considerable emphasis on Japan's success in combining a free market structure with indicative planning, and argues that post-war Japanese development was strongly assisted by a favourable international environment. His discussion of post-war recovery factors also differs from Shinohara in giving particular weight to the political and social reforms that accompanied economic reconstruction. The dissolution of the *zaibatsu*, the improvement of wages and working conditions, and above all the abandonment of large-scale military expenditures were, he argues, the foundations on which the 'economic miracle' was built. In this sense, from the vantage point of the 1960s and 1970s, Ōkita was able to reaffirm the analysis put forward by his economic brains-trust of 1945-6, and to suggest that the reforms which they had supported had indeed helped to achieve an unimaginable rate of economic recovery and expansion (Ōkita 1980a: 93-147; Ōkita 1961a: 20-1).

FOREIGN TRADE AND ECONOMIC GROWTH: KANAMORI HISAO (1924-   ) AND KOJIMA KIYOSHI (1920-   )

Shinohara Miyohei's analysis of the causes of high growth was itself to inspire controversy amongst Japan's modern economists. In particular, Shinohara's emphasis on the role of low wages in supporting Japan's export competitiveness seemed to point to a pessimistic view of Japan's future growth potential, and was strongly contested by some theorists. This debate helped to focus attention on foreign trade and its impact on Japanese growth, and encouraged a search for the origins of Japan's impressive export performance in the post-war period.

A leading participant in the debate was a prominent colleague of Ōkita Saburō's in the Economic Planning Agency, Kanamori Hisao. Kanamori had entered the EPA in the early 1950s, at a time when the Korean War boom was collapsing and the Japanese economy was entering a phase of recession. In an atmosphere of general pessimism, however, he developed a strong faith in the capacity of the Japanese economy to achieve future growth. Kanamori's economic approach, which was an empirical rather than a highly theoretical one, was influenced by the work both of Shimomura Osamu and of Shinohara Miyohei, and was refined during the three years (from 1958 to 1960) that he spent as a research student at Oxford University (see Kanamori 1968a: 221-7). After his return from Oxford, Kanamori rose rapidly within the EPA, and as head of its National Research Section, was responsible for the Economic White Papers of 1964, 1965, and 1966. These covered the years in which Japan was moving towards the liberalization of its rather highly protected trade system, and it was therefore natural that Kanamori's research should concentrate particularly on the issue of trade.

By the mid-1960s, it was possible to observe the fulfilment of

Shimomura Osamu's prophecy of high growth combined with an improving balance of trade. Yet this situation contradicted conventional economic wisdom, which suggested that the level of imports is determined by domestic GNP growth while the level of exports is determined by world GNP growth. If this were true, of course, any country experiencing abnormally high growth would also expect to find its imports rising more rapidly than its exports.

In explaining Japan's ability to avoid the pitfalls of a deteriorating trade balance, Kanamori relied more on Shinohara's than on Shimomura's analysis, but at the same time he modified and supplemented Shinohara's theory in a number of significant ways. In the first place, the notion of low wages as a factor in Japan's export competitiveness needed some refinement in the context of the 1960s. During the years of high economic growth, Japanese wages had in fact been rising more rapidly than wages in most other industrialized countries, but as Kanamori emphasized, productivity in Japan had been rising still faster, thus resulting in declining wage costs (wages divided by productivity) (Kanamori 1970: 225–58). This 'wage lag', however, was, in Kanamori's view, only part of the explanation for Japan's export performance. Equally important was the nature of the structural changes occurring in the Japanese economy. By comparison with other countries, Japan's growth was relatively 'unbalanced'. Growth, in other words, was heavily concentrated in a few areas of manufacturing (e.g. chemicals and machinery) – precisely those areas for whose products world demand was most income-elastic and most rapidly expanding (Kanamori 1968b: 311–18; Kanamori 1970: 261–3). At the same time, Japan's industrial growth involved the introduction of new equipment and technology which not only increased labour productivity, but was also more efficient in its use of raw materials and energy. Demand for natural resources was therefore growing more slowly than industrial production, and this trend was helping to hold down the level of raw material imports (Kanamori 1970: 264–7).

The relationship between structural change and export growth was even more strongly emphasized by another leading trade theorist of the 1950s and 1960s, the Hitotsubashi economist Kojima Kiyoshi. Unlike Kanamori Hisao, Kojima wholly rejected Shinohara's analysis of the role of low wages in Japan's export expansion, claiming that cheap labour had been a significant factor only for brief periods of Japan's economic history (Kojima 1958: Chaps 3–5; for an assessment of Shinohara's and Kojima's views, see Minami 1986: 246–7). In place of Shinohara's theories, Kojima attempted to construct a model of export development in late industrializing countries, integrating the comparative advantage theories of Ricardo, Heckscher, Ohlin, and Samuelson with the trade theory of the Japanese economist Akamatsu Kaname.

The problem with traditional Ricardian comparative advantage, Kojima pointed out, was its static nature. Countries were assumed to have a fixed endowment of resources, and this endowment was said to determine the product that each country could most advantageously export. However, as Heckscher, Ohlin, and Samuelson had shown, the processes of economic development, and of trade itself, altered the resource endowment of nations by increasing or decreasing the supply of labour and capital available for production. As a result of these shifts in supply, the comparative advantage of nations would change over time, with new export goods appearing while older exports diminished in importance.

The continuous change in the structure of exports was related to a cycle of product development which had been described by Akamatsu Kaname during the 1940s. Very briefly, Akamatsu's model runs as follows: in late industrializing countries like Japan, a new product (such as manufactured textiles) begins by being a major import item. Then a phase of import substitution occurs, with domestic manufacture of the product expanding rapidly; finally, the product is transformed into an export item, while imports and domestic manufacture shift towards new, more sophisticated manufactured goods. This wedge-shaped movement of a product through the economy, from the import side to the export side, was depicted by Akamatsu as resembling the 'pattern of geese in flight' (*gankō keitai*), a name that is now commonly used to indicate the cycle he analysed.

By putting together the theory of dynamic comparative advantage and Akamatsu's 'flying geese' model, Kojima was able to present an alternative to Shinohara's analysis of the relationship between exports and development in Japan. Rather than looking at long-term aggregate trends in trade and wages (as Shinohara had done), Kojima isolated a series of successive phases within which new patterns of exports emerged. (The dates of these phases, according to Kojima, were 1901–19, 1919–29, 1929–37, and 1945 onwards.) During the early part of each phase there were unstable years of transition, when imports tended to exceed exports. As new industries were established, however, a period of steady economic growth and rising exports ensued, each wave of industrial development leaving Japan with a more complex, diverse, and sophisticated export structure (Kojima 1958: Chap. 10). The conclusions to be drawn from this analysis were clearly optimistic ones: rising wages need no longer be seen as threatening export competitiveness and thus undermining high growth. On the contrary, wage increases would shift Japan's comparative advantage towards more capital-intensive goods, and at the same time expand the domestic market for sophisticated manufactured products, so initiating a new migration of 'flying geese' which would ultimately enhance the quantity and quality of Japanese exports.

In more recent works, Kojima has extended these ideas to justify the role of Japanese foreign investment in less-developed Asian countries. Japanese multinational companies, according to Kojima, tend to invest along the lines of comparative advantage, exporting labour-intensive technologies to countries such as Thailand and the Philippines, where labour is relatively abundant. In this respect they differ from US multinationals, whose investment, based on sophisticated know-how and patented technology, more often 'contradicts the comparative advantage pattern of trade and decreases the volume of trade' (Kojima 1978: 139). Japanese direct overseas investment, according to this view, assists less-developed countries to shift the focus of their production and exports step by step from agricultural or labour-intensive goods to more complex capital-intensive manufactures. In this way, Japanese multinationals can be seen as 'exporting' Japan's successful model of economic development to nations at a less advanced stage of industrialization (Kojima 1978: Chap. 7).

NEO-CLASSICAL THEORY AND THE CRITIQUE OF JAPANESE ECONOMIC POLICY: KOMIYA RYŪTARŌ (1928–   )

The theories of free trade and comparative advantage could be used, as they were by Kojima, to paint a positive picture of Japan's growth potential and of the overseas activities of Japanese enterprises. But in a country whose government in fact imposed considerable restrictions on the free flow of trade and capital, they could also become a weapon in the critique of government policy. This critical use of neo-classical theory is most evident in the writings of the Tokyo University academic Komiya Ryūtarō, who had emerged by the late 1960s as one of the leading exponents of modern economic theory in Japan.

Komiya's numerous writings cover an extraordinarily wide range of economic research. He has published studies of foreign trade and investment, economic policy, the role of savings in Japanese economic growth, and (as we have seen) the involvement of economists in government. Through many of these works, however, there runs a connecting theme: a theme of scepticism towards the benefits of government planning and intervention (so enthusiastically described by economists like Ōkita), and a belief that high growth had occurred as much despite as because of the policies of the Japanese government. To use Komiya's own words, his objective has been to escape from the dichotomy whereby

> those who are critical of the government as well as of the present Japanese economic system fondly underestimate the nation's viability, placing incessant emphasis only upon negative aspects of growth, while the defenders of the present politico-economic system tirelessly propagate the apparent success of government policies, particularly the well-publicised Income-Doubling Plan.
>
> (Komiya 1966a: xi)

In Komiya's view, the sources of Japan's high growth lay largely in factors beyond the control of government policy. Amongst the most important of these factors was the unusually high level of savings, which provided the capital for investment in the newly expanding industries of the 1950s and 1960s. One of Komiya's best-known papers traces the origins of this frugality to a variety of peculiarities inherent in the Japanese social structure, among them the age-related pay system, the widespread payment of biennial bonuses to employees, and the underdeveloped state of consumer credit (Komiya 1966b).

Komiya's attitude to the effects of government intervention is particularly apparent in his studies of trade and foreign investment. In characteristic neo-classical fashion, the free movement of goods and capital is presented as providing the maximum benefit to the welfare of all countries, and policies that protect domestic industries or limit the inflows of foreign capital are seen as being justified only in the most exceptional circumstances (Komiya and Amano 1972: Chaps 7, 8, and 16). Komiya was therefore a vigorous critic of the government's cautious attitude towards the opening of the economy to foreign investment. Writing in 1967, when the first moves towards capital liberalization were under way, Komiya argued that Japanese companies had little reason to fear the arrival of foreign multinationals, and that the inflow of foreign capital would result in the transfer of foreign managerial resources and skills to Japan. Komiya was particularly scathing about the frequently expressed fear that foreign companies would be unresponsive to 'administrative guidance' (i.e.

the informal methods by which the government sought to influence
the behaviour of major Japanese companies).

> Many people cite, as an undesirable consequence of capital
> liberalisation, the fact that it will make administrative guidance
> and voluntary control by corporations more difficult. But, to my
> mind, if this effect is strongly marked it will not be a disadvantage
> but will rather be one of the greatest advantages of liberalisation.
> (Komiya 1970: 228)

Administrative guidance, Komiya asserted, was a particularly
undesirable form of government intervention because it violated the
principle that economic policies should operate according to universal
and objective criteria, and should rely on indirect means (such as
taxes), rather than direct government orders, to influence the
behaviour of producers and consumers.

Komiya's assessment of Japanese economic policy was not wholly
negative. There was at least one respect in which he agreed with
Ōkita's positive assessment of indicative planning: by bringing
business people, officials, and others together to discuss the state of
the economy, the planning and industrial policymaking system had
helped to speed the dissemination of economic information and so
to assist rational decision-making (see Komiya 1975a: 221). In other
respects, however, Komiya found much to criticize. Despite the
existence of an indicative planning system, economic policies had
frequently been ill-coordinated and mutually contradictory. So-called
'infant industry' protection policies had frequently become a means
of feather-bedding mature but inefficient industries, while the areas
of manufacturing that flourished were often the ones which had
received little encouragement or support from the government.
Moreover, Komiya argued, government policies tended to favour the
interests of certain large enterprises while ignoring the interests of the
consumer. As a result, economic equity was diminished and the industrial structure had become increasingly unbalanced. These problems
manifested themselves in phenomena such as worsening environmental
pollution (Komiya 1975a: 218–26; see also Komiya 1975b).

The growing influence of Komiya's ideas in the late 1960s and
early 1970s was symptomatic of declining faith in the post-war neo-
classical-Keynesian synthesis. As deepening economic and social
problems foreshadowed the imminent collapse of high growth, so the
axioms of post-war modern economics came under growing attack,
not only from Komiya's anti-interventionist perspective but also from

those who used modern economic methods to serve more radical philosophies.

OLIGOPOLY AND INDUSTRIAL GROWTH:
MIYAZAKI YOSHIKAZU (1919–   )

A vital part of this new, critical approach was a questioning of the fruits of high economic growth itself. The modern economists whose work we have considered so far have, for the most part, focused their attention on the causes of rapid economic growth in Japan. It is true that their writings have at times touched on problems inherent in the growth process: Ōkita, for example, refers to the undesirable consequences of industrial dualism, while Komiya emphasizes the negative effects of certain government economic policies (Ōkita 1980a: 123–4). Nevertheless, the implicit assumption has generally been that rapid growth will result in improved welfare. Factors that stimulate growth have therefore usually been seen in a positive light.

By the late 1960s, however, there were increasing reasons to question the equation 'growth = greater welfare', and indeed to have reservations about that entire sense of optimism which pervaded post-war modern economics. Although real wages were indeed increasing quite rapidly – at an annual rate of 3.8 per cent in the first half of the 1960s and 8.8 per cent in the second – rising land prices and the low level of public investment in social infrastructure (housing, sewerage, recreational facilities, etc.) meant that improvements in the standard of living were uneven. Some aspects of the quality of life in fact deteriorated as cities grew more congested and commuters faced longer and more crowded journeys to work.

The most vivid illustration of the power of growth to cause death and disease rather than health and well-being came from the numerous cases of industrial pollution that caught the public attention in the late 1960s and early 1970s. Their names were soon to become as familiar as a litany of wartime battles: Minamata, Yokkaichi, Niigata, Kawasaki. To an increasing number of Japanese people it appeared that the benefits of industrial development had been absorbed by the ever-growing giant corporations whose office blocks dominated the central city landscapes, while ordinary individuals had gained a disproportionately small share of the benefits of growth. This deepening disillusionment with the goal of GNP growth expressed itself in political phenomena such as the student riots of the late 1960s and the election of socialist municipal governments in many major

A HISTORY OF JAPANESE ECONOMIC THOUGHT

cities. In the realm of economic theory, the changing popular mood meant that particular interest came to be focused on those economists who took a sceptical and questioning approach to assumptions of growth as a measure of economic 'success'.

The economists whose work we shall consider in the final section of this chapter have two things in common. Both have contributed to the development of economic theory by bringing together insights from Marxian and modern thought, and both have placed considerable emphasis on the social costs imposed by the Japanese growth process. Of the first of these economists, Miyazaki Yoshikazu, it has been said that

> Miyazaki's basic viewpoint can be said to be a Marxian critique of capitalism, but his special characteristic is that, in confronting the arguments introduced by so-called modern economics, he had absorbed these arguments and constructed his criticism from within their framework.
>
> (Murakami Yasusuke, quoted in Saeki and Shibagaki 1972: 69–70)

From another perspective, we can see Miyazaki's work as a precursor to the radical Keynesianism which was to achieve increasing influence in Japan after the oil crisis of 1973. At the same time, it is clear that Miyazaki draws considerable inspiration from American Marxists like Paul Baran and Paul Sweezy and from their liberal compatriots, most notably John Kenneth Galbraith.

Miyazaki's principal criticism of post-war modern economists was that their analysis of the causes of growth failed to pay adequate attention to the structural phenomena that supported Japan's extraordinarily rapid rate of post-war industrial development. While Shinohara, Ōkita, and others produced lists of diverse and largely unconnected growth factors (favourable trade conditions, industrial dualism, adaptability to new technology, etc.), Miyazaki attempted to show how growth was based on the peculiar structure of post-war Japanese big business. In this structure he identified two crucial elements: the reliance of large firms on indirect financing such as bank loans, rather than on share issue or self-financing through retained profit; and the tendency of Japanese enterprises to form groups (*keiretsu* or *kigyō shūdan*) centred around a major city bank. These two characteristics were, of course, inseparably interrelated, for enterprise groups provided the mechanism by which bank loans were chanelled to certain favoured large corporations.

Miyazaki noted, however, that unlike the pre-war *zaibatsu*, post-war enterprise groups did not concentrate their activities in one particular field, such as mining, heavy industry, or commerce, but rather sought to fill every major niche within the expanding economy. This resulted in the phenomenon that he labelled 'one-settism', whereby each *keiretsu* attempted to ensure that it controlled a complete 'set' of companies spanning every major industrial area. If a new industry emerged as an important locus of development (as did petrochemicals in the late 1950s, and oil exploration in the early 1970s) every *keiretsu* would simultaneously move to secure a foothold in that industry, and the consequences would be fierce competition and, not infrequently, excess capacity (Miyazaki 1966; see also Miyazaki 1980).

According to Miyazaki's analysis, however, the 'one-set' group structure, which had its origins in *zaibatsu* dissolution and the financial policies of the Occupation era, was a powerful impetus to growth from the 1950s onwards. The secret of its effectiveness lay in the way in which it at once promoted and regulated competition. 'One-settism' encouraged intense rivalry between the various *keiretsu* groups, while at the same time creating barriers to non-*keiretsu* firms wishing to enter expanding industrial areas. The growth of the *keiretsu* was also enhanced by their ability to 'internalize external economies': that is, to capture the multiplier effects of new investment (in terms of demand for raw materials, equipment, parts, etc.) within their own enterprise group (Miyazaki 1980: 71-3).

Yet if the group structure was a key to understanding Japan's economic growth, it was also a key to understanding the undesirable social consequence of growth. In his widely read study *Oligopoly* (*Kasen*, 1972), Miyazaki suggested that the Japanese enterprise structure represented no more than an extreme case of a trend that was apparent in many industrialized nations:

> a trend by which ownership and control [of enterprises], which was once united in the hands of the individual, comes, via a phase of dissolution, to be reunited in the hands of the company.
>
> (Miyazaki 1972: 21)

Miyazaki argued, in other words, that the tendency towards separation of ownership from control – analysed during the 1930s and 1940s by such writers as Adolf Berle, G.C. Means, and James Burnham – had given way to a phase of development in which large enterprises were increasingly coming to be both owned and controlled by other large enterprises. Japan's *keiretsu* offered an outstanding illustration of this process. Here the leading financial and industrial *keiretsu*

157

companies not only held shares in and provided loans to other group members, but were also able to influence the latters' management strategies by the use of interlocking directorates, or by placing their own appointees in key managerial positions (Miyazaki 1972).

With the emergence of this new corporate structure, however, the fundamental postulate of neo-classical economics – that free competition would lead to the optimum allocation of resources – had lost most of its force. The division of labour and the allocation of resources was now largely administered and controlled within enterprise groups. The ideology of neo-classical economics therefore obscured the reality of a growing 'autocracy of the corporation'. In the past the enterprise had served the interest (albeit a narrow and sectional interest) of the owner or shareholder, and was also to some extent obliged to meet the interests of the consumer, but the corporate structure embodied in the *keiretsu* threatened to create companies that served no interests but their own. The new enterprise group existed 'neither for shareholders, nor for employees, nor for consumers, nor for society, but . . . singlemindedly for the growth and benefit of the company itself' (Miyazaki 1972: 72). It is therefore entirely appropriate that Miyazaki should begin his study of oligopoly with a discussion of recent Japanese pollution cases, for his analysis suggested that the oligpolistic structures that promoted Japan's rapid growth were also precisely the structures that, by promoting the unfettered pursuit of corporate expansion, had created environmental degradation and urban blight.

BEYOND GNP: TSURU SHIGETO (1912–   )

Tsuru Shigeto, like Miyazaki Yoshikazu, is one of those economists whose work defies ready categorization. I have postponed discussion of his ideas until the end of this chapter not because they are unimportant (on the contrary, they have had a very great influence upon post-war Japanese economics) nor for chronological reasons (Tsuru is in fact older than many of the economists whose work has already been outlined), but because Tsuru's career seems to bring together so many of the themes which we have touched on in the past two chapters.

Japanese economists have often been accused of cliquishness and factionalism. Critics both within Japan and overseas have spoken of their failure to communicate with foreign researchers, their reluctance to move between the worlds of academia and public administration, and above all their inability to conduct discourses that cross the ideological divide between Marxism and modern economics. These criticisms may have some basis in fact, but examples of scholars such as Tsuru clearly show that the failing is not a universal one.

The international flavour of Tsuru's work was established during his student years. He spent the period from 1933 to the outbreak of the Pacific War at Harvard, studying with Joseph Schumpeter, Alvin Hansen, Wasily Leontief, and others (Odaka 1976). Although Tsuru returned to Japan in 1942, he retained close links with the international economic community, not only in the United States but also in Europe and less-developed Asian countries. In the post-war period he was a frequent participant in international conferences, and published books and articles in English, French, and German. His international and electic approach to his subject is illustrated by the quotations from Burke, Ruskin, and Emerson that punctuate his works, and it is characteristic of his style that he should commence his 1971 critique of GNP as a measure of welfare with a particularly apt passage from Saint-Exupery's *Le Petit Prince*.

During the Second World War and early Occupation period Tsuru worked as a government official, first in the Ministry of Foreign Affairs and later in the Economic Stabilization Bureau, of which he was first vice-minister. In these roles, as we have seen, he took part in the deliberations of the Foreign Affairs Special Research Council, and became chief author (with Ōkita and Shimomura) of Japan's first Economic White Paper. Tsuru's left-wing political position, however, made it increasingly difficult for him to work within the institutions of government, and in 1948 he moved into academia, taking up a senior research position at Hitotsubashi University (Odaka 1976: 430).

This relatively varied career has no doubt contributed to the breadth of Tsuru's research interests and intellectual vision. In terms of fundamental philosophy Tsuru is a Marxian rather than a modern economist, but he is one who can, as it were, speak the language of both tribes, and who has therefore been a participant in some of the modern economic debates discussed in this chapter. One of his most important contributions in this area was to the controversy over the Shimomura thesis, and particularly over Shimomura's hypothesis on the production coefficient of capital. Shimomura, it will be remembered, claimed that during the early 1950s, the ratio of increases in private fixed investment to increases in output had been approximately 1:1. His calculations, however, were based on investment statistics provided by the government's Annual Survey of Corporate Enterprises (*Hōjin Kigyō Tōkei Nenpō*). As Tsuru observed, these statistics were misleading, since they gave the book value of private fixed investment and not its productive capacity. The book value of machinery would normally depreciate at a given percentage each year, while its actual efficiency might remain unchanged for many years. In order to obtain an accurate picture of changes in capacity and their impact on growth, it was therefore necessary to have some estimate of the age structure of machinery and equipment in use, and to convert the nominal figures of the Corporate Enterprises Survey into real terms (Tsuru 1959: 98–9; Tsuru's arguments are also discussed in Shinohara 1962: 133–7).

Tsuru's approach to the statistical problems of the Shimomura thesis reflects a more fundamental concern which forms a connecting theme within many of his major economic writings. This is a concern for the distinction between the real and the value aspects of the economic system. All economies, Tsuru argues, are constrained by limited supplies of certain essential productive factors such as labour, land, and non-reproducible raw materials. Once we begin to measure these factors in price terms, however, we superimpose upon the real system a set of exchange values that will vary, depending on whether the economy we are examining is a feudal, capitalist, or socialist one. It is precisely because Marxism recognizes the distinction between the real structure and the value structure, while modern economics often obscures it, that Tsuru favours the Marxian approach to the analysis of economic problems. 'The most outstanding contribution of Marx as a social scientist', he states,

> may be said to have been to distinguish clearly between these two aspects, and to draw implications from them, and depict an historical evolution of a society from the tension caused by the contradictions between them.
>
> (Tsuru 1976a: 186)

This preference for the Marxian vision of the economy does not, however, preclude an appreciation of the merit of certain modern economic ideas, particularly the ideas of theorists such as Schumpeter and Keynes (see for example Tsuru 1983). Tsuru's approach is always a comparative one, seeking to define the strengths and weaknesses, on the one hand, in modern and Marxian economic theory and, on the other, in capitalist and socialist economic systems. Thus the contrast he draws between Marxian aggregates (the concepts of constant and variable capital, surplus value, etc.) and Keynesian aggregates (income, savings, consumption, etc.) shows that each may have its part to play in certain types of analysis. Marx's aggregates, for example, operate over the long term and ignore the 'parametric adjustments' caused by temporary shifts in supply and demand, while the Keynesian system is more sensitive to such short- to medium-term fluctuations. At the same time, however, the Keynesian schema operates in net terms, that is by focusing on inputs to and outputs from the economic system. This allows it to be used in a way that leaves the internal workings of the economy unexamined, something which is impossible when Marxian aggregates, operating as they do in gross terms, are the basis of analysis. Consequently

> the Marxian aggregates depict the bone structure, as it were, of the capitalistic circular flow as seen through x-ray, whereas the Keynesian aggregates show us the delineation of our subject matter as projected on one dimensional plane.
>
> (Tsuru 1976b: 80)

Tsuru's comparison between the capitalist and the socialist economy is also carefully balanced and considered. Although he inherits from Marx a view that economic theory should serve as a basis for political practice. Tsuru's advocacy of socialism is not a rigid or dogmatic one. Capitalism, he admits, is 'capable of raising [the] welfare of the working class', though 'it does so only when it does not conflict with the overriding interests of capital' (Tsuru 1976c: 28). Centrally planned economies, on the other hand, may 'operate with a certain degree of ruthlessness in carrying out a program of crude priorities where a number of industries . . . are pushed to the maximum often without regard to rational cost' (Tsuru 1976c: 30). Tsuru's practical prescriptions for the Japanese economy are therefore gradualist ones. In the early post-war period he spoke of the need for a steady expansion of publicly-owned development projects – based perhaps on models like the US Tennessee Valley Authority – and his more recent works have continued to emphasize the potential for a gradual socialization, both of economic stocks and economic flows, as a means of driving a socialist wedge into the heart of the capitalist system (see Tsuru 1958: 52–7; Tsuru 1983: 161).

The combination of a firm grasp on modern economic theory and a sharp eye for the defects of that theory enabled Tsuru to become a leading figure in the emerging criticism of high growth in Japan. As the dark side of the 'economic miracle' became increasingly apparent in rising prices and worsening pollution, support for the government's development strategies weakened and the media began to spread the new, defiant catch-cry of '*kutabare GNP*' ('to hell with GNP'). This popular sentiment was given theoretical substance by Tsuru's studies, which analysed the economic roots of the deepening international environmental crisis, and pointed to the growing divergence between, on the one hand, human welfare measured in real terms, and, on the other, the value measurements embodied in GNP statistics (Tsuru 1976d; Tsuru 1972; Tsuru 1975).

Tsuru's argument was that in a certain phase of capitalist development, GNP growth rates had indeed provided a reasonable approximation to the growth of real wealth. However, the increasing importance of economic externalities and the decline of consumer sovereignty were making this approximation less and less accurate. In a series of criticisms that have since gained widespread acceptance, Tsuru indicated some of the absurdities inherent in GNP measurement: the fact, for example, that geographical and social necessities may ensure that some regions have higher GNP than others without this in any way representing higher welfare. (The sale of heaters in a cold country will boost GNP, as will the sale of burglar alarms in a country with a high crime rate.) Similarly, institutionalized waste, built-in obsolescence, and political or social arrangements that inflate prices (such as the Japanese land tax and planning laws) will all help to raise the level of GNP (Tsuru 1976: 80–8; Tsuru 1972: 108–18).

Tsuru's solution to the deficiencies of GNP statistics was not to replace GNP with some other index of welfare increases, as other economists have done, but rather to argue for an analysis that would distinguish the stock of 'social wealth' from the flow of 'income'. It was the former, consisting of accumulated reserves of capital, social infrastructure, natural resources, and so on that, Tsuru argued, was the real determinant of human welfare. Rather than measuring the flow of income, which might in fact represent a depletion of the wealth, economists concerned with quality of life should therefore seek to refine methods for measuring rises or falls in the social stock. Through this analysis Tsuru, who had contributed to many of the debates of the high-growth era, also helped to build the foundations for some of the significant theoretical developments of 'post-high-growth' Japan, developments that we shall examine in the following chapter.

THE COLLAPSE OF THE NEO-CLASSICAL–
KEYNESIAN SYNTHESIS

In the years from the end of the Second World War to the early 1970s, neo-classical and Keynesian ideas, which had had such a tentative hold in pre-war Japan, acquired very great influence in Japanese economic thought. To a large extent, these ideas were absorbed from the works of economists such as Harrod, Samuelson, and Kuznets. Non-Marxian economics in Japan, as in the United States, therefore came to be dominated by the paradigm of neo-classical-Keynesian synthesis. The intellectual framework of this synthesis was readily acceptable in post-war Japan, where high growth seemed to justify an optimistic vision of capitalism, and where the free market was modified by considerable government intervention (even though this intervention was seldom of the typical Keynesian demand-stimulating variety). As a result, modern economics in 1950s and 1960s Japan was not much concerned with the more philosophical or highly theoretical aspects of economics. Most of its practitioners were content to work within imported ideological and theoretical parameters, and to concentrate on the application of theory to the practical problems of understanding Japan's remarkably rapid industrial growth.

By the beginning of the 1970s, however, the basis not only of high growth, but also of this comfortable intellectual edifice was crumbling. Japanese economists were therefore forced to redirect their attention to the most essential and fundamental questions of economic theory – even to the meaning of the term 'economics' itself. Just as Japan was finding it increasingly hard to rely on imported technology, so there came to be a growing sense that Japanese economics, rather than accepting and adapting imported theories, would need to contribute to the generation of new paradigms to meet the problems of a changing economic environment.

6

Contemporary Japanese economic thought

It may seem paradoxical that at the very time when Japan has at last achieved unchallenged status as an economic great power, Japanese economic thought should have entered a period of profound crisis. Yet in fact the 'success' itself is surely a significant reason for the crisis.

Economic maturity has brought with it an end to the rapid growth of the post-war decades. Rising costs of labour and land, growing competition from the newly industrializing Asian countries, and the increasing need for Japan to undertake its own research and development were already, by the late 1960s, making it unlikely that high growth rates could be sustained indefinitely. At the same time, the expanding economic power of Japan and Western Europe was undermining the US-dominated international economic order and was to lead in the early 1970s to the collapse of the Bretton Woods system. This was followed by the first oil crisis, which caused acute economic disruption in Japan and plunged the industrialized world into the most severe recession since 1945.

Quite abruptly, the immediate task for analysts of the Japanese economy ceased to be the search for causes of high growth, and became the pursuit of solutions to economic crisis. Yet it was precisely at this point that confidence in the management strategies of modern (and particularly of Keynesian) economics began to crumble. The Japanese government, which had little need for Keynesian demand-stimulation during the 1950s and 1960s, introduced a strongly stimulative budget in the wake of the yen revaluation of 1970–1, only to find that this provoked severe inflation. Declining growth rates and increasing demands for welfare and military spending led to large budget deficits. Even unemployment levels, although still low by international standards, began to rise as the Japanese economy faced problems of industrial restructuring at home and resurgent protectionism overseas.

MONETARISM IN JAPAN:
SUZUKI YOSHIO (1913–) AND SHIMPO SEIJI (1945–)

One reaction to the economic crisis in Japan, as in other industrialized countries, was a turning away from Keynesianism towards the revitalized monetarist ideas of economists such as Milton Friedman. These ideas had indeed begun to receive a sympathetic hearing in Japan in the early 1960s, when Milton Friedman visited Tokyo for discussions with Ōkita Saburō and other leading Japanese economists. Friedman challenged the dominant Japanese schools of growth analysis, which (in Keynesian fashion) tended to view the money supply as an important factor in growth only to the extent that changes in money supply brought about changes in the rate of interest. Against this perspective, Friedman argued that movements in the quantity of money could directly trigger price changes and alterations in the level of real economic activity.

Friedman's critique of accepted economic wisdom made a deep impression on some of the younger generation of bureaucratic economists, such as Suzuki Yoshio of the Bank of Japan (see Suzuki 1986: 117, 139), but failed to undermine the overwhelming authority of Keynesians like Shimomura and Ōkita during the high growth era. By the mid-1970s, however, the young generation were entering positions of importance in the Japanese economy, and Japan's changed economic circumstances created a fertile environment for attacks on the growth theories of the 1960s. Monetarist ideas were popularized in books and magazine articles by leading bureaucratic economists and by academics, like Keiō University's Katō Hiroshi (Kan) (b. 1926) and it was hardly surprising that Milton and Rose Friedman's popular work, *Free to Choose*, quickly became a bestseller in Japan (Tsujimura 1986: 25).

The leading Japanese monetarists have in general been concerned less with the pursuit of major theoretical innovations than with the verification, adaptation, and modification of US monetarist theory in the light of Japanese experience. Thus Suzuki Yoshio and others have undertaken detailed studies on the relationship between money supply, prices, and growth in Japan, while Shimpo Seiji of the Economic Planning Agency has applied Friedman and Phelps's 'natural rate of unemployment' hypothesis to Japan. Predictably,

165

Suzuki's studies confirmed the causal relationship between movements in the money supply and movements in industrial production (Suzuki 1964; Suzuki 1986: 139–44), while Shimpo's offered support for the notion of a natural level of unemployment which could not, in the long run, be reduced by policies of aggregate demand expansion. (According to Shimpo, this level has been steadily rising in the Japanese case, from around 1.5 per cent in 1972 to around 2.5 per cent in the mid-1980s; see Shimpo 1979: Chap. 8; Shimpo 1988: Chaps 2 and 6.) Shimpo has also conducted analyses of the Japanese economy using the rational expectationist model developed by the US Federal Reserve Bank (the so-called 'St. Louis Model') (see Shimpo 1977).

Despite their reliance on US economic theory, however, Japanese monetarists have been cautious in their assessment of US economic practice. In this they reflect a subtle shift in opinion which affects political as well as economic thought in contemporary Japan. As trade friction has intensified, monetarists and others on the right of the political spectrum have tended to become more critical of the United States, and more willing to emphasize the virtues of the Japanese system itself. This critique of the United States, however, contains two distinct strands. Orthodox monetarists for the most part focus their attention on the competitive, free-market aspects of the Japanese economy. Thus Suzuki argues that Japan has been 'less monetarist in rhetoric than either the United States or Great Britain, but far more monetarist in practice' (Suzuki 1986: xiv), and suggests that the flexibility of its wage rates and labour markets makes the Japanese economy particularly responsive to sound monetary policy (Suzuki 1987: Chap. 6). By contrast, some of the 'post-modern' economists whose work we shall consider later in this chapter extend the argument far beyond market structures, and explain Japan's economic strength in terms of history, institutions, and culture.

ADMINISTRATIVE REFORM VERSUS DOMESTIC DEMAND EXPANSION

In many ways monetarists like Suzuki, Shimpo, and others are the heirs to the 'government economists' of the 1960s. Given their positions in the administrative system, it is inevitable that the views they express should exert influence on economic policy. In fact, monetarist influence began to make itself felt as early as 1974–5, when a new tone entered the Japanese government's White Papers on the Economy.

166

These annual publications have from time to time provided popular catch-phrases which neatly encapsulate new directions in economic policy and economic ideology; the White Paper issued in the autumn of 1974 offered such a phrase in its very title: 'Beyond a Growth Economy'. In the context of soaring import costs, a 16 per cent inflation rate, and a substantial budget deficit, the 1974 White Paper signalled the official abandonment of the policies of growth promotion, and a shift of emphasis towards economic stability and stringent anti-inflationary measures. This theme was continued the following year, when the Economic White Paper spoke of two courses open to Japan. The first, a return to the high-growth policies of the past, would lead to 'instability and inflation', while the second required

> the nation to endure severe trials in creating a new economic structure. The choice is up to us, the Japanese people, but we owe it to the coming generations to endure such trials.
>
> (White Papers of Japan 1975: 26)

This sense of sobriety, restraint, and of a redefining of economic objectives persisted throughout the 1970s and was eventually to attain its clearest expression in the policy of 'administrative reform' (gyōsei kaikaku), announced by the government in 1981. 'Administrative reform' must be understood in the context not only of developments in economic thought, but also of the political circumstances of Japan in the early 1980s. The ruling Liberal Democratic Party (LDP) at this time held power only by the slenderest of majorities, and this situation made it electorally unthinkable for the government to reduce the budget deficit by significantly raising taxes (Sawa 1984: 44). The government therefore turned to the alternative strategy of reducing expenditure by streamlining administration. The pursuit of 'small government' was to be accompanied (as in other countries) by the privatization of public corporations and the deregulation of sectors such as finance and telecommunications.

Needless to say, the policy of administrative reform did not win universal support. Marxian economists rejected the notion that budgetary improprieties and excessive government intervention were major causes of Japan's economic problems. On the contrary, they saw these problems as symptoms of a much wider crisis of capitalism whose origins lay in excess capital accumulation and in the changing structure of international economic relations. Reductions in government expenditure were merely a device for shifting the burden of economic crisis (a crisis created by subordination to the United States and by the 'high growth' policies of the monopoly capital system) onto the shoulders of the working class and of all labouring people.

(Tokita 1982: 192)

From a non-Marxian perspective, the concept of administrative reform was also subjected to critical scrutiny by economists like Itō Mitsuharu (b. 1927) of Kyoto University. Itō did not deny the need to reduce government expenditure, but questioned whether administrative rationalization was an effective means of achieving this reduction. According to Itō, the fundamental cause of expanding budget deficits was to be found in the perpetual lavishing of government funds on an ever-growing variety of regional projects – a process that constituted a vital part of the Liberal Democratic Party's vote-gathering strategy. The solution to the financial problems of the nation therefore lay in political reform and a strengthening of regional economic autonomy (Itō 1984: 96–104).

In the end, however, support for the policy of administrative reform was undermined not so much by the arguments of its critics within Japan as by external factors. Although the budget deficit was not eliminated, the level of government borrowing was reduced between 1980 and 1985, and financial stringency together with wage restraints virtually eliminated inflation by the mid-1980s. But throughout those 'severe trials' predicted by the 1975 Economic White Paper, a moderate rate of growth was maintained mainly through the growth of overseas demand. Exports as a percentage of Japan's GNP rose from around 10 per cent to around 13 per cent between the late 1970s and mid-1980s, and by 1985 Japan's trade surplus with the United States had soared to almost US $40 billion. In order to reduce this massive imbalance, Japan's trading partners – the United States in particular – began to demand that the Japanese government expand imports by reflating the economy.

The Japanese response to these demands took the form of a number of proposals for domestic demand expansion (*naiju kakudai*). In 1984 the prominent LDP politician Miyazawa Kiichi put forward a plan (deliberately reminiscent of Ikeda's policies of the 1960s) for the 'doubling of national assets'. Though somewhat thin on practical detail, the Miyazawa plan implied that domestic growth could be stimulated by policies to improve Japan's stock of social capital (housing, sewerage, parks, etc.). Two years later, broadly similar ideas were reiterated in the government-commissioned Maekawa

Report, which argued that urban redevelopment, tax reductions, and shorter working hours were essential to revitalize domestic demand and reduce international trade friction.

These proposals sparked a heated debate between Japanese Keynesians and monetarists, with many of the growth advocates of the 1960s, as well as the 1970s Friedmanites, taking sides. As one might expect, domestic demand-stimulation won strong support from economists such as Kanamoni Hisao, who argued that higher growth would not only reduce conflict with Japan's major trading partners, but would also generate increased tax revenue and so reduce the need for government borrowing (Tahara 1984: 31–2). It was also not surprising that Shimpo Seiji, Katō Hiroshi, and others of like mind should see increased public spending as a recipe for inflation, and should insist that growth could be promoted only by removing government restraints on private business initiative (Katō 1984: 180–1; Shimpo 1988: 48–9). From a similar perspective, the Nagoya University economist Iida Tsuneo suggested that the major cause of trade friction was the failure of the US government to curb its own expenditure. The size of Japan's trade surplus was such, Iida calculated, that massive and unsustainable levels of growth would be needed to generate the domestic demand necessary to eliminate it. Japan's surplus must therefore be seen not as something to be eliminated within a few years, but rather as a phase in the long-term cycles of the rise and fall of nations.

> Many countries at some time experience a 'sudden rise to power'. These countries achieve faster rates of growth and development than others, and at the same time demonstrate exceptionally strong export competitiveness, which results in consistently maintained export surpluses. However this 'rise to power' does not last for ever, and must some day come to an end. Such was the case of Britain in the nineteenth century and the United States from the early twentieth century until (perhaps) the first half of the 1960s. And such, it seems, is the case of Japan today.
>
> (Iida 1986: 68)

A somewhat more unexpected note of opposition to demand-stimulation, however, came from the chief prophet of 1960s growth, Shimomura Osamu. While agreeing with the monetarists that the most urgent task of the mid-1980s was restraint of government spending, Shimomura also cast doubts on the 'asset doubling' proposal from a different perspective. Japan's economy, he claimed, had now

169

developed to the point at which further high growth, rather than fulfilling fundamental human needs, would merely result in the proliferation of trivial and wasteful consumer products. At the same time, the endless pursuit of growth could only result in the exhaustion of non-renewable natural resources. The improvement of social capital should not therefore be seen as a means of expanding demand and stimulating growth. Instead, it should be achieved by a reordering of economic priorities within the framework of very low – or even zero – growth (Saitō and Shimomura 1984).

THE CRISIS OF ECONOMIC THEORY

Shimomura's disillusionment with the fruits of growth is in a sense symptomatic of the state of economics in 1970s and 1980s Japan. It illuminates the fact that behind the debates over the relative merits of administrative reform or domestic demand expansion, a far more profound intellectual crisis was taking shape, one that was confined neither to Japan nor to 'modern' economics, but which crossed both national and ideological boundaries.

One part of this crisis seems to be related to the widening gap between academic economics and the concerns of everyday life. Not only in the neo-classical school, but also in some branches of Marxian economics, minute specialization and the increasing use of mathematics and technical jargon have made large areas of recent economic theory inaccessible to the ordinary reader. In this respect, Japanese economists are rather less to blame than economists in many other countries, since Japan has a long and excellent tradition of popular economic journalism. Yet even in Japan the gap between expert and lay-person deeply felt. Takeuchi Kei observes that in the immediate post-war years, Japanese economists were principally concerned with issues such as poverty and unemployment, which most people could readily relate to their own experience. The present economic debates, however, more often concern budget deficits, exchange rates, or trade surpluses – issues that have a much less direct and recognizable impact on daily existence (Takeuchi 1987: 32). *Keizai*, Takeuchi suggests, has become more and more obsessed with *keikoku* (administering the nation), and less and less concerned with *Saimin* (relieving the sufferings of the people) (Takeuchi 1986: 44).

A second source of theoretical confusion lies in the changing industrial and economic structure itself. Whether or not we accept that developed nations are experiencing an 'information revolution', there is little doubt that many branches of the economy are under-going extremely rapid technological change. This change, which involves computer-based automation, the development of new communications systems, and the emergence of highly knowledge-intensive industries, is occurring particularly rapidly in Japan (and is, of course, part of the reaction to the economic impasse described at the beginning of this chapter). But the growing com-modification of knowledge, which lies at the heart of contemporary technological change, has created serious theoretical challenges to conventional notions of price and value (both neo-classical and Marxian) – challenges which economists have not yet satisfactorily answered.

The most fundamental source of crisis, however, is probably the transformation of scientific knowledge itself. Economists of all ideological persuasions have long taken pride in the fact that their discipline is the most rigorously 'scientific' of the social sciences. Yet the notion of science on which it was founded was essen-tially the Newtonian physics of the nineteenth century. As the theoretical premises of Newtonianism have gradually been eroded, so the very intellectual foundations of economics have been exposed to questioning. If, as seems likely, the universe itself is not a giant machine whose workings can be objectively revealed by human observation and experimentation, how much less likely it is that the human observer will be able to discover objective and universal laws guiding the operation of the economic system. This recognition has resulted in a growing awareness that 'the pre-vailing economic theory is the other side of the coin to a country's normative values' (Sawa 1984: 46). In other words, modern eco-nomic thought does not represent a steady advance towards a perfect understanding of immutable economic phenomena, but is instead an ideological product of the Western industrial world in a particular phase of its historical development (see Sawa 1982).

There is therefore a sense that existing theories are reaching a point of deadlock, and that we are on the threshold of a profound reshaping of economic thought. In some quarters this seems to have produced an anticipation of a single revolutionary paradigm which, like Keynesianism in the 1930s, will transform our under-standing of the economic structure. Given the complexity and diversity of contemporary economics, however, it is perhaps more realistic to suggest the emergence of several distinct new approaches to economic theory, which will point to a number of different possible directions out of the current crisis of economic theory. Recent developments in Japanese economic thought indicate some possible forms which these new approaches may take.

The most significant reaction to the crisis of the 1970s and 1980s is perhaps an awareness of the need for a rethinking of the boundaries of economics itself. There is now a growing recognition that neo-classical economics, in presenting the economy as an integrated and self-contained mechanism, neglected the crucial interaction of this mechanism with other systems, such as the cultural heritage, political institutions, and the natural environment. Two issues in particular have revealed the need to extend the frontiers of economic thought. The first is the environmental crisis, which emerged as a major economic and social issue in the late 1960s and early 1970s. In order to confront this crisis economists have found it necessary to pursue their analysis beyond the bounds of the market system, and to reassess the economic significance of the free goods and services generated by the processes of nature or of social interaction. The second is the trend towards a 'post-industrial' or 'information' society. In their attempts to define the underlying causes and implications of this trend, Japanese scholars have been obliged to recognize that the study of information as a commodity cannot be wholly divorced from an understanding of the role that information plays in human relationships, institutions, and cultures.

During the debates on these issues, therefore, certain shifts have occurred in the ideological boundaries between modern and Marxian thought. Many of those writers who have defended the merits of the existing economic order have done so less by emphasizing the benefits of the free market (in the fashion of their orthodox monetarist colleagues) than by stressing the benefits of contemporary business strategies and government policies. They have also often focused attention on organizational or cultural arrangements peculiar to Japan. Their analysis, in other words, has tended to be institutional and sometimes implicitly nationalist, rather than adhering strictly to the principles of economic liberalism.

Marxian writers, on the other hand, have faced a somewhat different set of intellectual difficulties. Marxism has always been quick to recognize the inseparable links between the economic, the social, and the political, and for Marxist economists, the main problem has rather been the application of radical political economy to new problems such as the environmental crisis and the growth of the service economy. Many academic economists in Japan continue to work within a relatively traditional Marxian framework, but some of the best recent analysis has come from writers who are willing to question traditional notions of proletarian revolution, the imminent collapse of capitalism, and even the labour theory of value itself.

At the same time, some of the most influential criticisms of the existing economic order have come not from Marxian economists at all, but from scholars who derive a large part of their analytical approach from modern economics. On the one hand, post-Keynesians like Uzawa Hirofumi, drawing much of their inspiration from the British Cambridge school, have rediscovered and refined that strand of critical analysis evident in the work of Keynes and some (though by no means all) of his followers. On the other, economists like Morishima Michio have begun to question one of the most fundamental postulates of traditional economic theory, both Marxian and modern: the notion that a single theoretical model may be used to analyse all capitalist economies. In this sense, it seems that the universalist theory of modern economics may begin to give way to more modest post-modern 'little theories' – theories that recognize the inability of an all-encompassing mathematical model to capture economic behaviour in a meaningful way.

THE ECONOMICS OF DIVERSITY:
MORISHIMA MICHIO (1923–   )

A good deal of Morishima's world view is conveyed by his contribution to the debate on Japanese military expenditure which filled the pages of popular magazines in the late 1970s and early 1980s. In response to a series of articles calling for an expanded military capacity to meet the Soviet threat, Morishima argued that it was absurd for a small nation like Japan to contemplate a military confrontation with such a great power as the USSR. Japan's best method of defence, Morishima suggested, lay not in increased arms expenditure, but in closer political, economic, and cultural co-operation with other nations, both capitalist and socialist. If, indeed, the Japanese people were ever confronted with the imminent reality of a Soviet invasion, the only sane response would be to lay aside their red and white Rising Sun banners and to go out to meet the invader carrying two flags – one white and the other red (Morishima 1979). The comment is typical not only of Morishima's occasionally irreverent sense of humour, but also of the genuine dislike of nationalism and dogmatism expressed in much of his work.

Although the roots of his thought lie in modern economic theory, Morishima is one of those who, like Okishio, Miyazaki, Tsuru, and

173

others, have fruitfully brought together insights from modern and Marxian theory. It may be no coincidence, however, that his theories, like Tsuru Shigeto´s, have been developed in the course of a rather unusual academic career. After research at Oxford and Yale, and a period as professor at Osaka University, Morishima moved out of the sphere of Japanese academia and in 1970 was appointed to a professorship at the London School of Economics. In that capacity he has become the Japanese economist whose work is perhaps best known internationally: he is, for example, the only Japanese scholar included in Mark Blaug's survey *Great Economists Since Keynes* (Blaug 1985: 175–6). Paradoxically, however, his early, highly theoretical writings have given way to research that increasingly pertains to the specific economic and social problems of Japan.

Until the early 1970s, Morishima's contribution to theoretical economics consisted in essence of the application of modern mathematical techniques (particularly those developed by John von Neumann) to a wide range of economic problems. The value of the mathematics used by Morishima was its ability to encompass a more complex, and thus more realistic, picture of the economy than that contained in earlier mathematical models. In his *Theory of Economic Growth*, for example, Morishima demonstrated how von Neumann's system could be used to overcome problems relating to the treatment of capital goods in conventional growth theory. While existing neo-classical theory assumed that capital was freely transferable from one firm to another, and that it declined in productive capacity by a steady rate each year, the techniques employed by Morishima were able to handle a more difficult real world in which capital goods are non-transferable and lose their efficiency in an uneven way (Morishima 1969).

Morishima's mathematical approach, however, was applicable not only to neo-classical but also to Marxian theory. Although approaching Marxism from an essentially agnostic perspective, Morishima, like Okishio and Koshimura, demonstrated that many aspects of the internal logic of Marxian economics were sufficiently rigorous to survive restatement in highly mathematical terms. Marx's model of extended reproduction, for example, could, with slight modification, be used to shed light on the unstable growth of capitalist economies (Morishima 1973: Chaps 10 and 11). In relation to the Marxian labour theory of value, Morishima's results were somewhat more ambiguous. By replacing the traditional system of equations with a system of simultaneous inequalities, Morishima was able to offer mathematical proof of the 'generalized fundamental Marxian theorem' that 'positive exploitation is necessary and sufficient for the system to have positive growth capacity as well as to guarantee capitalists positive profit' (Morishima and Catephores 1978: 172). But this proof could only be obtained by paring Marx's theories down to an essential minimum, and by abstracting from them such problems as the analysis of an economy in which labourers possess different levels of skill (Morishima 1973: Chap. 14; Morishima and Catephores 1978: Chap. 2). In spite of these problems, however, Morishima's analysis was welcomed by many Marxian economists, and has contributed to the evolving debate between adherents of the traditional labour theory of value and the so-called neo-Richardians who use Sraffa's economics as a basis for criticizing that theory (see Morishima and Catephores 1978: Chap. 2; Steedman 1981).

Morishima's avoidance of ideological partisanship is evident not only in his contributions to pure theory, but also in his comments on the practical workings of socialist and capitalist economies. Both, he suggests, contain elements of 'irrationality' since they distribute the surpluses generated by production according to dogmatic criteria: capitalism generally assumes that all profits should revert to investors, while socialism assumes that they should be distributed to employees. This irrationality could be avoided, Morishima argues, if a system of shadow pricing were used to impute profits to scarce factors of production, whether they be capitalists, managers, or workers. In practice, he implies, both capitalism and socialism appear to be moving cautiously in this direction – capitalism by introducing bonuses for workers, and some socialist economies by levying charges for the use of capital. In this sense, the ideological distance between the two systems may be more imagined than real (although it should be emphasized that the workers' bonuses common in countries like Japan are far from conforming to Morishima's notion of the 'rational' distribution of profits) (Morishima 1976: Chap. 3).

The comparison of socialist and capitalist systems is one element in Morishima's gradual movement away from the extreme abstraction of mathematical economics, and towards the study of contemporary national economies in all their diversity and complexity. By 1976 he was writing that 'mathematical economic theory has recently become more and more abstract, transparent and sterile' (Morishima 1976: viii). The lively and original student texts that he published in the 1970s and 1980s therefore attempted to focus on 'the way in which the real economy operates and the best way to bring about a change in the direction of this operation' (Morishima 1984: viii).

In order to achieve this realism, it was necessary to abandon the assumption of a united body of theory applicable to all contemporary economic systems:

> The real economy is not managed by an abstract ethereal being known as *Homo economicus*. Countries may share a capitalist economy, but their historical experience and cultural traditions differ, and the lives, beliefs and modes of behaviour of their people are certainly not the same. . . . Furthermore . . . countries can also react in a different manner to the same stimulus. When the difference in reaction is not more than a matter of degree it is possible to handle these economies with models of the same type using different numerical values and coefficients (parameters) constituting the framework, but where reactions are qualitatively different they have to be analysed using quite separate models.
> (Morishima 1984: 2–3).

This analysis suggests two future directions. One (the more theoretical) involves the construction of several distinct models to fit the distinct categories of modern economies, while the other (more empirical) direction requires the detailed historical analysis of specific cases (Morishima 1976: 25–6). Morishima's approach to the first path – the construction of models of diversity – has relied on a reordering of the accepted post-war integration of Keynesian and neo-classical economics: where Samuelson and his followers saw the two theories as applicable (in varying circumstances) to every capitalist economy, Morishima sees them as applicable to different types of economy. Walrasian neo-classicism is best suited to 'flexprice economies', which depend heavily on primary production, while Keynesianism (supplemented by the theories of Michael Kalecki) is most appropriate to highly industrialized 'fixprice economies' (Morishima 1976: Chaps 6 and 7; Morishima 1984: 32–7).

Within these two broad groupings, however, Morishima allows room for further diversity based on historical, cultural, and social differences. The most extreme departure from his early theoretical and mathematical methods is represented by his 1982 study, *Why has Japan 'Succeeded'*? In this book he abandons mainstream economics altogether, and turns wholeheartedly to culture and history, seeking to construct a variant of Weberian theory that would explain Japan's development in terms of the impact of Confucianism and Shintoism. The success of this endeavour is very debatable, but, to be fair, it needs to be seen in the context of a period in which many Western governments (including Britain's) were caught up in a sudden and ill-considered frenzy of enthusiasm for initiating the policies of Japanese enterprise and government. Morishima's book, addressed primarily to a British audience, suggests that the cultural factors that prompted Japanese growth were not only specifically Japanese, but have also resulted in undesirable social consequences, among them a lack of international perspective and a subservience to established authorities (Morishima 1982: 194–201). His study therefore illustrates a revival of interest among economists in the cultural dimensions of development; it also represents an honest effort to counteract Western over-enthusiasm for the achievements of the Japanese econmic system.

ENVIRONMENTAL CRISIS AND THE THEORY OF SOCIAL CAPITAL: MIYAMOTO KENICHI (1930–   )

While Morishima attacks the cultural deficiencies that he believes have been reinforced by the process of Japan's economic development, other writers have concentrated their criticisms on the social deprivation caused by unbalanced industrial growth. As we have seen, growing awareness of urban problems and environmental pollution was already by the late 1960s stimulating new developments in critical theory from a Keynesian as well as a Marxian perspective (see pp. 158–63). But although these negative effects of growth undermined the optimistic vision of post-war modern economics, they also created considerable intellectual difficulties for radical economists. The new forms of deprivation apparent in the affluent Japan of the 1960s and 1970s did not show any signs of fuelling the fires of revolution, nor even of resulting in any sharpening of the lines of class antagonism, within or outside the workplace. On the contrary, they seemed to create a more complex and subtle pattern of social conflict than that foreseen by earlier generations of Marxian analysts. In their attempts to comprehend the irony of privation in the midst of plenty, Japanese economists were therefore obliged to turn a critical eye to some of the most fundamental assumptions of traditional theory.

Miyamoto Kenichi of Osaka City University, approaching the problem from a Marxian perspective, has found it necessary to reassess the conventional Marxist concept of immiseration. The process described by Marx, by which exploitation results in the absolute impoverishment of the workers, is defined by Miyamoto as constituting 'original' (*kongenteki*) or 'classical' (*kotenteki*) immiseration,

177

and as being typical of the early stages of capitalist development. By contrast, contemporary (*gendaiteki*) immiseration typically manifests itself in problems such as pollution, urban congestion and decay, or chronic inflation (Miyamoto 1981a: 135–8). Unlike classical immiseration, whose effects were borne by the proletariat alone, these modern problems influence all sections of society, even though it is usually the poor who experience them most painfully and directly. Moreover, contemporary immiseration cannot be solved simply by a redistribution of wealth after the processes of production have occurred. For this reason it is to be found in socialist as well as capitalist countries – in nations that possess, as well as those that lack, progressive welfare policies (Miyamoto 1981a: 141–2).

In order to find the causes of and solutions to contemporary immiseration, Miyamoto suggests that we must turn our attention to the role of the state and of social capital in the economic system. Miyamoto firmly rejects Uno Kōzō's vision of a 'pure capitalism' in which the state plays no role. On the contrary, he emphasizes the crucial, though evolving, function of the state in all stages of capitalist development:

> to erase the figure of the state from the economic processes of pure capitalism, and to deny the state as an object of economic enquiry is surely to be poisoned by bourgeois ideology.
>
> (Miyamoto 1981a: 53)

Emphasis on the state also involves emphasis on that area of the economy which has so often been neglected both by Marxian and modern economists: the social infrastructure that lies outside the realm of private ownership. In his influential study *The Theory of Social Capital (Shakai Shihonron)* Miyamoto analyses the 'common labour processes' (*ippan rōdō shūdan*) which do not directly create commodities, but constitute essential preconditions for the emergence of a commodity economy. These include the provision of land, water, transport, and communications: goods and services that are necessary to the process of 'common social consumption' (*shakaiteki kyōdō shōhi*), whereby societies recreate themselves from one generation to another (Miyamoto 1976: 11–40). Indeed, Miyamoto suggests that Marx's reproduction schema should be supplemented by a separate sector (which Miyamoto designates by the letter O) representing capital and consumer infrastructure. The size of the O sector, Miyamoto argues, will determine the level of surplus labour that may be extracted in the course of commodity production (Miyamoto 1981a: 81–2).

Common labour processes of the type described by Miyamoto have at all times been characterized by peculiarities that make them ill-adapted to private ownership, and the state has therefore been their chief provider since the earliest phases of capitalism. This aspect of the state's economic function, however, has become very much more important with the development of monopoly capitalism since the early twentieth century. In words that recall the writings of Kurt Zieschang and of the Japanese structural reform theorists, Miyamoto emphasizes the growing 'socialization' of capitalism, and the consequent inter-penetration of private capital and the state. Increasing horizontal and vertical integration within industry, for example, makes individual firms more heavily reliant on transport and communications networks. Twentieth-century capitalism has also encouraged massive urbanization and qualitative changes in the nature of the city, which in turn have demanded enormous social expenditures on urban infrastructure (Miyamoto 1976: 73–9, 102–23). At the same time, however, Miyamoto argues that the character of public expenditure itself has changed. Public works projects are contracted out to private enterprise on a massive scale, and even those that remain in the hands of the state come to be organized along the lines of profit-making ventures – a process that Miyamoto describes as 'the commercialization of the state' (*kokka no kigyō-ka*).

The ultimate irony of this process is that the state's investment in 'public' projects ultimately becomes the major cause of the deteriorating quality of life. The expressways and airports constructed with taxpayers money, ostensibly to meet social needs, do more damage to the living environment for ordinary citizens than do the activities of private industry itself (Miyamoto 1981b: 198–214). In this situation, Miyamoto proposes, it is necessary to reassess the meaning of 'public works'. More radically, it is also necessary to devise a new system for the pricing of both privately and publicly-produced goods and services, a system that will be based on 'social-use value'. Although this concept is not very fully developed in Miyamoto's writing, he does imply that social-use value may be evolving within capitalism to replace the labour value upon which traditional Marxian theory is based:

> Marx stated that, as mechanisation progressed, human labour would come to play only a subsidiary part in the total production process. Eventually, a higher level of production might be reached where, as in the case of automation and robotics, human labour would be whole excluded. In this case, the system of production based

upon exchange value would break down. Such a level has not yet been attained. However, the share of productive workers in the total industrial workforce has shrunk to a mere 20–30%, and the public sector has grown to have a great influence on economic activity. In such present circumstances, we may perceive signs that Marx's higher stage of production has begun to arrive, and that a new scale for the measurement [of value] will be needed.

(Miyamoto 1981a: 308–9)

THE ECONOMICS OF DISEQUILIBRIUM:
UZAWA HIROFUMI (1928–)

Miyamoto Kenichi, although writing within a Marxian framework, derives inspiration also from non-Marxist economists such as John Kenneth Galbraith. Amongst the sources on which he draws are the writings of one of the most eminent of contemporary Japanese economists, Uzawa Hirofumi. It is interesting to place Uzawa's writings side by side with Miyamoto's because, although they deal with similar issues and at times reach rather similar conclusions, Uzawa arrives at these conclusions from an intellectual background very different from Miyamoto's.

Much of Uzawa's early work, which was carried out as a researcher and university teacher in the United States, appears to fit without too much difficulty into the mainstream of post-war US neo-classical economics. His most famous contribution to this field was the extension of neo-classical growth models to the analysis of a two-sector economy, in which conditions of production in the investment goods sector differ from those in the consumption goods sector (Uzawa 1962). On one level, this theoretical work could already be seen as revealing a fundamental divergence from the standard neo-classical view of the economy, for it implies the existence not of a homogeneous society in which capital and labour are merely substitutable factors of production, but of a society divided into classes of capitalists and labourers. In practice, however, this aspect of Uzawa's growth model was not amplified, and his analysis was quite readily incorporated into the burgeoning literature on dualistic economic development (see for example Kelley, Williamson, and Cheetham 1972).

During the early 1960s Uzawa made numerous other contributions to the development of mathematical economics, particularly in the field of linear and non-linear programming, and in 1964 he was appointed professor of economics at the University of Chicago. It was after his return to Japan in 1968, however, that the critical emphasis in Uzawa's economic ideas began to become increasingly apparent. In part this reflects the influence of the Cambridge school, and in particular of Joan Robinson, with whom Uzawa had worked closely for a number of years and whose writings he has translated into Japanese. More importantly, however, the increasingly radical tone of his writing indicates a reaction to those contradictions of Japanese growth that were also addressed by Marxian economists like Miyamoto: the contradictions of a society in which high levels of nominal wealth coexist with a poor quality of life for a large proportion of the population.

Uzawa's critique of contemporary capitalism, however, does not imply an acceptance of Marxian ideas, but rather involves an attempt to revive and develop the radicalism of Keynesian thought which had to a large extent been lost in the post-war evolution of modern economics. His objective, in other words, is to sharpen the definition of an alternative both to Marxism, with its excessive reliance on dogma and on the centralized power of the state, and to neo-classicism, with its unrealistic vision of a rational *homo economics* 'devoid of cultural or historical identity' (Uzawa 1986: 21).

A central focus of this project has been the delineation of a theory of the economy which gives adequate weight to the importance of social capital. As Uzawa emphasises, it is precisely the neglect of social capital which constitutes one of the crucial flaws in neo-classical thought. The neo-classical paradigm assumes that resources are privately owned, and that the goods and services they generate are distributed by the mechanisms of the market. Although modern economists like Paul Samuelson have given some attention to the issue of public goods, their analyses have never been incorporated into the central hypotheses of neo-classical theory, and remain little more than studies of a curious but peripheral 'special case' (see Uzawa 1974: 121-6).

Uzawa's view of the economy, on the contrary, begins by recognizing the essential interdependence of two categories of economic resources

The first category consists of private resources which are in the hands of, and may be freely used by, individual economic actors: i.e. so-called private capital. On the other hand, there is a second category consisting of property which is not in the hands of private economic actors but is held in common by society as a whole: i.e.

socially controlled common resources in the broad sense, or, more correctly, social overhead capital.

(Uzawa 1974: 120)

This social overhead capital can, Uzawa proposes, be further categorized in three forms: natural capital (air, water, etc.), social capital (roads, bridges, etc.), and institutional capital (laws, administrative systems, etc.) (Uzawa 1974: 124).

The distinction between private and social capital provides the starting point for Uzawa's analysis of the contemporary economy. Just as Miyamoto suggests that Marx's reproduction schema should be expanded to include the 'general labour process', so Uzawa demonstrates that the production function of modern economics can be rearranged to encompass social overhead capital. Uzawa's analysis, however, goes considerably further than Miyamoto's in terms of the development of formal mathematical models (Uzawa 1975: 9–22).

The crucial characteristic of Uzawa's vision of the economy is the emphasis that it places on the balanced accumulation and allocation of social capital. The economic model devised by Uzawa implies not only that it is possible to define optimal patterns of investment in and distribution of social capital, but also that such patterns are vital to the creation of a healthy and equitable economy. In some instances, this may mean that it is necessary to devise pricing systems to limit access to certain scarce social resources. However, access to such resources is often an economic and social necessity as well as an important means of diminishing inequality. From this perspective it becomes essential that the stock of social capital should be maintained and expanded as human use of such capital increases (Uzawa 1975; see also Uzawa 1974: 123–53).

It is the failure to maintain this balance between the accumulation of social and private capital which, Uzawa argues, lies at the root of contemporary economic dislocation. Rejecting the comfortable visions of equilibrium so popular in modern economics, Uzawa returns to the harsher original Keynesian view, in which economic equilibrium is seen as a happy accident rather than a permanent condition of the capitalist economy. The phase of prosperity and near-equilibrium that existed in most of the Western industrialized world in the 1950s and 1960s was sustained, according to Uzawa, by a variety of economic and political circumstances, but a particularly important factor was an adequate stock of social capital in the broadest sense of the phrase.

.I⅜t is a condition of equilibrium that an appropriate balance should be maintained between social overhead capital and private capital. At such times in general circumstances the stability of market equilibrium can be guaranteed, and both the nominal and real distribution of income will have an inherent tendency towards equalisation.

(Uzawa 1986: 250)

The forces of industrial growth and competition unleashed during the 1960s, however, resulted in the collapse of this equilibrium and in the ensuing age of disequilibrium the destabilizing pressures identified by Keynes have been aggravated by the growing separation of fixed capital from financial capital, production from speculation (Uzawa 1986: 147–83). To find a path out of the present phase of instability, it is not enough to rely on conventional demand stimulation through public works policies. In an analysis which resembles Miyamoto's, Uzawa observes that the Japanese government's public works projects have largely been oriented to the needs of private industry, and justified on narrowly commercial grounds. Such projects, while adding to the stock of 'social capital' in its most restricted sense, may actually result in a net loss of that more broadly defined 'social overhead capital' which includes the natural environment. The implication is that contemporary ills of the capitalist system can be cured only by a radical reorientation of priorities away from private growth and accumulation and towards social equity and an improved quality of life.

It is perhaps ironic that Uzawa's defence of a mixed economy should coincide with a strong trend towards privatization in Japan and in many other industrialized nations. It is also particularly piquant that the central symbol in his critique of the contemporary economic system should be that emblem of Japan's industrial success: the automobile. (His most influential popular work is entitled *The Social Costs of the Automobile* [*Jidōsha no Shakaiteki Hiyō*].) In many ways, however, his writings reflect an important aspect of the best of modern Japanese economic thought: an ability to range knowledgeably and yet critically across the fields of neo-classical, Keynesian, and Marxian theory. More unusually perhaps, Uzawa's writings also combine complex mathematical modelling with a strong sense of the social and philosophical dimensions of economics. Here at least, despite Takeuchi's observations, the *saimin* element of *keizai* has not been forgotten.

183

SOCIAL VALUES AND INDUSTRIAL GROWTH:
MURAKAMI YASUSUKE (1931–   )

The path out of crisis charted by both Miyamoto and Uzawa relies, in somewhat different ways, on the reshaping of traditional economic analysis to encompass the so-called 'free goods' created by nature and by society. Other economists, however, starting from a very similar analysis of the present as a watershed in economic development, have put forward ideas that point in quite different directions.

Murakami Yasusuke resembles Uzawa not only in being a professor at Tokyo University, but also in being a modern economist who has made significant contributions to mathematical economics: Murakami's major contributions relate to the use of turnpike theorems in input-output analysis (see Tsukui and Murakami 1979). But Murakami, like Uzawa, is also concerned with the philosophical basis of modern economics, and with the importance of extending this basis to encompass political and social phenomena. The resemblance does not end there, for Murakami's analysis of the crisis of industrial capitalism shows certain similarities to Uzawa's. In his widely read study *The Maladies of Industrial Society (Sangyō Shakai no Byōri*, 1975) Murakami proposes that this crisis is composed of three main elements: first, the changing values associated with the age of mass consumption; second, the ecomomic constraints imposed by the limits of the earth's natural resources; and third, the growth of conflict between developed and less-developed countries (Murakami 1975: 3–32). While Uzawa's analysis focuses mainly on the second of these problems, Murakami is most interested in the consequences of the first.

In order for economics to deal with the challenges of a changing economic system, Murakami argues that it is necessary to reverse the divergence between the economic and the political which has been characterisitc of modern economics, and to recreate the discipline of 'political economy'. He is, however, highly critical of many of those (including the neo-Marxists) who regard themselves as political economists. Reintegration, in Murakami's eyes, is a delicate process that must be achieved without disturbing the intellectually rigorous nature of existing modern economics (Murakami 1975: 319). The key problem of such an integrated analysis is that the economic system, unlike the physical world around us, is a 'self-organizing [*jiko soshiki*] system': in other words, those who analyse the economic structure are at the same time part of the structure which they are analysing. Therefore, in the very process of examining and comprehending the economic system, they alter the way in which that system works (Murakami 1975: 355–9).

In *The Maladies of Industrial Society* Murakami speaks, in somewhat obscure terms, of the need for a 'meta-analytical' (*chō-bunsekiteki*) approach to this ever-changing, self-organizing system. In some of his later works, however, the possible nature of such a meta-analysis becomes clearer. In particular, he uses a critique of rational expectationism as a means of emphasizing the need for a more realistic study of the way in which human expectations about the economy affect the way in which the economy itself evolves. As Murakami emphasizes, the expectations of individuals or firms are not based on linear extrapolations of existing economic trends. Instead, they involve assumptions about a wide range of unpredictable, externally generated variables, including social and political variables. What is needed, therefore, is a supra-economic model, or, in other words, 'a political economy of expectations' (Murakami 1985: 236).

The formulation of such a model of the impact of human expectations remains, however, a task for the future. In the meanwhile, Murakami's thought integrates the social and political with the economic in a rather more traditional way: through the analysis of social values and their role in promoting or retarding industrial growth. From this perspective, his work can be seen as a modern addition to a long tradition of economic and social thought reaching back through writers such as David McClelland, Talcott Parsons, and Elton Mayo to Joseph Schumpeter and Max Weber. What makes Murakami's contribution a distinctly contemporary one, however, is its emphasis on the declining efficacy of 'Western' values and its analysis of 'Japanese' values as having been particularly adaptable to twentieth-century industrialization.

As already mentioned, Murakami identifies the roots of contemporary economic crisis as lying above all in the changing value systems associated with mass consumption. The freeing of human beings (at least in developed countries) from a continual struggle for physical survival, and the coming of an age of increased leisure, have sundered the nexus of values that supported the industrialization of Europe and North America. The essential feature of this nexus was the interaction of 'instrumental activism' (*shudanteki nōdōshugi*) and 'individualism' (*kojinshugi*). Instrumental activism (a term borrowed from Talcott Parsons) implies the ability of human beings to define distant goals and work rationally towards them. Murakami accepts the view that it was Protestanism that served to link this cultural trait into a mutually reinforcing relationship with individualism. Even when religious faith weakened, instrumental activism and individualism worked symbiotically as long as human beings were forced to struggle for material well-being. With the emergence of mass consumption and mass education, however, the link between the two has been broken, and individualism has become a mere pursuit of personal satisfaction rather than an endeavour to better one's well-being and status through hard work and frugality (Murakami 1975: Chaps 5–8; see also Murakami 1986: 219–20).

When Parsonian sociology was at the peak of its influence in the 1950s and early 1960s, there was widespread acceptance that rationalism, activism, and individualism were at once uniquely Western Protestant values and essential prerequisites for industrialization. Industrialization and modernization were therefore synonymous with Westernization. Murakami, however, while accepting that certain values, most notably 'instrumental activism', are essential for modern industrial growth, denies the need for industrialization to be supported by a philosophy of individualism:

> There are two paths by which the nexus of values for industrialisation may be created. One is the path which reinforces instrumental activism with individualism. This is achieved through the mediation of Protestant-type religions which, while separating man from God, place one in direct communion with the other. The alternative path is a path of collectivism where the power of the political system is used to direct society as a whole towards industrialisation.
>
> (Murakami 1975: 177)

This second path, by which instrumental activism is reinforced through collectivism, is of course the path taken by Japan. In Japan's case, the crucial driving force behind modernization was the cohesive force of the family (or quasi-family) group. The state was able to foster and utilize the sense of group solidarity originally centred around the stem family (*ie*), and harness this to the common cause of resisting and competing with the power of the West (Murakami 1975: Chap. 9). This theory of the cultural basis of Japan's industrial growth has led Murakami into some substantial, if controversial, research on the history and social anthropology of the Japanese family. The point emphasized in these studies is that traditional family values were not naturally transposed into modern institutions such as the company, but rather that family collectivism was deliberately re-created and re-shaped to suit the needs of different phases of economic evolution (Murakami 1984: particularly pp. 339–63). It should be noted,

186

however, that in recent works Murakami does not propose Japanese 'familism' as the only alternative to the Western individualist path to industrialization. Rather, he implies that there may also be a 'Chinese periphery' alternative, an 'Indo-Hispanic' alternative, and an 'Islamic' alternative, although all of these appear to be grouped with Japanese familism in the category of 'activism plus collectivism' rather than 'activism plus individualism' (Murakami 1986: 226–33).

It will be obvious from this brief summary that Murakami's ideas are, from one pespective, part of an intellectual current that is particularly powerful in contemporary Japan. The main characteristics of this current are an emphasis on the uniqueness of the Japan value system, an identification of Japanese values with collectivism and the family (*ie*), and a belief in the decline of the Western value system (which in turn is identified with individualism). Perhaps the best-known proponent of these ideas is the philosopher Umehara Takeshi, whose recent works speak of the need for a rediscovery of traditional Japanese culture as a means of overcoming the cultural stagnation of the West. Murakami's view of Japanese social values, it should be said, is a more cautious one than Umehara's, for Murakami observes in Japan a weakening of collectivism and a loss of national goals, and suggests that Japan itself may prove to be as vulnerable as the West to 'the maladies of industrial society'. However, Murakami evidently agrees with Umehara in perceiving traditional Japanese collectivism as something desirable. In this sense, he differs from Morishima Michio, whose analysis of the cultural sources of Japan's economic success stresses the undesirable social and political consequences of the collectivist ethos in Japan (Morishima 1979). Murakami, despite some criticism of the contemporary state of Japanese culture and society, appears to believe in the possiblity of a 're-creation of a new family-type collectivism' based on a new national goal, which will replace the obsolete aim of catching up with the West. At the same time he cautions that this new collectivism should not be based (as pre-war nationalism was) on political confrontation with foreign nations (Murakami 1975: 208–10).

To outside observers, the enthusiasm of economists like Murakami and Morishima for cultural explanations of economic development may seem a little puzzling. In the United States since the mid-1960s, Parsonian-style analyses of the cultural preconditions for industrialization have to a large extent fallen from favour. The very economic successes of countries like Japan, South Korea, and Singapore undermined many of their hypotheses and created a more fundamental doubt about the usefulness of assigning labels such as 'individualistic' or 'collectivist' to large, complex, and rapidly changing societies.

On reflection, however, the popularity of such ideas in Japan is not surprising. They arise not only from Japan's own economic success but also from the weakening hold of the idea that Western culture and Newtonian science represent the irrefutable culmination of human development. In one sense, Murakami's theories serve as a useful corrective to the traditional Weberian or Parsonian approach, since they point to the possibility of a diversity of cultural patterns in industrialization. On the other hand, their insistence on Japanese collectivism and on the need for integration and the formulation of national goals runs some risk of strengthening stereotyped images of Japan overseas and, however unintentionally, of feeding precisely that stream of reviving nationalism which Murakami himself deplores.

THE INFORMATION NETWORK SOCIETY: IMAI KENICHI (1931-)

Murakami is only mildly optimistic about the ability of the Japanese system to generate new goals for economic development, and gives little indication of the forms that these goals might take. Other Japanese economists, however, have been more positive and outspoken in outlining their visions of future directions for the Japanese economy, and for industrialized market economies as a whole. Perhaps the most influential of these prophets of the emerging economic structure is the Hitotsubashi professor Imai Kenichi, who has collaborated with Murakami on studies of the information economy (Imai *et al.* 1970).

Imai, in common with many well-known Japanese writers (such as the engineer Hayashi Yūjirō and the futurologist Masuda Yoneji) defines the future goal of the economy as the creation of an 'information society' – or, to use Imai's own term, an 'information network society' (*jōhō nettowāku shakai*). The main driving force behind the emergence of this new socioeconomic order is the contemporary wave of technological innovation, evident particularly in the fields of microelectronics, computer and communications technology, and biotechnology. According to Imai these innovations are likely to bring about significant changes in the relationship between human beings and machines, and between human beings and nature. Consequently, 'we cannot but think that these new technologies will fundamentally alter the system of industrial society' (Imai 1983: 24).

Simultaneous with these technological changes, Imai perceives a shift in the world view of the scientific disciplines, away from the paradigm of Newtonian science and towards the 'new science' of Prigozhine and others. This new science, with its emphasis on the concepts of information, time, and irreversible processes, is gradually beginning to influence economic thought, and clearly plays some part in the shaping of Imai's own ideas (Imai 1984: 40–4).

The central features of Imai's vision of the information network society are the declining significance of economies of scale and the growing importance of links between organizations of various types. The main factor in reversing the previous tendency towards increasing economies of scale is the application of microelectronics to industrial production. The new, microelectronically-controlled equipment is better adapted to the small-scale production of diverse products than to the mass production of a uniform product. It is, moreover, often relatively small-scale and inexpensive, and therefore tends to lower barriers of entry to new industrial areas (Imai 1984: 140). At the same time, the emergence of mature industrial societies in which basic human needs are fulfilled is leading (as Murakami also observes) to a greater diversity of consumer demand. This fragmentation of the market creates a wide range of specialized niches that can best be filled by relatively small-scale enterprises. Small firms also have the advantage of being able to respond with greater sensitivity to slight changes in the economic environment, and may therefore be particularly well adapted to survival in a high-technology society. This does not mean, of course, that the large enterprise will cease to exist (although even within large firms there may be an increasingly fine division of tasks between different sections). Rather, there will be a reversal of the trend towards the growing domination of capitalist economies by giant firms, and the creation of a more diverse industrial structure (Imai 1983: 32–4; Imai 1984: 135–41 and 156–66).

The increasingly minute inter-firm and intra-firm division of labour will of itself necessitate the development of improved connections between one section or enterprise and another. Such links serve to carry signals from one part of the economy to another, in much the same way as the nervous system carries messages from one part of the body to another. Without such a connecting network, it would be impossible for the constituent elements of the system (firms) to react effectively to changes in other sections of the economic structure. Networks are also particularly essential in the sphere of research and development, where significant innovation increasingly depends on the communication of knowledge between private and public research centres and between different scientific disciplines (Imai 1984: 119–20; Imai 1987).

Traditionally, the links that hold together the economic system, have been of two types: markets (M), in which decisions are based on price signals (M_1) and which participants are free to enter and leave at will (M_2); and organizations (O), in which decisions are made within a power structure (O_1) and participants are tied into long-term relationships with one another (O_2). The hallmark of the information network society, Imai suggests, is the growing inter-penetration of markets and organization. For example, companies, while still operating within a market framework, may find their decisions influenced by the advice of government or of a parent or related company. Similarly, firms that are nominally independent of one another may find themselves linked into long-term relationships by, for example, joint research projects. Using the two characteristics of markets and organizations listed above, Imai illustrates the new types of intermediate organization using the diagram shown in the figure below. He emphasizes, however that the new non-market links

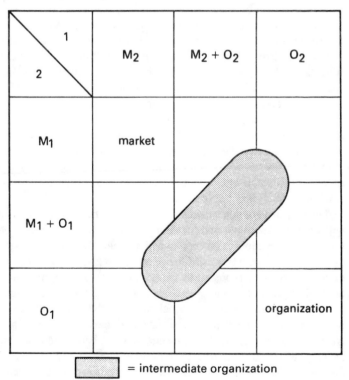

Source: Imai, 1983, p.38

190

between firms are likely to be loose connections (co-operation in the areas of staff, research, etc.) rather than the more conventional, tight connections (interlocking shareholdings and directorates, etc.). A theme that recurs throughout Imai's works is the notion that new communication technology will ease the creation of such loose connections between firms (Imai 1983: 36–40; Imai 1984: 145–7; see also Imai 1986: 140–2).

In general, Imai's view of the information network society is an optimistic one. He expresses doubts about the impact of new technologies on employment and about the growth of consumer demand for the products of these technologies, but he nevertheless presents the emerging social order as one in which diversity and flexibility will prevail, and enterprises will be increasingly responsive to the needs of consumers (Imai 1984: 165–6). Imai, moreover, sees the Japanese industrial system as especially well placed to adopt the structures necessary for successful survival in the information age. The interpenetration of market and organization that Imai describes is already quite well advanced in Japan, and Japanese firms have been skilled in communicating information both within and between organizations. In particular, Imai claims that an effective upward flow of information – from the point of sale to the planning and design headquarters – has made Japanese enterprises highly responsive to market trends (Imai 1984: 119; see also Imai 1983). In a sense, therefore, the old industrial system with its giant managerial corporations comes to be identified particularly with the United States, while the new information network society is identified particularly with Japan.

> When the transport and communications infrastructure of the U.S. was completed in the 1880s . . . mass production and mass distribution made a tendency towards monopoly become suddenly apparent. In the words of Harvard professor A. Chandler, this provided the occasion for the invisible hand of the market to be replaced by the visible hand of giant enterprise. . . .
> Is it not probable that in Japan, after the completion of the future information communication infrastructure, the reverse of this U.S. experience will occur? In other words, we may perhaps escape from the existing dominance of the visible hand, and move towards a world where a new invisible hand is supported by that imperceptible substance, information.
>
> (Imai 1984: 205–6)

TECHNOLOGY AND ECONOMIC THOUGHT:
SAWA TAKAMITSU (1942–)

Not all Japan observers, however, share Imai's optimistic attitude towards the impact of technological change on the economy. On the political left, not surprisingly, greater attention has been paid to the role of computerization in destroying jobs and skills. Debates in Japan have closely paralleled European and US 'de-skilling' debates, with some writers perceiving a growing gap between a technocratic élite and the mass of low-skilled workers, while others accept Serge Mallet's predictions of the emergence of a technically skilled and militant 'new working class' (see Mallet 1975; Ōmori and Hiroe 1984; Aomi 1984).

From a somewhat different point of view, theories on the information society have been analysed and criticized by Kyoto University's Sawa Takamitsu, who is widely regarded as one of the most innovative of the younger generation of economic thinkers. Sawa, as we have already seen, has been a trenchant critic of the positivist notion of economics as a value-free 'science' and has focused his attack particularly on the Popperian 'piecemeal engineering' approach which he sees as characteristic of post-war American economic thought. In Sawa's view, economics is a cultural product, whose development can be understood only by a careful examination of its technological, social, and political context. While he agrees with Imai in emphasizing the decentralized network structure of new computer technology, Sawa sees these technologies not as revitalizing the free market economy, but rather as revitalizing the ideology of perfect competition.

In an intriguing speculative study, which ranges over topics from psychiatry to robotics and from early modern European thought to the rise of the American yuppie, Sawa draws a parallel between the development of computer technology and the recent evolution of economic thought (Sawa 1987: 124–43). During the 1960s and early 1970s, computerization involved centralized processing by very large machines whose use was controlled by a small élite of technical specialists. This structure not only reflected but also promoted the concept of capitalist planning, in which the state was seen as having a growing role in collecting and processing economic information, and was expected to use this information to correct the imperfections of the market. Since the early 1970s, however, the trend has been towards decentralized processing, using small-scale machines and communications networks of the type described by Imai. The new system, Sawa suggests, mirrored and reinforced the world view of rational expectationism, according to which each individual was seen as having access to perfect information, and the state was viewed as an impediment rather than a necessary supplement to the market mechanism (Sawa 1987: 126–7).

The change in economic philosophies, however, was only part of a wider transformation of ethical values. Using phrases that often recall the writings of Murakami, Sawa speaks of an 'age of moral vacuum' (*rinriteki kūhaku ki*) and of the decay of individualism from a creative force to a narrow antisocial selfishness. Murakami, however, regarded these trends as a product of mass consumer society, and saw them as being particularly well exemplified by the self-indulgent student movement of the late 1960s and early 1970s. For Sawa, on the contrary, 1960s radicalism was precisely a symptom of the wider social concerns that, he believes, are being lost in the information age. His 'moral vacuum', conversely, is symbolized by the young US graduates who choose to turn their talents to acquiring quick fortunes on the stockmarket rather than devoting them to the development of new technologies or to the solution of social problems (Sawa 1987: 181–6). Sawa identifies the source of this new egotism as lying in the shift from a 'stock' to a 'flow' society. Whereas economies based on manufacturing depended on the accumulation of capital and knowledge, Sawa argues that the information economy depends primarily on access to a perpetual flow of knowledge – knowledge whose value is inherently transient. The flow economy discourages the traditional values of accumulation and frugality. At the same time, declining faith in the power of the state to ameliorate the injustices of the market economy alters the basis of economic and political individualism.

> The individualism which was the motive force of industrial society was in essence quite different from the individualism of the 'soft' [i.e. information] society. In the individualism of the 'soft' society one can perceive none of the ideological depth of the old individualism, which was born of the desire for freedom from oppression and a hatred of absolutism. The division between individualism and selfishness has thus become indistinct.
>
> (Sawa 1987: 143)

Sawa, moreover, has little faith in the ability of the Japanese economy or of Japanese culture to provide answers to the problems he outlines. Indeed, he argues that Japan is in many ways particularly vulnerable to the dilemmas of the information age. Here his analysis focuses on the tendency for recent technological change to be accompanied by a shift of employment from manufacturing to service industries. This trend is reinforced by the growth of the multinational enterprise, and by the relocation of many manufacturing activities from developed nations (such as Japan and the United States) to the newly industrializing countries of East and South-East Asia. While many economists have seen overseas investment as an important means of reducing trade friction between Japan and other industrialized nations, Sawa argues that this 'hollowing of the economy' (*keizai no kūdōka*) may paradoxically aggravate international trading problems. Foreign investment, as he notes, tends to increase the share of capital, and decrease labour's share, in the national income. This in turn reduces the marginal propensity to consume, thus raising the rate of capital accumulation and restricting the demand for imports (Sawa 1987: 208–9).

In the longer term Sawa perceives a rather bleak future for Japan as an exporting nation. Japan's success as an exporter of industrial products — particularly consumer durables - has depended primarily on the nation's ability to mass-produce reliable goods at low cost. The shift towards an information society, however, implies that services and commodified information will become increasingly important as earners of export revenue. But these 'soft' commodities are for the most part highly culturally specific, and Japan's ability to export such products is likely to be hampered (as the case of the computer software industry already reveals) by its linguistic and cultural isolation from the major industrialized markets (Sawa 1987: 152–550). Sawa also casts doubt on the ability of the information and service industries to absorb the mass of labour released from manufacturing by new technology and the changing international division of labour (Sawa 1987: 189–200).

Sawa's picture of the future, however, is not entirely grim, for he predicts that the very problems indicated by his analysis will provoke changes in economic theory and economic policy. Several aspects of the contemporary crisis in particular are seen as providing potential stimuli to the emergence of a reincarnated and restructured Keynesianism. These include the evident failure of the floating exchange rate system to solve international trade imbalances; the mounting debt burden of less-developed nations; the growing inability of the United States to fund such essential 'international public goods' as the United Nations and the International Monetary Fund; and the increasing need for Japan to reverse the 'hollowing' of its economy and to stimulate domestic demand (Sawa 1987: 161–8). In other words, just as the economic crisis of the 1930s focused attention on the failures of the free market within industrialized nations, so the current economic crisis is focusing attention on the failures of the free market at an international level. The solution, which Sawa points to (without spelling out its details), is a new 'global Keynesianism' involving a closer co-operation not only between advanced industrialized societies such as Japan and the United States, but also between the nations of the First World and those of the Third World (Sawa 1987: 224–31).

CONCLUSIONS

Within the present ferment in Japanese economic thought, the outlines of future directions are beginning to become clear. The most important common feature linking the economists whose ideas we have considered here is their rejection of the conventional, relatively narrow interpretation of 'economic' phenomena. Each in his own way has tried to overstep the boundaries that have confined most modern economic thought, in Japan and elsewhere, and to reintegrate the economic with aspects of the political, the social, and the cultural. In place of the relatively insular economism which was characteristic not only of much neo-classical thought, but also of some Keynesians and Uno-style Marxists, there appears to be an attempt to rediscover lost elements of that earlier concept of 'political economy' or *keikoku saimin*.

However, there is no sign of the evolution of a new synthesis that might dominate future Japanese thought in the way that the neo-classical–Keynesian synthesis dominated post-war American economics. Instead, many of the old sources of divergence and controversy have acquired renewed significance in the context of present-day economic problems. In particular, two pairs of polarities that have haunted the history of Japanese economic thought continue to shape the nature of contemporary debates. The first is the contrast between faith in the free market and belief in the need for state planning. These two positions may be seen as defining the extremes of a continuum on which we can locate contemporary thinkers like Suzuki, Imai, Uzawa, and Miyamoto just as we can locate Meiji economists or even late Tokugawa thinkers such as Kaiho Seiryō and Satō Nobuhiro.

The second axis on which we can situate participants in the controversy of the 1980s is the continuum that runs from universalism

195

to particularism. As we have seen, a recurring debate in the analysis of the Japanese economy has concerned the extent to which Japan must be seen as being unique or exceptional. Just as the pre-war debates between the *Rōnō* school and the *Kōza* school can be defined in terms of tendencies towards universalism or particularism, so we can see differences between Uzawa and Murakami, Sawa and Imai as being partly explicable in these terms.

The continuing search for new paradigms to encompass the problems of a changing economic order is therefore likely to lead Japanese economists in diverse directions. For some, it will involve a reaffirmation of the power of capitalism to generate solutions to its own problems, while for others it will lead to demands for a radical reshaping of the political and economic system. Some will look for internationally valid answers to the common crises of mature industrialism, while others will turn inward to rediscover the economic significance of specifically Japanese institutions and values.

In these debates, however, there will undoubtedly be one quite new element which must not be ignored. Throughout the 300 years of history surveyed in this book the writings of Japanese economic thinkers have received little attention in other countries. Although since the mid-nineteenth century Japan has imported and assimilated an enormous volume of foreign economic ideas, the economic controversies that have raged within Japan might, for all the interest they attracted abroad, have been conducted within a soundproofed room. But Japan is now a country whose economic policy has immense significance for the international system. To the extent that Japanese economic thought influences the nature of Japanese economic policy, it is no longer possible for economists elsewhere to neglect the ideas that are current in Japan. Whatever the future directions taken by Japanese economic debates, therefore, there will surely be a growing number of foreign observers following them – perhaps with concern, perhaps with hope, but always with interest.

BIBLIOGRAPHY

Ackroyd, Joyce (ed.) (1979) *Told Round a Brushwood Fire: The Autobiography of Arai Hakuseki*, Princeton: Princeton University Press.

Akamatsu, Kaname (1950) *Sekai Keizai no Kōzō*, Tokyo: Reimei Shobō.

Albritton, Robert (1986) *A Japanese Reconstruction of Marxist Theory*, London: Macmillan.

Althusser, Louis (1977) *For Marx* (trans. B. Brewster), London: New Left Books.

Andō, Yoshio (1979) *Kindai Nihon Keizaishi Yōran*, Tokyo: Tōkyō Daigaku Shuppankai.

Aoki, Michio (1976) 'Tsuchiya Takao', in K. Nagahara and M. Kano (eds), *Nihon no Rekishika*, Tokyo: Nihon Hyōronsha.

Aomi, Tsukasa (1984) 'Ōtomēshon to Rōdō no Mirai', *Yūbutsuron Kenkyū* 10: 81–93.

Arai, Hakuseki (1977) *Arai Hakuseki Zenshū*, Tokyo: Kokusho Kankōkai.

Bell, J.F. (1960–1), 'Origins of Japanese academic economics', *Monumenta Nipponica* 16: 263–87.

Bellah, Robert N. (1957) *Tokugawa Religion: The Values of Pre-Industrial Japan*, Glencoe: Free Press.

—— (1978) 'Baigan and Sorai: Continuities and discontinuities in eighteenth-century Japanese thought', in T. Najita and I. Scheiner (eds), *Japanese Thought in the Tokugawa Period 1600–1868*, Chicago: University of Chicago Press.

Bernstein, Gail Lee (1976) *Japanese Marxist: A Portrait of Kawakami Hajime*, Cambridge, Mass.: Harvard University Press.

Blacker, Carmen (1969) *The Japanese Enlightenment: A Study of the Writings of Fukuzawa Yukichi*, Cambridge: Cambridge University Press.

Blaug, Mark (1985) *Great Economists Since Keynes*, Brighton: Harvester Press.

Böhm-Bawerk, Eugen von (1949) *Karl Marx and the Close of his System*, New York: Augustus M. Kelley.

Bowen, R.W. (1980) *Rebellion and Democracy in Meiji Japan*, Berkeley: University of California Press.

Braisted, W.R. (1976) *Meiroku Zasshi: Journal of the Japanese Enlightenment*, Tokyo: Tokyo University Press.

Bronfenbrenner, Martin (1956) 'The state of Japanese economics', *American Economic Review* 46: 389–98.

Butter, Irene H. (1969) *Academic Economics in Holland 1800–1870*, The Hague: Martinus Nijhoff.

Caldwell, Malcolm (1977) *The Wealth of Some Nations*, London: Zed Books.

Dazai, Shundai (1972) *Keizai Roku*, reprinted in *Nihon Shisō Taikei*, vol. 37, Tokyo: Iwanami Shoten.

Emmanuel, Arghiri (1972) *Unequal Exchange: A Study of the Imperialism of Trade*, New York: Monthly Review Press.

Fujii, Shōichi (1976) 'Noro Eitarō', in K. Nagahara and M. Kanō (eds), *Nihon no Rekishika*, Tokyo: Nihon Hyōronsha.

Fukuda, Tokuzō (1922) *Shakai Seisaku to Kaikyū Tōsō*, Tokyo: Kaizō Sha.
Gide, Charles and Rist, Charles (1913) *A History of Economic Doctrines from the Time of the Physiocrats to the Present Day* (trans. R. Richards), Boston: D.C. Heath.
Goonatilake, Susantha (1984) *Aborted Discovery: Science and Creativity in the Third World*, London: Zed Books.
Gotō, Yōichi (1976) 'Kumazawa Banzan no Shōgai to Shisō no Keisei', in *Nihon Shisō Taikei*, vol. 30, Tokyo: Iwanami Shoten.
Hattori, Shisō (1955) 'Sangyō Shihon no Keisei', in S. Hattori, *Ishinshi no Hōhō*, Tokyo: Riron Sha.
Hilferding, Rudolf (1949) *Böhm-Bawerk's Criticism of Marx*, New York: Augustus M. Kelley.
Honjō, Eijirō (1965) *Economic Theory and History of Japan in the Tokugawa Period*, New York: Russell and Russell.
—— (1966) *Nihon Keizai Shisōshi Kenkyū*, vols 1–2, Tokyo: Nihon Hyōron Sha.
Hoston, Germaine A. (1984) 'Marxism and Japanese expansionism', *Journal of Japanese Studies* 10 (1): 1–30.
—— (1986) *Marxism and the Crisis of Development in Prewar Japan*, Princeton: Princeton University Press.
Hu, Jichuang (1984) *Chinese Economic Thought Before the Seventeenth Century*, Beijing: Foreign Languages Press.
Ihara, Saikaku (1959) *The Japanese Family Storehouse* (trans. G.W. Sargent), Cambridge: Cambridge University Press.
Iida, Tsuneo (1976) 'The lineage of Japanese economics', *Japanese Economic Studies* 4 (4): 63–80.
—— (1986) 'Naiju Kakudai Ron wa Pinto Hazure de Aru', *Sekai* (June): 59–69.
Ikuzawa, Kenzō (1957) *Kokusai Keizaigaku Josetsu*, Kyoto: Mineruba Shobō.
Imai, Kenichi (1984) *Jōhō Nettowāku Shakai*, Tokyo: Iwanami Shinsho.
—— (1986) 'Japan's industrial policy for high technology industry', in J. Patrick (ed.), *Japan's High Technology Industries*, Seattle: University of Washington Press.
—— (1987) 'Sōzōteki Inobēshon no Soshikika', *Economics Today* (Tokyo) 5: 36–61.
Imai, Kenichi et al. (1970) *Jōhō to Gijutsu no Keizai Bunseki*, Tokyo: Nihon Keizai Kenkyū Sentā.
—— (1983) *Nihon no Sangyō Shakai: Shinka to Henkaku no Dōtei*, Tokyo: Chikuma Shobō.
Inoue, Harumaru (1947) 'Nihon Nōgyō Shihonshugika Mondai', *Keizai Hyōron* (Aug.–Sept.): 1–15.
—— (1957) 'Shokuminchiteki Jūzoku to Han-Hōkenteki Tochi Shoyū Seido', in H. Ogura (ed.), *Nihon Shihonshugi Kōza*, vol. 10, Tokyo: Iwanami Shoten.
Ishida, Baigan (1972) *Toi Mondō*, modern Japanese edition reprinted in *Nihon no Meicho*, vol. 18, Tokyo: Chūō Kōron Sha.
Itō, Mitsuharu (1984) *Keizaigaku wa Genjitsu ni Kotaeru ka*, Tokyo: Iwanami Shoten.
Itō, Tōju (1976) 'Banzan no Gakumon to Shisō', in *Nihon no Meicho*, vol. 11, Tokyo: Chūō Kōron Sha.

Itoh, Makoto (1980) *Value and Crisis: Essays on Marxian Economics in Japan*, London: Pluto Press.

Johnson, Chalmers (1965) *An Instance of Treason: The Story of the Tokio Spy Ring*, London: Heinemann.

—— (1982) *MITI and the Japanese Miracle*, Stanford: Stanford University Press.

Kaiho, Seiryō (1970) *Keiko Dan*, reprinted in *Nihon Shisō Taikei*, vol. 44, Tokyo: Iwanami Shoten.

Kajinishi, Mitsuhaya, Katō, Toshihiko, Ōshima, Kiyoshi, and Ōuchi, Tsutomu (1960–70) *Nihon Shihonshugi no Botsuraku*, vols 1–8. Tokyo: Tōkyō Daigaku Shuppankai.

Kanamori, Hisao (1968a) *Tsuyoi Taiyō: Nihon Keizai no Seichō Ryoku*, Tokyo: Daiyamondo Sha.

—— (1968b) 'Economic growth and exports', in L. Klein and K. Ohkawa (eds), *Economic Growth: The Japanese Experience Since the Meiji Era*, Homewood, Ill.: Richard D. Irwin.

—— (1970) 'Keizai Seichō to Kokusai Shūshi', in H. Kanamori (ed.), *Bōeki to Kokusai Shūshi*, Tokyo: Nihon Keizai Shinbun Sha.

Kanda, Fuhito (1983) *Senryō to Minshushugi*, Tokyo: Shōgakkan.

Kata, Tetsuji (1962) *Nihon Shakai Keizai Shisōshi*, Tokyo: Keiō Tsūshin.

Katō, Hiroshi (1976) *Gendai Nihon no Kōkigyō*, Tokyo: Nihon Keizai Shinbun.

—— (1982) *Gyōkaku wa Nihon o Kaeru*, Tokyo: Bungei Shunjū Sha.

—— (1984) 'Fiscal reform comes first', *Japan Echo* 11 (4): 18–21.

Kawakami, Hajime (1945) *Shihonron Nyūmon*, Tokyo: Sekai Hyōron Sha.

—— (1965) *Bimbō Monogatari*, Tokyo: Iwanami Bunko.

Keiō Gijuku Daigaku Keizai Gakkai (ed.) (1959) *Nihon ni Okeru Keizai Gaku no Hyakunen*, Tokyo: Nihon Hyōron Shinsha.

Keizai Kikakuchō (ed.) (1961) *Kokumin Shotoku Baizō Keikaku*, Tokyo: Ōkurashō Insatsu Kyoku.

Kelley, Allen, C., Williamson, Jeffrey, G., and Cheetham, Russell J. (1972) *Dualistic Economic Development: Theory and History*, Chicago: University of Chicago Press.

Kirby, E. Stuart (1952) 'The reception of Western economics in the Orient', *Quarterly Journal of Economics* 66 (3): 409–17.

Kita, Ikki (1971) *Nihon Kaizō Hōan*, Tokyo: Bideo Shuppan.

Koizumi, Shinzō (1966) *Fukuzawa Yukichi*, Tokyo: Iwanami Shinsho.

—— (1967–72) *Kachi Ron to Shakaishugi*, reprinted in *Koizumi Shinzō Zenshū* vols 1–26, Tokyo: Bungei Shunjū Sha.

Kojima, Kiyoshi (1958) *Nihon Bōeki to Keizai*, Tokyo: Kokugen Shobō.

—— (1978) *Direct Foreign Investment: A Japanese Model of Multinational Business Operations*, London: Croom Helm.

Komiya, Ryūtarō (1966a) Editor's preface to R. Komiya (ed.), *Postwar Economic Growth in Japan*, Berkeley: University of California Press.

—— (1966b) 'The supply of personal savings', in R. Komiya (ed.), *Bōeki to Kokusai Shūshi*, Tokyo: Nihon Keizai Shinbun Sha.

—— (1970) Shihon Jiyūka no Keizaigaku, reprinted in Kanamori, Hisao (ed.) *Bōeki to Kokusai Shūshi*, Tokyo: Nihon Keizai Shinbunsha.

—— (1975a) 'Planning in Japan', in M. Bornstein (ed.), *Economic Planning, East and West*, Cambridge, Mass.: Ballinger.

Komiya, Ryūtarō (1975b) *Gendai Nihon Keizai Kenkyū*, Tokyo: Tokyo Daigaku Shuppankai.

—— and Amano, Akihiro (1972) *Kokusai Keizaigaku*, Tokyo: Iwanami Shoten.

—— and Yamamoto, Kōzō (1981) 'Japan: The officer in charge of economic affairs', in A.W. Coats (ed.), *Economists in Government*, Durham, N.C.: Duke University Press.

Kondō, Yasuo *et al.* (1953) 'Nōchi Kaikaku to Han-Hōkensei', in Inoue Harumaru (ed.), *Nihon Shihonshugi Kōza*, vol. 5, Tokyo: Iwanami Shoten.

Kosai, Yutaka and Ogino, Yoshitarō (1984) *The Contemporary Japanese Economy*, London: Macmillan.

Koshimura, Shinzaburō (1951) *Rōdō Kachi Setsu no Sūgakuteki Tenkai*, Tokyo: Sekishoin.

—— (1975) *Theory of Capital Reproduction and Accumulation* (trans. T. Ataka), Kichener, Ontario: DPG Publishing.

Kuhn, Thomas (1970) *The Structure of Scientific Revolutions* (2nd edn), Chicago: University of Chicago Press.

Kumazawa, Banzan (1971) *Shūgi Washo*, reprinted in *Nihon Shisō Taikei*, vol. 30, Tokyo: Iwanami Shoten.

—— (1976) *Shūgi Gaisho*, modern Japanese edition reprinted in *Nihon no Meicho*, vol. 11, Tokyo: Chūō Kōron Sha.

Kuranami, Seiji (1970) 'Kaiho Seiryō' in *Nihon Shisō Taikei*, vol. 44, Tokyo: Iwanami Shoten.

Kurihara, Hyakuji (1947) 'Nōchi Kaikaku Hō ni Kansuru Sho-Ronsetsu', *Shakai Kagaku* 7: 53–9.

—— (1951) *Gendai Nihon Nōgyō Ron*, Tokyo: Chūō Kōron Sha.

Lenin, Vladimir I. (1962) *The Agrarian Programme of Social Democracy in the First Russian Revolution*, reprinted in V.I. Lenin, *Collected Works*, vol. 13, London: Lawrence and Wishart.

Lidin, Olof (1973) *The Life of Ogyū Sorai*, Lund: Student Litterature.

Lie, John (1987) 'Reactionary Marxism: The end of ideology in Japan', *Monthly Review* 38 (11): 45–51.

List, Friedrich (1928) *The National System of Political Economy*, London: Longmans Green.

Mallet, Serge (1975) *The New Working Class* (trans. Andree and Bob Shepherd), Nottingham: Bertrand Russell Peace Foundation.

Mandel, Ernest (1971) *Late Capitalism*, London: Verso Press.

Maruyama, Masao (1961) *Nihon no Shisō*, Tokyo: Iwanami Shinsho.

—— (1974) *Studies in the Intellectual History of Tokugawa Japan* (trans. M. Hane), Tokyo: Tokyo University Press.

Marx, Karl (1976) *Capital*, vols 1–3, London: Penguin Books/New Left Review.

Masamura, Kimihiro (1965) 'Gendai Nihon no Marukusushugi: Kokka Dokusen Shihonshugi Ron', in K. Nagasu and B. Tomizuka (eds), *Gendai no Shihonshugi Kan*, Tokyo: Shiseidō.

—— (1968) *Gendai Nihon Keizai Ron*, Tokyo: Nihon Hyōron Sha.

Matsuura, Tamotsu (1972) 'Marginalism in Japan', *History of Political Economy* 4, (2): 533–50.

McEwan, J.R. (1962) *The Political Writings of Ogyū Sorai*, Cambridge: Cambridge University Press.

Medvedev, Roy (1979) *The October Revolution*, London: Constable.

Mill, John Stuart (1973) *Principles of Political Economy*, London: A.M. Kelley.

Minami, Ryōshin (1986) *The Economic Development of Japan: A Quantitative Study*, London: Macmillan.

Miyamoto, Kenichi (1969) *Nihon no Toshi Mondai*, Tokyo: Chikuma Shobō.

—— (1976) *Shakai Shihon Ron* (2nd edn), Tokyo: Yūsankaku.

—— (1981a) *Gendai Shihonshugi to Kokka*, vol. 4 of *Gendai Shihonshugi Bunseki*, Tokyo: Iwanami Shoten.

—— (1981b) *Nihon no Kankyō Mondai* (2nd edn), Tokyo: Yūsankaku.

Miyazaki, Yoshikazu (1966) *Gendai Nihon no Keizai Kōzō*, Tokyo: Shin Hyōron.

—— (1967) *Gendai no Shihonshugi*, Tokyo: Iwanami Shinsho.

—— (1972) *Kasen*, Tokyo: Iwanami Shinsho.

—— (1980) 'Excessive concentration and the formation of *Keiretsu*', in K. Sato (ed.), *Industry and Business in Japan*, New York: M.E. Sharpe and Croom Helm.

Morishima, Michio (1969) *Theory of Economic Growth*, Oxford: Clarendon Press.

—— (1973) *Marx's Economics: A Dual Theory of Value and Growth*, Cambridge: Cambridge University Press.

—— (1976) *The Economic Theory of Modern Society*, Cambridge: Cambridge University Press.

—— (1979) 'Shin "Shin Gunbi Keikaku Ron",' *Bungei Shunjū* 57 (7): 94–121.

—— (1982) *Why Has Japan 'Succeeded'? Western Technology and the Japanese Ethos*, Cambridge: Cambridge University Press.

—— (1984) *The Economics of Industrial Society*, Cambridge: Cambridge University Press.

—— and Seton, F. (1961) 'Aggregation on Leotief matrices and the labour theory of value', *Econometrica* 29 (2): 203–20.

—— and Catephores, George (1978) *Value, Exploitation and Growth*, Maidenhead: McGraw-Hill.

Murakami, Yasusuke (1975) *Sangyō Shakai no Byōri*, Tokyo: Chūō Kōron Sha.

—— (1984) '*Ie* Society as a pattern of Civilisation', *Journal of Japanese Studies* 10 (2): 281–363.

—— (1985) 'Kitaino Seiji Keizaigaku e no Josetsu', in S. Fukuchi and Y. Murakami (eds), *Nihon Keizai no Tenbō to Kadai*, Tokyo: Nihon Keizai Shinbun Sha.

—— (1986) 'Technology in transition: two perspectives on industrial policy', in H. Patrick (ed.), *Japan's High Technology Industries*, Seattle: University of Washington Press.

Nagasu, Kazuji (1965) *Kokusai Jidai no Nihon Keizai*, Tokyo: Kawade Shobō.

—— (1973) *Kōzō Kaikaku Ron no Keisei*, Tokyo: Gendai no Riron Sha.

Najita, Tetsuo (1972) 'Political economism in the thought of Dazai Shundai (1680–1747)', *Journal of Asian Studies* 31 (4): 821–39.

—— (1978) 'Method and analysis in the conceptual portrayal of Tokugawa intellectual history', in T. Najita and I. Scheiner (eds), *Japanese Thought in the Tokugawa Period 1600–1868*, Chicago: University of Chicago Press.

Nakamura, Hajime (1986) *A Comparative History of Ideas*, London: Kegan Paul.

Nakamura, Takafusa (1981) *The Postwar Japanese Economy: Its Development and Structure* (trans. Jacqueline Kaminski), Tokyo: Tokyo University Press.

Nakayama, Ichirō (1972a) *Junsui Keizaigaku*, reprinted in *Nakayama Ichirō Zenshū*, vol 1, Tokyo: Kōdan Sha.

—— (1972b) ' "Keinzu Ippan Riron Kaisetsu" Zensho: Shunpētā to Keinzu', reprinted in *Nakayama Ichirō Zenshū*, vol. 1, Tokyo: Kōdan Sha.

Naniwada, Haruo (1938–41) *Kokka to Keizai*, vols 1–4, Tokyo: Nihon Hyōron Sha.

—— (1973) *Kindai Nihon Shakai Keizai Shisō Shi*, Tokyo: Maeno Shoten.

Nawa, Tōichi (1948) 'Kokusai Kachi Ron', *Keizai Shichō* 7: 1–37.

—— (1950), 'Gaikoku Bōeki to Rijun Ritsu', *Sekai Keizai*, May and July.

Nihon Kyōsantō (1978) *Nihon Kyōsantō no Gojū Nen*, Tokyo: Nihon Kyōsantō Chūō Iinkai Shuppan Kyoku.

Nihon Rōdō Nenkan (1985) *Nihon Rōdō Nenkan*, Tokyo: Ōhara Shakai Kenkyūjo.

Noguchi, Yukio (1977) Dissecting the Finance Ministry – Bank of Japan Dynasty, *Japan Echo* 2: 4.

Norman, E.H. (1949) *Ando Shoeki and the Anatomy of Japanese Feudalism*. Transactions of the Asiatic Society of Japan. Tokyo.

Noro, Eitarō (1983) *Nihon Shihonshugi Hattatsu Shi*, vols. 1–2, Tokyo: Iwanami Bunko.

Odaka, Kōnosuke (1976) 'Commentary', in S. Tsuru (ed.), *Towards a New Political Economy: The Collected Works of Tsuru Shigeto*, vol. 13, Tokyo: Kodan Sha.

Ogyū, Sorai (1973) *Seidan*, reprinted in *Nihon Shisō Taikei* vol. 36, Tokyo: Iwanami Shoten.

Ohkawa, Kazushi and Rosovsky, Henry (1973) *Japanese Economic Growth: Trend Acceleration in the Twentieth Century*, Stanford: Stanford University Press.

Oka, Mitsuo and Yamazaki, Ryūzō (1983) *Nihon Keizaishi: Bakuhan Seido no Keizai Kōzō*, Kyoto: Mineruba Shobō.

Okishio, Nobuo (1963) 'A mathematical note on Marxian theorems', *Weltwirtschafliches Archiv* 91: 287–99.

—— (1965) *Shihonsei Keizai no Kiso Ron*, Tokyo: Sōbun Sha.

Ōkita, Saburō (1959a) 'Nihon Keizai no Seichō Ryoku to "Shin Chōki Keizai Keikaku",' in Kinyū Zaisei Jijō Kenkyūkai (ed.), *Nihon Keizai no Seichō Ryoku: 'Shimomura Riron' to Sono Hihan*, Tokyo: Kinyū Zaisei Jijō Kenkyūkai.

—— (1959b) 'Keizai Seichō Ryoku to Seichō Jitsugen no Seisaku Ron', in Kinyū Zaisei Jijō Kenkyūkai (ed.), *Nihon Keizai no Seichō Ryoku: 'Shimomura Riron' to Sono Hihan*, Tokyo: Kinyū Zaisei Jijō Kenkyūkai.

—— (1961a) *Nihon no Keizai Seisaku*, Tokyo: Yūki Shobō.

—— (1961b) *Nihon Keizai no Seichō to Kōzō*, Tokyo: Bungei Shunjū Sha.

—— (1970) 'Shigen Yunyū Koku Nihon o Jikaku Seyo', in H. Kanamori (ed.), *Bōeki to Kokusai Shūshi*, Tokyo: Nihon Keizai Shinbun Sha.

—— (1980a) 'Causes and problems of rapid growth in postwar Japan and their implications for newly developing countries', in S. Okita (ed.), *The*

Developing Countries and Japan: Lessons in Growth, Tokyo: University of Tokyo Press.
—— (1980b) 'The experience of economic planning in Japan', in S. Okita (ed.), *The Developing Countries and Japan: Lessons in Growth*, Tokyo: University of Tokyo Press.
Ōmori, Nobuyuki and Hiroe, Akira (1984) 'Maikuroerekutoronikusu-ka no Shinten to Rōdō no Shitsu', *Tokyo Gakugei Daigaku Kiyō* (Dec.): 47–64.
Ōno, Yoshihiko (1963) *Sengo Nihon Shihonshugi Ronsō*, Tokyo: Aoki Shoten.
Oser, Jacob and Blanchfield, William C. (1975) *The Evolution of Economic Thought*, New York: Harcourt Brace Jovanovich.
Ōshima, Kiyoshi and Enomoto, Masatoshi (1968) *Sengo Nihon no Keizai Katei*, Tokyo: Tōkyō Daigaku Shuppankai.
Ōuchi, Hyōe (1960) *Keizaigaku Gojūnen*, Tokyo: Tōkyō Daigaku Shuppankai.
—— (1963) *Nihon Keizai Ron*, vols 1 and 2, Tokyo: Tōkyō Daigaku Shuppankai.
—— (1975a) 'Nōchi Seido Kaikaku no Igi', reprinted in *Ōuchi Hyōe Chosaku Shū*, vol. 6, Tokyo: Iwanami Shoten.
—— (1975b) 'Nōson Minshukano Michi Chikakarazu', reprinted in *Ōuchi Hyōe Choshaku Shu*, vol. 6, Tokyo: Iwanami Shoten.
—— (1970) ' "Sengo Kaikaku" e no Futatsu no Apurōchi', *Shakai Kagaku Kenkyū* 21: 5–6, 177–89.
—— (1971) *Gendai Nihon Keizai Ron*, Tokyo: Tōkyō Daigaku Shuppankai.
Rangaswami, Aiyangar K.V. (1934) *Aspects of Ancient Indian Economic Thought*, Benares: Benares Hindu University.
Reischauer, Edwin O. (1964) *Japan: Past and Present* (3rd edn), London: Duckworth.
Roberts, John G. (1973) *Mitsui: Three Centuries of Japanese Business*, New York: John Weatherhill.
Rowthorn, Bob (1980) *Capitalism, Conflict and Inflation*, London: Lawrence and Wishart.
Saeki, Naomi and Shibagaki, Kazuo (1972) *Nihon Keizai Kenkyū Nyūmon*, Tokyo: Tōkyō Daigaku Shuppankai.
Saitō, Seiichirō and Shimomura, Osamu (1984) 'Setting priorities for asset accumulation', *Japan Echo* 11 (4): 11–17.
Sakisaka, Itsurō (1958) *Nihon Shihonshugi no Shomondai*, Tokyo: Shiseido.
Satō, Nobuhiro (1926) *Satō Nobuhiro Kagaku Zenshū*, Tokyo: Iwanami Shoten.
—— (1977a) *Kondō Hisaku*, reprinted in *Nihon Shisō Taikei*, vol. 45, Tokyo: Iwanami Shoten.
—— (1977b) *Suitō Hiroku*, reprinted in *Nihon Shisō Taikei*, vol. 45, Tokyo: Iwanami Shoten.
Sawa, Takamitsu (1982) *Keizaigaku to wa Nan Darō ka*, Tokyo: Iwanami Shinsho.
—— (1984) 'The paradigm of the high growth period', *Japan Echo* 11 (4): 37–47.
—— (1987) *Bunka to Shite no Gijutsu*, Tokyo: Iwanami Shoten.
Scalapino, Robert, A. (1983) *The Early Japanese Labour Movement*, Research Monographs no. 5, Berkeley: University of California.
Sekine, Thomas T. (1975) '*Uno-Riron*: A Japanese contribution to Marxian

political economy', *Journal of Economic Literature* 8: 847-77.

Shaw, Loretta L. (1922) *Japan in Transition*, London: Church Missionary Society.

Shimazaki, Takao (1977) 'Satō Nobuhiro: Jinbutsu Shisō narati ni Kenkyū Shi', in *Nihon Shisō Taikei*, vol. 45, Tokyo: Iwanami Shoten.

Shimomura, Osamu (1958) *Keizai Seichō Jitsugen no Tame ni*, Tokyo: Kōchikai.

—— (1959a) 'Nihon Keizai no Kichō to Sono Seichō Ryoku', in Kinyū Zaisei Jijō Kenkyūkai (ed.), *Nihon Keizai no Seichō Ryoku: 'Shimomura Riron' to Sono Hihan*, Tokyo: Kinyū Zaisei Jijō Kenkyūkai.

—— (1959b) 'Nihon Keizai no Seichō Ryoku Sairon', in Kinyū Zaisei Jijō Kenkyūkai (ed.), *Nihon Keizai no Seichō Ryoku: 'Shimomura Riron' to Sono Hihan*, Tokyo: Kinyū Zaisei Jijō Kenkyūkai.

—— (1959c) 'Okita Saburō Shi no Sairon o Ginmi Suru', in Kinyū Zaisei Jijō Kenkyūkai (ed.), *Nihon Keizai no Seicho Ryoku: 'Shimomura Riron' to Sono Hihan*, Tokyo: Kinyū Zaisei Jijō Kenkyūkai.

—— (1962) *Nihon Keizai Seichō Ron*, Tokyo: Kinyū Zaisei Jijō Kenkyūkai.

Shimpo Seiji (1977) 'Monetarisuto Moderu ni Yoru Sutagufurēshon no Kaimei', *ESP*, December.

—— (1979) *Gendai Nihon Keizai no Kaimei*, Tokyo: Tōyō Keizai Shinpōsha.

—— (1988) *Ikita Nihon Keizai Nyūmon*, Tokyo: Nihon Keizai Shinbunsha.

Shinohara, Miyohei (1961) *Nihon Keizai no Seichō to Junkan*, Tokyo: Sōbun Sha.

—— (1962) *Growth and Cycles in the Japanese Economy*, Tokyo: Kinokuniya.

—— (1964) *Keizai Seichō to Kōzō*, Tokyo: Kokugen Shobō.

—— (1968) 'Patterns and some structural changes in Japan's postwar industrial growth', in L. Klein and K. Ohkawa (eds), *Economic Growth: The Japanese Experience Since the Meiji Era*, Homewood, Ill.: Richard D. Irwin.

Shiozawa, Yūten (1986) 'Marukusu Keizaigaku no Sakufu: Uno Kōzō to Keizaigaku no Genzai', *Shisō* 747: 17-35.

Smith, D. Howard (1974) *Confucius*, London: Paladin.

Smith, T.C. (1955) *Political Change and Industrial Development in Japan: Government Enterprise 1868-1880*, Stanford: Stanford University Press.

—— (1959) *The Agrarian Origins of Modern Japan*, Stanford: Stanford University Press.

Spiegel, H.W. (1971) *The Growth of Economic Thought*, Durham, N.C.: Duke University Press.

Steedman, Ian (1981) *Marx After Sraffa* London: Verso Press.

Sugihara, Shirō (1980) *Nihon Keizai Shisōshi Ronshū*, Tokyo: Mirai Sha.

—— (1984) *Nihon no Ekonomisuto*, Tokyo: Nihon Hyōron Sha.

Sugiyama, Chuhei (1977) 'The development of economic thought in the Meiji era (1868-1912) of Japanese modernisation', *Les Actes du Cinquieme Congress International d'Histoire Economique* 1: 182-97.

—— and Mizuta, Hiroshi (1988), *Enlightenment and Beyond: Political Economy Comes to Japan*, Tokyo: University of Tokyo Press.

Sumiya, Etsuji (1967) *Nihon Keizaigaku Shi*, Kyoto: Mineruba Shobō.

Sumiya, Mikio and Taira, Koji (1979) *An Outline of Japanese Economic History: Major Works and Research Findings*, Tokyo: University of Tokyo Press.

Suzuki, Yoshio (1964) *Nihon no Tsūka to Bukka*, Tokyo: Tōyō Keizai Shimpōsha.

—— (1980) *Money and Banking in Contemporary Japan*, New Haven: Yale University Press.

—— (1986) *Money, Finance and Macroeconomic Performance in Japan*, New Haven: Yale University Press.

—— (1987) *Sekai no naka no Nihon Keizai to Kinyū*, Tokyo: Tōyō Keizai Shimpōsha.

Tahara, Soichirō (1984) 'Six views on the asset-doubling plan', *Japan Echo*, 11 (4): 29–36.

Taira, Koji (1970) 'Factory legislation and management modernisation during Japan's industrialisation', *Business History Review* 44: 84–109.

Takahashi, Kamekichi (1927) 'Nihon Shihonshugi no Teikokuteki Chii', *Taiyō* (April): 1–44.

Takata, Yasuma (1940) *Seiryoku Setsu Ronshū*, Tokyo: Nihon Hyōron Sha.

Takekoshi, Yosaburō (1967) *The Economic Aspects of the History of the Civilization of Japan*, vols 1–3, London: Dawsons of Pall Mall.

Takeuchi, Kei (1986) 'Keizaigaku no Yūutsu', *Sekai* (June): 43–58.

—— (1987) '"Nihon no Keizaigaku" – Yūkōsei no Kaifuku o', *Sekai* (Feb.): 31–44.

Tamanoi, Yoshirō (1971) *Nihon no Keizaigaku*, Tokyo: Chūkō Shinsho.

Thompson, E.P. (1978) *The Poverty of Theory*, London: Merlin Press.

Tokita, Yoshihisa (1982) *Gendai Shihonshugi to Rōdōsha Kaikyū*, vol. 5 of *Gendai Shihonshugi Bunseki*, Tokyo: Iwanami Shoten.

Trezise, Philip H. and Suzuki, Yukio (1976) 'Politics, government and economic growth in Japan', in H. Patrick and H. Rosovsky (eds), *Asia's New Giant: How the Japanese Economy Works*, Washington, D.C.: Brookings Institution.

Tsuchiya, Takao (1937) *Nihon Shihonshugi Ronshū*, Tokyo: Ikusei Sha.

—— (1977) *An Economic History of Japan*, Philadelphia: Porcupine Press.

Tsujimura, Kōtarō (1984) *Nihon no Keizaigakusha-tachi*, Tokyo: Nihon Hyōron Sha.

—— (1986) 'Naiju Kakudai no Keizaigaku', *Sekai* (June): 23–42.

Tsukatani, Akihiro (1980) *Kindai Nihon no Keizai Shisōshi Kenkyū*, Tokyo: Yūsankaku.

Tsukui, Jinkichi and Murakami, Yasusuke (1979) *Turnpike Optimality in Input-Output Systems*, Amsterdam: North-Holland Publishing.

Tsunoda, Ryūsaku *et al.* (1964) *Sources of Japanese Tradition*, vols 1–2, New York: Columbia University Press.

Tsuru, Shigeto (1958) 'The strengths and weaknesses of Japan's economy', in S. Tsuru (ed.), *Essays on Japanese Economy*, Tokyo: Kinokuniya.

—— (1959) 'Nihon Keizai no Seichō Ryoku to Keiki Junkan', in Kinyū Zaisei Jijō Kenkyūkai (ed.), *Nihon Keizai no Seichō Ryoku: 'Shimomura Riron' to Sono Hihan*, Tokyo: Kinyū Zaisei Jijō Kenkyūkai.

—— (1972) *Kōgai no Seiji Keizaigaku*, Tokyo: Iwanami Shoten.

—— (1975) 'Kōdo Seichō Ron e no Hansei', in S. Tsuru (ed.), *Tsuru Shigeto Chosaku Shū*, vol. 4, Tokyo: Kōdan Sha.

—— (1976a) 'Marx and the analysis of capitalism: a new stage on the basic contradiction?' in S. Tsuru (ed.), *Towards a New Political Economy: The Collected Works of Shigeto Tsuru*, vol. 13, Tokyo: Kōdan Sha.

—— (1976b) 'Keynes versus Marx: The methodology of aggregates', in S. Tsuru (ed.), *Towards a New Political Economy: The Collected Works of Shigeto Tsuru*, vol. 13, Tokyo: Kōdan Sha.

—— (1976c) 'Merits and demerits of the mixed economy in economic development: Lessons from India's experience', in S. Tsuru (ed.), *Towards a New Political Economy: The Collected Works of Shigeto Tsuru*, vol. 13, Tokyo: Kōdan Sha.

Tsuru, Shigeto (1976d) 'In place of GNP', in S. Tsuru (ed.), *Towards a New Political Economy: The Collected Works of Shigeto Tsuru*, vol. 13, Tokyo: Kōdan sha.

—— (1983) *Taisei Henkaku no Seiji Keizaigaku*, Tokyo: Shin Hyōron.

Uchino, Tatsurō (1980) 'Fūsetsu to Dorama no Sanjū Yonen', *Tōyō Keizai* 25 (August) 98–106.

—— (1983) *Japan's Postwar Economy*, trans. Mark A. Harbison, Tokyo, New York and San Francisco: Kōdansha International.

Uno, Kōzō (1950) *Keizai Genron*, vol. 1, Tokyo: Iwanami Shoten.

—— (1952) *Keizai Genron*, vol. 2, Tokyo: Iwanami Shoten.

—— (1959) *Marukusu Keizaigaku Genriron no Kenkyū*, Tokyo: Iwanami Shoten.

—— (1963) *Keizaigaku no Hōhō*, Tokyo: Hōsei University Press.

—— (1964) *Keizai Genron* (2nd edn), Tokyo: Iwanami Zensho.

—— (1969) *Shihonron no Keizaigaku*, Tokyo: Iwanami Shinsho.

—— (1980) *Principles of Political Economy* (trans. Thomas T. Sekine), Sussex: Harvester Press.

Usami, Seijirō (1957) 'Jūzoku Keizai to Dokusen Shihon', in H. Ogura (ed.), *Nihon Shihonshugi Kōza*, vol. 10, Tokyo: Iwanami Shoten.

Uzawa, Hirofumi (1962) 'On a two-sector model of economic growth', *Review of Economic Studies* 30: 105–18.

—— (1974) *Jidōsha no Shakaiteki Hiyō*, Tokyo: Iwanami Shinsho.

—— (1975) 'Optimum investment in social overhead capital', in E.S. Mills (ed.), *Economic Analysis of Environmental Problems*, New York: Columbia University Press.

—— (1986) *Kindai Keizaigaku no Tenkan*, Tokyo: Iwanami Shoten.

Varley, H. Paul (1974) *Japanese Culture: A Short History*, Tokyo: C.E. Tuttle.

Wakayama, Norikazu (1950) *Hogo Zeisetsu*, reprinted in *Wakayama Norikazu Zenshū*, Tokyo: Tōyō Keizai Shinpōsha.

White Papers of Japan (1975–6), Tokyo: Japan Institute of International Affairs.

Wilson, George M. (1969) *Radical Nationalist in Japan: Kita Ikki 1883–1937*, Cambridge, Mass.: Harvard University Press.

Yamada, Moritarō (1934) *Nihon Shihonshugi Bunseki*, Tokyo: Iwanami Shoten.

—— (1949) 'Nōchi Kaikaku no Rekishiteki Igi', in Tokyo Daigaku Keizaigakubu (ed.), *Sengo Nihon Keizai no Sho-Mondai*, Tokyo: Yūsankaku.

Yamaguchi, Muneyuki (1971) 'Hashimoto Sanai, Yokoi Shonan: Hansonjo, Tōbaku Shisō no Igi to Genkai', in *Nihon Shisō Taikei*, vol. 55, Tokyo: Iwanami Shoten.

Yamazaki, Masukichi (1981) *Nihon Keizai Shisōshi: Nihonteki Risō Shakai e no Michi*, Tokyo: Kōbundō Shuppan.

Yokoi, Shōnan (1971a) *Iryo Ōsetsu Taii*, reprinted in *Nihon Shisō Taikei*, vol. 55, Tokyo: Iwanami Shoten.

—— (1971b) *Kokuze Sanron*, reprinted in *Nihon Shisō Taikei*, vol. 55, Tokyo: Iwanami Shoten.

Yokoyama, Gennosuke (1972) *Nihon no Kasō Shakai*, Tokyo: Meiji Bunken.

Index

'a prosperous country and a
strong army' 41–2, 45
administrative reform 167
agriculture: as basis of economy
4, 16–18, 84–5; as basis of
wealth 9; Japanese 20th
century 86–7; labour
productivity 109;
restructuring of 105; *see also*
rural economy; taxation
Akamatsu Kaname 115–16, 151
Althusser, Louis 88, 117
American influence 136–8,
165–6
analysis of contemporary
conditions 120–1, 121–6
Ancient Learning (Kogaku) 20,
39
Andō Shōeki 3, 28
Arai Hakuseki (1657–1725)
13–14, 19, 21–5, 59
Arisawa Hiromi 99, 143, 146
Aristotle 8
Association for Social Policy,
established in Germany in
1872 63–4
Association for the Study of
Social Policy, established
1896 64–9, 76

backwardness factor 124–5, 148
balance of payments 138–40
Bandeau, Abbé 12
Bansho Shirabesho 46, 49
Baran, Paul 156
Bastiat, Frédéric 49, 53
Bellah, Robert 28
Berle, Adolf 157
Blaug, Mark 174
Böhm-Bawerk, Eugen von 89–90
Booth, Charles 77
Bortkiewicz, L. von 111–12
Brentano, Lujo (1844–1931) 68
Bronfenbrenner, Martin 129–30
Buckle, H.T. 52

Buddhism 15
Burke, Edmund 159
Burnham, James 157

capital liberalization 153–4
capitalism: collapse of 120, 123;
compared with socialism 161,
175; Japanese 83–8; post-war
106–11; stages of 97 *see also*
stage theory; state monopoly
122–9, 168, 179
Carey, Henry Charles
(1793–1879) 59–60
Central Labour Council 134
Chandler, A. 191
Christian missionaries 74
class struggle 80, 97, 121, 177
classical economics 49–52, 60,
62
collectivism, family 186–8
commerce: restructuring of 105;
state participation in 34–8;
value of 27–30
comparative advantage 61,
114–16, 151–2
Confucian philosophy 8, 11–14,
30, 52; Chu Hsi school
(Shushigaku) 12–13, 15, 20;
innovations in 15–16
constitution, new (1947) 106
Cournot, A.A. 136
Cromwell, Oliver 59
currency: convertible and
unconvertible 53–4, 57;
recoinages 19, 23–4; reform
54
cycle of product development 151

Dazai Shundai (1680–1747)
25–6, 32
decentralized network structure
189–92
demand deficiency 139, 148
demand expansion, domestic
168–9

INDEX

pure socialism 97
Putiatin, Admiral 39

quantity theory of money 23, 25
Quesnay, François 7, 12, 17, 60

Ranis, Gustav 137
Rathgen, Karl 65
Realist school (Jitsugaku) 39
Reischauer, E.O. 73
reproduction schema 178-80
Ricardo, D. 59, 114-16, 151
rice: basis of economic system 8-9; as medium of exchange 17
Robinson, Joan 181
Rōnō school 75, 82, 85-8, 106, 109, 116, *see also* Kōza/ Rōnō debate
Roscher, W. 47
Rowntree, B. Seebohm 77
Rowthorn, Robert 114
rural economy 87; capitalist relations in 109; commercialization of 32, 56-7; *see also* agriculture; taxation
rural poverty 15-16, 31, 72, 77; *see also* poverty
Ruskin, John 159

Saeki, Naomi 141
Saint-Exupéry, Antoine de 159
Sakisaka Itsurō (1897-1985) 86-7, 103
Samuelson, Paul 136, 138, 151, 176, 181
Satō Nobuhiro (1769-1850) 3, 31, 34-8, 41, 78, 195
Sawa Takamitsu (b. 1942) 192-6
Schmoller, Gustav von (1838-1917) 62-3, 65, 136
Schumpeter, Joseph (1883-1950) 89-93, 136, 159-60, 185
Sekine, Thomas 119-20
Shibagaki Kazuo 141
Shimomura Osamu (b. 1910) 134, 138-40, 145, 147-50,

159-60, 165, 170
Shimpo Seiji (b. 1945) 165-6, 169
Shingaku 27-8
Shinohara Miyohei (b. 1919) 125, 135, 137, 141-5, 148, 150-1
Shōwa (1926-89) *see* inter-war period
Shōwa Research Association, established 1936 100-1, 134
Shundai 14
Smith, Adam 3, 7, 12, 50, 52, 60, 100
Smith, Howard 11
social capital theory 178-9, 181-3
Social Policy School 86
social problems, economic causes of 63, 65
social values 184-8, 193
Socialist ideas *see* Marxism
Socialist Party 106, 127
Sraffa, Piero 112, 175
stage theory 118, 120-1, 123 *see also* capitalism, stages of
state, role of 66-7, 178, 192-3
state intervention 4, 41-2, 45-6, 54, 58, 61, 63, 67, 100, 125-6, 133, 153
state monopoly capitalism 122-9, 168, 179
state-controlled economy 34-8
status system 9, 11, 15, 18; ideal 35-6
structural change, and export growth 150-1
structural reform theory 126-9
subordination thesis 109-10
Sugi Kōji 59
Sūkra 8
Suzuki Yoshio (b. 1913) 165-6, 195
Sweezy, Paul 104, 156

Taguchi Ukichi (1857-1905) 55, 66
Taishō period (1912-26) *see* inter-war period

212